Effective Learning and Teaching in Social Policy and Social Work

Written to meet the needs of teachers, lecturers, tutors and trainers, this is *the* guide to understanding the key issues in learning and teaching in social policy and social work – as well as related areas such as probation, criminology and early childhood studies.

The field of social welfare is constantly changing, and this book is an accessible text covering the core concerns critical to educators teaching in these disciplines. Key areas covered include curriculum planning, design and delivery of teaching, assessment, promoting inclusion, e-learning, inter-professional practice and continuing professional development. International perspectives and the impact of globalisation are also considered.

Written for undergraduate- and postgraduate-level teaching, less experienced teachers looking for authoritative, expert guidance will find this title indispensable, as will more experienced educators seeking material for reflection and innovative teaching practice.

Hilary Burgess is Senior Lecturer in the School for Policy Studies, University of Bristol, UK, and Learning and Teaching Adviser to the Subject Centre for Social Policy and Social Work, UK (SWAP), Higher Education Academy.

Imogen Taylor is Professor of Social Work and Social Care at the University of Sussex, UK, Co-Director of SWAP and is a National Teaching Fellow.

Effective Learning and Teaching in Higher Education series

Effective Learning and Teaching in Law
Edited by Roger Burridge, Karen Hinett, Abdul Paliwala and Tracey Varnava

Effective Learning and Teaching in Business and Management
Edited by Bruce Macfarlane and Roger Ottewill

Effective Learning and Teaching in Mathematics and its Applications
Edited by Joseph Kyle and Peter Kahn

Effective Learning and Teaching in Medical, Dental and Veterinary Education
Edited by John Sweet, Sharon Huttly and Ian Taylor

Effective Learning and Teaching in Social Policy and Social Work
Edited by Hilary Burgess and Imogen Taylor

Effective Learning and Teaching in Engineering
Edited by Caroline Baillie and Ivan Moore

Effective Learning and Teaching in Computing
Edited by Alastair Irons and Sylvia Alexander

Effective Learning and Teaching in Social Policy and Social Work

Edited by
Hilary Burgess and Imogen Taylor

RoutledgeFalmer
Taylor & Francis Group

LONDON AND NEW YORK

First published 2005
by RoutledgeFalmer
2 Park Square, Milton Park, Abingdon, Oxon OX14 4RN

Simultaneously published in the USA and Canada
by RoutledgeFalmer
270 Madison Avenue, New York, NY 10016

RoutledgeFalmer is an imprint of the Taylor & Francis Group

© 2005 Hilary Burgess, Imogen Taylor and individual contributors

The right of Hilary Burgess, Imogen Taylor and individual
contributors to be identified as the Author of this Work has been
asserted by them in accordance with the Copyright, Designs and
Patents Act 1998

Typeset in Bembo by
Florence Production Ltd, Stoodleigh, Devon
Printed and bound in Great Britain by
TJ International Ltd, Padstow, Cornwall

British Library Cataloguing in Publication Data
A catalogue record for this book is available from
the British Library

Library of Congress Cataloging in Publication Data
    Effective learning and teaching in social policy and social
    work/[edited by] Hilary Burgess and Imogen Taylor
        p.cm – (Effective learning and teaching in higher
        education series)
    Includes bibliographical references and index.
    1. Social policy – Study and teaching (Higher)   2. Human
    services – Study and teaching (Higher)   3. Social work
    education.   I. Burgess, Hilary, 1954–   II. Taylor, Imogen.
    III. Series: Effective learning and teaching in higher education.
    HN29.E35 2004
    361.2'5 – dc22   2004006777

ISBN 0–415–33495–0 (hbk)
ISBN 0–415–33496–9 (pbk)

Contents

About the editors and specialist contributors

Editors

Hilary Burgess is Senior Lecturer in the School for Policy Studies, University of Bristol, where she led the development of a problem-based learning curriculum for the Diploma in Social Work, called Enquiry and Action Learning (EAL). She was programme director from 1990 to 1996. She has published extensively on social work education, and her work on EAL has been widely referred to nationally and internationally. Since 2000 she has been seconded to the UK Learning and Teaching Support Network Subject Centre for Social Policy and Social Work (SWAP) as learning and teaching adviser. Through this she has developed a leading role in national developments in social work education, including membership of the Department of Health Project Group on Practice Learning for the Reform of Social Work Education in England (2002–3).

Imogen Taylor is Professor of Social Work and Social Care at the University of Sussex, where she has led the development of the new BA Social Work (a joint degree with the University of Brighton), followed by the MA Social Work. Prior to this she was Senior Lecturer at the University of Bristol, having qualified as a social worker in Toronto where she practised before joining the Faculty of the School of Social Work there. Imogen is Co-Director of the UK Learning and Teaching Support Network Subject Centre for Social Policy and Social Work (SWAP). She has published extensively on the topic of learning and teaching in social work, including her book *Developing Learning in Professional Education: Partnerships for Practice* (1997), and is a member of the Editorial Board of *Social Work Education*. Imogen was awarded a National Teaching Fellowship in 2003.

Specialist contributors

Melanie Ashford is Senior Research Fellow for SWAP, based at the University of Southampton. Her background is in developing flexible learning materials and e-learning and her interests include the effective use of technology for learning, work-based learning, networking and online tutoring.

Bill Beaumont is Lecturer in Social Work in the School for Policy Studies, University of Bristol. Previously, he worked as a probation officer in London and for the National Association of Probation Officers. As well as teaching about anti-oppressive practice, offending, substance misuse and homelessness on the social work programme, he teaches criminology and criminal justice policy on the social policy programme. His writing and research have focused on adult offenders and the probation service.

Peter Beresford is Professor of Social Policy and Director of the Centre for Citizen Participation at Brunel University. He is Chair of Shaping Our Lives, the national user-controlled organization core-funded by the Department of Health to improve the effective involvement of service users and the quality of support they receive. He is a long-term user of statutory mental health services and is actively involved in the psychiatric system survivor movement.

Sarah Cemlyn is Senior Lecturer in the School for Policy Studies, University of Bristol, where she has taught on the social work programmes since 1991. She has research interests in policy and practice relating to minority groups, including gypsies and travellers, and asylum seekers, and in approaches that examine power relationships such as community work and human rights perspectives.

Viviene E. Cree is Senior Lecturer in the School of Social and Political Studies and Associate Dean (Admissions), College of Humanities and Social Science, at the University of Edinburgh. Viviene is a qualified social worker and practice teacher who worked for 16 years in statutory and voluntary social work agencies before moving into social work teaching in 1992. She has written and published widely on social work education and practice, most recently *Becoming a Social Worker* (2003), Routledge, London.

Beth R. Crisp is Senior Lecturer in Social Work at the University of Glasgow. She has extensive experience of developing and teaching both on campus and with distance education students in Australia, and has also worked with colleagues in the Glasgow School of Social Work to redevelop the social work degree programmes. She co-authored a Knowledge Review for the Social Care Institute for Excellence (SCIE) on learning and teaching methods of social work assessment.

Pam Green Lister is Lecturer in Social Work at the University of Glasgow. She teaches on social work and social policy programmes in the areas of social work theory and practice, and child abuse. Her research interests include learning and teaching approaches to social work education and child abuse. She co-authored a Knowledge Review for SCIE on learning and teaching methods of social work assessment.

Pat Higham is Professor of Social Work and Social Care and Associate Dean, Academic Planning and Quality, in the Faculty of Economics and Social Sciences at the Nottingham Trent University. She was a member of the Department of Health Project Group for Continuing Professional Development, Registration, and Post Qualifying Studies.

Zoë Irving is Lecturer in Comparative Social Policy in the Department of Sociological Studies, University of Sheffield, having previously worked at Leeds Metropolitan University where she was Course Leader. She has undertaken research on teaching social policy with Pat Young for SWAP.

Karen Lyons is Professor of International Social Work at the University of East London, where she runs an MA ISW (International Social Work) programme. She gained experience of European and international social work through exchange programmes, consultancy and research, and the latter currently includes a European study of knowledge creation through doctoral work.

Sue Orton is Research Fellow and Learning and Teaching Adviser for SWAP and supports staff development for e-learning in the Social Work Department at the University of Sussex. Her interests concern the impact of e-learning developments on staff skills, including facilitation, emotional intelligence and group leading and learning.

Malcolm Payne is Director, Psychosocial and Spiritual Care, St Christopher's Hospice, London. He was Professor and Head of Applied Community Studies at Manchester Metropolitan University for fifteen years and is the author of works on social work theory, education, management and multi-professional teamwork.

Jackie Rafferty holds a University of Southampton Senior Research Fellowship and is Director of the Centre for Human Service Technology (CHST) in the School of Social Sciences and also Director of SWAP, the Learning and Teaching Support Network Subject Centre for Social Policy and Social Work. With a background in community development, she has researched and published extensively on information and communication technologies in social work education and practice.

Bob Rotheram is E-Learning Development Manager in the Centre for Academic Practice at the Nottingham Trent University. He has long experience of teaching social work and social policy, and has a special interest in the use of computers in education. He won a National Teaching Fellowship in 2002.

Duncan Scott is Research Fellow at the Centre for Applied Social Research, Department of Sociology, University of Manchester. He designed and co-directed field placements for social policy students and a linked two-module course at the University of Manchester 1976–2002.

Steven M. Shardlow is Professor of Social Work at the University of Salford, Director of Salford Centre for Social Work Research and Professor II in Social Work at Bodø University College, Norway. He is founding Editor-in-Chief of the *Journal of Social Work*. His research, consultancy and publications cover a range of fields, including evidence-based policy and practice, professional ethics, international practice, comparative practice in the social professions, social work education and practice learning.

Judith Thomas is Senior Lecturer at the University of the West of England where she is programme leader for the BSc Social Work. She has also managed the Regional Practice Learning Centre and the Self Assessment in Professional and Higher Education Project (SAPHE), funded by the Higher Education Funding Council for England (based at Bristol University). She is a member of the research team evaluating the interprofessional curriculum in the Faculty of Health and Social Care.

Pat Young is Senior Lecturer in Social Policy at the University of the West of England and a Learning and Teaching Adviser for SWAP at the University of Bristol. She has taught social policy in further and higher education since 1980 and is the author of a popular social policy textbook. She directed a research project on teaching in social policy for SWAP with Zoë Irving.

Acknowledgements

We would like to thank all the people who have contributed in many different ways to this book. First and foremost, our thanks to colleagues in SWAP, the Learning and Teaching Support Network Subject Centre for Social Policy and Social Work, now part of the Higer Education Academy. They have contributed their ideas and experience by writing some of the chapters and through team discussions; they have also encouraged and supported us throughout all stages of production. A considerable number of other educators (academics, practice teachers and service users) have helped us in our thinking about learning and teaching in social policy and social work, and the kind of book we wanted to produce. We would also like to acknowledge the contribution to our understanding of teaching and learning made by students (past and present), through their responses, challenges and ideas. Our families have also supported us during the preparation of this book.

Finally, we would like to thank Sally Brown, former Series Editor for the *Effective Learning and Teaching* books, and the staff at Taylor & Francis for commissioning us to edit this book.

Abbreviations

AASW	Advanced Award in Social Work
AOP	anti-oppressive practice
APEL	Accreditation of Prior Learning
ASW/MHA	Approved Social Worker/Mental Health Award
BMS	benchmark statements
CAIPE	Centre for the Advancement of Interprofessional Education
CASE	Collaborative Studentships from the ESRC
CCETSW	Central Council for Education and Training in Social Work
CHIME	Centre for Health Informatics & Multiprofessional Education
COBALT	Community Based Learning Teamwork
CPD	continuing professional development
CSWE	Council on Social Work Education
DH and DoH	Department of Health
DipSW	Diploma in Social Work
EAL	Enquiry and Action Learning
EASSW	European Association of Schools of Social Work
EBL	enquiry-based learning
EHE	Enterprise in Higher Education
EISS	European Institute of Social Security
ERASMUS	European Community Action Scheme for the Mobility of Students
ESRC	Economic and Social Research Council
EU	European Union
GSCC	General Social Care Council
HE	higher education
HEFCE	Higher Education Funding Council for England
HEI	higher education institution
HESA	Higher Education Statistics Agency
HMSO	Her Majesty's Stationery Office

IASSW	International Association of Schools of Social Work
ICSW	International Council of Social Welfare
IFSW	International Federation of Social Workers
ILTHE	Institute for Learning and Teaching in Higher Education
IMF	International Monetary Fund
INGO	international non–governmental organization
IPAOP	Inequality, Power and Anti-Oppressive Practice (name of module)
IPE	interprofessional education
IT	information technology
JISC	Joint Information Systems Committee
LGA	Local Government Association
LTSN	Learning and Teaching Support Network
MLE	managed learning environment
NCWE	National Council for Work Experience
NHS	National Health Service
NHSU	University for the National Health Service
NI	Northern Ireland
NIMHE	National Institute for Mental Health in England
NOPT	National Organisation for Practice Teaching
NOS	National Occupational Standards
NVQ	National Vocational Qualification
OeE	Office of the e-Envoy
OHP	overhead projector
OTiS	Online Tutoring Skills Project
OU	Open University
PBL	problem-based learning
PDP	personal development planning
PEPBL	Project on the Effectiveness of Problem Based Learning
PFI	private finance initiatives
PIPE	Promoting Interprofessional Education Project
PPP	public private partnerships
PQ	post-qualifying
PQ1	Post-Qualifying Requirement
PQCCA	Post-Qualifying Award in Child Care
PQSW	Post-Qualifying Award in Social Work
PRTL	Post-Registration Training and Learning
PTA	Practice Teaching Award
QAA	Quality Assurance Agency
RAE	Research Assessment Exercise

SAPHE	Self Assessment in Professional and Higher Education Project
SCIE	Social Care Institute for Excellence
SCLDI	Social Care Leadership Development Initiative
SCoP	Standing Conference of Principals (of Higher Education Colleges)
SCOPT	Scottish Organisation for Practice Teaching
SENDA	Special Educational Needs and Disability Act
SIP	Sociologists in Placements
SRHE	Society for Research into Higher Education
SSI	Social Services Inspectorate
SWAP	Subject Centre for Social Policy and Social Work
TOPPS	Training Organisation for Personal Social Services
TRIPLE	Three Centre Research on Interprofessional Practice in Learning and Education
UEL	University of East London
UKeU	United Kingdom e-university
UN	United Nations
UWE	University of the West of England
VLE	virtual learning environment
WE	work experience
WUN	Worldwide Universities Network

Introduction

Hilary Burgess and Imogen Taylor

Aim of the book

This book emerges from our shared interest in and commitment to developing a discipline-based pedagogy in social policy and social work. As editors we have benefited from our collaboration over almost a decade in developing the scholarship of learning and teaching. This led us in 2000 to be involved in developing the Subject Centre for Social Policy and Social Work (SWAP), one of twenty-four discipline-based Subject Centres established by the UK Higher Education Funding Councils to promote high-quality learning, teaching and assessment in the disciplines. SWAP has, along with the Institute for Learning and Teaching in Higher Education (ILTHE), become established as a leading force in pedagogical development in the UK. Both form part of the new Higher Education Academy, established in 2004.

Our experience of working with the Subject Centre and the extensive range of educators from both disciplines who have contributed to and benefited from the work of SWAP have further enabled us to write for and edit this book. Our work with the SWAP team has brought us into contact with departmental key contacts, individual academics and stakeholder groups. We have facilitated and brokered a range of activities including conferences, workshops and consultations. The SWAP website (www.swap.ac.uk) provides a wealth of information, news and event, supported by a monthly e-bulletin and bi-annual newsletter.

We are concerned to redress the fact that, in terms of academic priorities, teaching and learning have, for some time, been the poor relatives to research, particularly in vocational subjects such as ours where applied research has not been valued in the Research Assessment Exercise. Pedagogic research has not been easily accessible, and discipline-specific pedagogic research is under-funded and unevenly developed. Professional development for teaching has had, until recently, a low profile, and teaching has often been an individual-ized and private activity. Teaching on professional programmes in some universities has also been a devalued activity, compared to teaching in the traditional disciplines. If, however, we value learning, and wish to ensure that students have the best opportunity to develop their knowledge, understanding, skills and value base to enable them in turn to improve the service provided to service users and carers, then teaching and learning must be given a higher profile and priority.

Social policy and social work

The disciplines of social policy and social work share some important charac-teristics, both in terms of their history and focus, and they also diverge in significant ways. The links include similar histories in higher education, which may be reflected in co-location within one department or school in some universities, and formal links through cost centres. They also share a panel for the Research Assessment Exercise, and the Quality Assurance Authority Benchmark Statement, both powerful drivers in the fields of research and teaching respectively. Furthermore, they have a common focus on social welfare and social exclusion; this is reflected in collaborative research, and also in the development of interdisciplinary teaching. However, there are also significant differences, of which perhaps the most striking is the professional focus of social work education, and the consequent close relationship with employers together with regulation by external accrediting bodies and govern-ment funders (further explored in Chapter 1).

We were particularly struck by the returns to the SWAP survey of academics teaching social policy and social work in higher education in the UK, of whom 24 per cent identified themselves to be engaged in teaching both social policy and social work (SWAP, 2002). This picture of conver-gence and differentiation has proved challenging, yet immensely interesting as we have sought to identify commonalities and contrasts. In many areas, both disciplines have much to learn from each other.

Audience

This book is aimed at both experienced and new academics teaching social policy and social work in higher education. We hope that new academics will benefit from the overview it provides of education in these disciplines, providing both contextual information to explain current policies and approaches, and ideas that can be adapted for use in a range of teaching contexts. For more experienced academics, we hope the book will enable them to reflect on some of the key challenges in learning and teaching that they will have encountered, and provide some new ways of addressing these.

In both disciplines, but particularly social work, a considerable number of sessional staff are employed to contribute to programmes. Increasingly, educators in social work include not only lecturers and practitioners, but users and carers. We hope that these staff too will benefit from this discussion of learning and teaching in social policy and social work. Students may also be interested in reading this book as, increasingly, as stakeholders they have opportunities for debate about how their education is conducted, and the dilemmas that must be resolved in the design and delivery of programmes.

While written primarily for a UK audience, we anticipate that this book will also be of interest to educators from social work, social policy and related disciplines in other countries. As we can see in the two chapters on globalization and international perspectives, Chapters 12 and 13, many of the concerns and questions about both education and practice are shared, and are directly transferable between contexts. Furthermore, examination of different approaches in different countries may serve to inform practice in one's own country.

Structure of the book

In Chapter 1, *Dancing on a moving carpet*, Hilary Burgess and Pat Young explore the fast-changing context of higher education and of professional practice. In Chapter 2, *Designing the curriculum*, the complex processes involved in curriculum planning are outlined by Hilary Burgess and Zoë Irving. Attention is drawn to the need for educators to balance coherence with opportunities for innovation and flexibility. Questions regarding participation in curriculum planning pave the way for Chapter 3, *Participation in social policy and social work learning*, in which Peter Beresford argues for the involvement of citizens (community groups and service users) in education for social work and social policy. The importance of this issue, in challenging the historical separation of the recipients of welfare from both the providers and educators, is underlined by its early placing in the book. In Chapter 4, *Promoting equality and inclusion*, Bill Beaumont and Sarah Cemlyn explore another set of issues of central importance for both disciplines, which share a tradition of questioning inequalities and oppressions. The chapter shows how this agenda can be addressed within higher education, in terms of institutional policy and practice within departments. An example is provided to illustrate the complexities of introducing students to this arena of learning.

Having set the stage for teaching and learning in social policy and social work, the next four chapters examine the fundamentals of educational practice. In Chapter 5, *Students learning to learn*, Viviene E. Cree shows how educators can help students to make the best use of their education through understanding the nature of learning. She argues that such best practice must be supported by the higher education institution itself. In Chapter 6, *Promoting interactive learning and teaching*, Hilary Burgess and Pat Young put the case for actively engaging students in their learning, and show how this can be put into practice in lectures, seminars, group work and experiential learning. The closely related, and often thorny, issue of assessment is addressed in Chapter 7, *Walking the assessment tightrope*, in which Beth R. Crisp and Pam Green Lister outline the key features for constructing a sound assessment strategy. Since there still tends to be an over-reliance on traditional essays as the standard assignment, they provide a range of examples of different methods. With eLearning rapidly gaining ground as an element of educational practice, Jackie Rafferty, Melanie Ashford and Sue Orton explore the opportunities for adoption of this approach in social policy and social work, as well as some of the barriers to implementation in Chapter 8, *Towards eLearning*. They provide an accessible guide to terminology and the issues for educators, with an emphasis on how technology can support learning, rather than being an objective in its own right.

Specific issues for social policy and social work educators are developed in the following chapters. In Chapter 9, *Developing learning beyond the campus*, Duncan Scott and Steven M. Shardlow examine the place of practice learning or placements in both disciplines. Despite a shared history of extra-mural learning, they argue that while social work has increasingly embraced 'practice' as a vehicle to achieve professional competence, social policy has retreated from this area of learning as part of its quest for academic status and identity. *Interprofessional education*, Chapter 10, is unusual in that its focus is primarily on social work, since these students are more likely to engage in learning with other professional groups such as nurses. Melanie Ashford and Judith Thomas consider the topic from the perspectives of policy, the institution, the educator and student, and summarize the dilemmas arising from implementation. In Chapter 11, Pat Higham and Bob Rotherham look at the particular issues in *Continuing professional development and education*. The need for postgraduate and post-qualifying programmes for both social work and social policy practitioners to reflect the concerns of both learners and employers is stressed.

Increasingly, the two disciplines relate to both global and international issues; these are explored in the next two chapters. In Chapter 12, *Globalization*, Zoë Irving and Malcolm Payne consider the implications for learning and teaching in social policy and social work, as economic, social and political systems across the world increasingly impact on social welfare in the UK. They discuss the educational consequences of the global context for education. In Chapter 13, *International perspectives*, Karen Lyons argues for the promotion of comparative and international perspectives. The aim is to produce welfare professionals who are more globally aware and able to work collaboratively with a view to improving welfare services for all users.

The book concludes with Chapter 14, *Developing the university as a learning organization*, in which Imogen Taylor argues that we cannot understand the development of learning and teaching by the individual educator without

1

Dancing on a moving carpet: the changing context

Pat Young and Hilary Burgess

Introduction

There is little doubt that the carpet under our feet is moving, as diverse and complex changes impact on the professional practice of academics who teach in higher education. Changing discipline requirements follow changing institutional policy or faculty configuration, compounded by changing government policy in higher education. For academics, who must continue to teach and to research, the experience could be likened to dancing on a moving carpet. The changes bring increased need for collaboration with a wider range of colleagues, and the challenge of mastering new dance steps includes co-ordinating those steps with new and unfamiliar partners. In this chapter we examine the nature of the moving carpet, with an analysis of key aspects of developments in higher education for lecturers in social policy and social work. Recognizing that change in the environment in which we work means modifying practice, the chapter offers an overview of new thinking about teaching as a form of professional practice and, in conclusion, suggests a model for self-management of change.

Conceptualizing change in higher education

There exists a growing armoury of descriptive and explanatory concepts for making sense of the changes in higher education. Hargeaves, for example, locates his understanding of developments affecting schoolteachers in the context of 'a powerful and dynamic struggle between two immense social forces: those of modernity and postmodernity' (Hargeaves, 1994: 8). Others have used the concepts of 'Fordism' and 'post-Fordism' as ways of making sense of changes in higher education (Rustin, 1994). This model begins with an analogy with changes in consumption and production of motor cars, typi-fied by the contrast between the mass consumption of identical products created by the mass production systems pioneered by the Ford motor company, and more recent developments of flexible production and differentiated and segmented consumption. The distinction between an elite and a mass system (Trow, 1992) has achieved wide currency as a means of summarizing a range of developments in higher education. Adopting these terms, Jackson writes of the current friction between a mass system and traditional elite values (Jackson, 1997). We begin by analysing this friction and offering means of reconcilia-tion through developing professional practice, bringing teaching practice more in line with the needs of a mass system, under pressure from various sources. Five areas of significant change impacting on lecturers are discussed to set the scene.

Changes in higher education – students

Most obviously, student numbers have increased. In 1965–6, 400,000 students were engaged in higher education; by 2001–2 the numbers had swelled to more than one million (statistics from the Higher Education Statistics Agency (HESA), reported in the *Times Higher Education Supplement*, 2002). The widening participation agenda has sought to challenge the traditional bias of higher education in favour of privileged groups. Social policy and social work are both subjects that have successfully attracted students from a wide range of backgrounds, both socially and educationally, with diverse needs.

The introduction of means–tested tuition fees in 1997 and the substitution of a system of loans for grants, together with widening participation, has changed and diversified students' life-styles. Most students in higher education now combine work with study, in some cases working almost full-time. Shorrock (2002) quotes a survey which found that 40 per cent of students in employment are working between 12.5 and 20 hours a week and concludes that 'having a job and studying is now considered to be part of the normal experience of higher education' (Shorrock, 2002: 53). Many students of social work and social policy also have family responsibilities. The proposed intro-duction of student loans, combined with 'top-up fees' for universities in England may further impact on the study/work balance for students (Department for Education and Skills, 2003).

Alongside changes in the wider society, and in the funding of education, attitudes have changed. Students tend to be more instrumental in their atti-tude to study, prioritizing assessed work that counts towards their final degree classification and keeping a sharp eye on the employment market. Kneale (1997: 119) talks of the rise of the 'strategic student' and suggests that staff recognize that not all students in the expanded higher education system are primarily academic and committed to all their modules. The spread of consumerism into public services documented by social policy writers (for example Clarke, 1998) has led to increased awareness within higher education of students as 'customers', seeking 'value' for their own, or their parents', monies.

Changes in higher education – resourcing

The expansion of higher education has taken place in a time of cost constraints in public spending as a whole, and the unit funding of students has dropped from £7,500 in 1989–90 to less than £5,000 in 2003–4 (HESA statistics, *Times Higher Education Supplement*, 2002). The White Paper *The Future of Higher Education* (Department for Education and Skills, 2003) reports a 36 per cent drop in funding per student between 1989 and 1997 (paragraph 1.31), with the decline in unit funding only reversed in 2000–1. In most programmes, lower unit funding has increased the ratio of students to staff (Jackson, 1997). The impact of this financial squeeze has been felt in terms of resources for students (buildings, libraries, technology), but most significantly in terms of staff stress (Association of University Teachers, 2003).

Changes in higher education – accountability

Greater numbers of students and higher levels of public expenditure on universities, together with the increased significance attached to higher education, have brought greater pressures for external control and intervention in the work of academics. The Quality Assurance Agency (QAA) describes the increase in external regulation in the following quotation:

> When the HE [higher education] system was small and largely uniform, and made a relatively small claim on public funds, reliance upon implicit, shared assumptions and informal networks and procedures (for quality assurance) may have been possible, and sufficient. But with the rapid expansion of numbers of students and institutions, the associated broadening of the purposes of HE, and the considerable increase in the amount of public money required, more methodical approaches have had to be employed.
>
> (QAA, 1998, quoted in Becher and Trowler, 2001: 6)

The methodology employed by the QAA on behalf of the Higher Education Funding Councils from 1997 had a strong emphasis on subject review (with a 24-point rating scale) and was criticized as heavy handed (see for example *Times Higher Education Supplement*, 22 September 2000). From 2003, the system in

England and Northern Ireland moved to one focused primarily on institutional audit, incorporating five discipline trails. In Scotland the focus is more on quality enhancement within institutions, with no discipline review. Henkel (2000) offers an overview of these issues.

Some sources write of a move to 'professionalize' the activity of teaching (Huber, 1999; Light and Cox, 2001). Aspects of the professionalization of higher education teaching include training for newly appointed staff, the creation of educational development units in most universities, and the establishment of the Institute for Learning and Teaching in Higher Education (ILTHE) and the Learning and Teaching Support Network (LTSN) subject centres, which are incorporated into the new Higher Education Academy.

The Research Assessment Exercise (RAE) and the linking of funding to research outputs has intensified pressures for all staff to be research-active and to publish extensively. Many staff with backgrounds in practice rather than research, and those in post-1992 universities with high teaching loads, have struggled to meet the demands of the research agenda. Cuthbert (2002: 36, citing McNay, 1997) suggests that the RAE has significantly changed the behaviour of 'institutions, faculties, schools, departments and individual academics'. The RAE is also thought to have impeded pedagogic research and scholarship (Yorke, 2003), which has not been valued on a par with discipline-based research by the panels. Further uncertainty lies ahead with the Roberts Review (suggesting research funding be concentrated in a small numbers of universities), and potential changes to the RAE itself.

Greater governmental demands for accountability and the spread of managerialism across the public sector have increased the administrative burden on academic staff. Quality assurance procedures have multiplied demands for paperwork and attendance at committees. The QAA has also introduced benchmarking statements for each discipline, codes of practice for ten areas, and programme specifications and progress files; while these may play an important role in quality provision, the time spent on formal procedures has been increased.

Changes in higher education – the nature of knowledge

Knowledge development and dissemination in all fields has increased. Thompson (1997) suggests that as new knowledge is acquired at a greater rate, it also more quickly becomes obsolete, an issue that may be more acute in social policy and social work than in most other subjects. The New Right in the 1970s and 1980s, and New Labour in the 1990s and into the new millennium, brought radical and wide-ranging policy changes in all aspects of social welfare and service configuration and organization. The boundaries between the public and private have become porous, extending the complex knowledge bases of social policy and social work from a primary focus on state welfare to an inclusion of a greater range of informal and non-statutory agencies. Devolution of power to the four countries of the UK, and to local agencies of governance, as well as the growing influence of globalization have further challenged lecturers in social policy and social work to keep abreast of theoretical and empirical developments in their subjects. Since both subjects also draw on other disciplines – economics, politics, sociology, law, psychology – the potential knowledge is exhilarating or daunting, depending on your perspective. Increased complexity in interprofessional education and the involvement of service users in teaching and research further increase the boundaries of underpinning knowledge.

Not only has there been acceleration in the rate of growth of knowledge, but also change in access to knowledge. The technical advances that brought computers to most academics' desks have enabled speedy and global access to rapidly growing quantities of information. Democratized access to knowledge challenges traditional power relations. Students as well as lecturers can access, and indeed create and disseminate information. As well as keeping up to date with subject content and incorporating skills development into the curriculum, lecturers are under pressure to learn and adopt educational applications of new technology, for example the virtual learning environments (VLEs) currently being introduced in many universities.

Changes in higher education – delivery modes

With expanded numbers of increasingly diverse students, and the opportunities offered by new forms of technology, higher education is no longer limited to those able to study full-time within the walls of the university. Recent decades have seen increasing diversity in delivery modes of higher education (Jackson, 1997), with an increase in part-time provision, forms of open learning using new technology (Candy 1997) and employment-based modes of study (Thompson, 1997). Becher and Trowler (2001: 3) refer to the 'borderless' nature of institutions as new 'knowledge media' enable universities to deliver distance teaching to large numbers of students across the globe. New developments such as the NHSU, which provides training and education for staff within the National Health Service, further challenge traditional conceptions of a university and of higher education.

In this context of competing demands and intensified pressures, lecturers may understandably be reluctant to radically overhaul teaching. However, struggling with approaches to teaching and learning developed for a very different context may be a more, rather than a less, stressful option. In the following section we consider how professional practice in higher education is changing in line with the developments examined above.

Changes in learning and teaching

This section examines key themes in developments in teaching and learning. We suggest these can offer a way of making sense of the turbulent times in which we teach, and contribute towards a framework for improving professional practice which can enable lecturers to swim with, rather than struggle against, the currents of change.

From didactic to active learning

Active learning seeks to encourage all students to employ the learning strategies of successful students. To explain this, Biggs (1999) employs a device for illustrating a key distinction between more and less academically successful students. Within the current student population, Biggs suggests that lecturers will encounter 'Susan' and 'Robert'. 'Susan' is 'academically committed' and learns in an 'academic way' (Biggs, 1999: 3). 'Robert', on the other hand, is 'less committed', 'possibly not as bright' and has a 'less developed background of relevant knowledge'.

The central justification for Biggs' approach to teaching is that Susan 'spontaneously' uses active learning, in the form of higher-order cognitive processes such as relating and theorizing, in teaching situations towards the 'passive' end of the teaching method continuum, such as lectures. Robert, however, does not. Biggs suggest that the large gap between Susan's and Robert's levels of engagement is significantly reduced by active methods such as problem-based learning, in which higher-order cognitive activities are not optional, but required.

Active learning also fits with the direction of social change in other aspects of society. In the media, the traditional roles of presenter and audience are being challenged with increasingly varied forms of participation. In other aspects of social life, rigid divisions in which less powerful members are discouraged from holding and expressing opinions are dissolving. Technological developments and the global re-location of industry mean that there is less demand for silent workers to carry out repetitive tasks in factories, and more need for social skills in service industries, where individual initiative and creative teamwork are needed for flexibility and innovation. In the public sector, active learning is reflected in the rise of the consumer and user participation.

From subject content to transferable skills

Current thinking in the educational literature displaces discipline or subject content from the centre stage and asserts the primacy of various kinds of 'transferable' skills. This theme is particularly relevant for social policy, since in social work education, skills development has always had a central place. The increase in the speed of change in knowledge makes it impractical to teach everything, and more important to develop skills for learning (Biggs, 1999). A shift of emphasis from content to skills can liberate lecturers from an obsessive and self-defeating chase for the holy grail of comprehensive and up-to-date subject knowledge.

From subject expert to reflective practitioner

Where previously an academic could rest on his or her reputation in research and publishing in the discipline, awareness of pedagogic issues and the ability to reflect on teaching practice is advocated for the contemporary lecturer. Changing times are best met with flexibility and adaptability, built on a secure framework of well-thought-out core values. This allows the maintenance of a sense of personal integrity with a willingness to make changes that are congruent with the environment and the needs of others.

The conception of students as customers of the university gives students a right to ask questions about their education, and lecturers a responsibility to answer. It is also the case that lecturers wishing to make changes to teaching, particularly in the direction of active learning, will need to engage in changing the culture of education in which students expect to be 'taught'. The lecturer needs to be able to articulate the reasoning behind the new approach to learning and teaching. Reflective practice is also crucial in terms of the move towards increased collaboration discussed below. The productive sharing of practice requires professional discourse. Expressions such as 'that seminar didn't work' or 'that lecture went badly' are limited in explanatory power and poor tools for improving practice. Strategies for peer observation of teaching may be an important first step in this.

From individualism to collaboration

In all areas of work, there is currently an emphasis on teamwork, and an awareness of the limitations of thinking in purely individual terms and the benefits of drawing on wider communities of practice (Wenger 1998). Light and Cox (2001) draw on Bennett's (1998) distinction between an 'autonomous' and a 'relational' model of academic being (quoted in Light and Cox, 2001: 39). The first model is one of 'insistent individualism' and is lodged in the idea of the self as individual and detached. There is 'inherent suspicion of the collaborative and the co-operative' by academics (Light and Cox 2001: 40). The alternative 'relational model' is seen as embedded in earlier academic traditions of a common sense of community and shared purposes.

The enthusiastic response to Wenger's (1998) conceptualization of 'communities of practice' shows the unmet need for an understanding of the relations between the individual and others at work. Martin (1999) argues that team learning goes way beyond the knowing or learning of any single member of the team, involving the development of a collective pool of knowledge out of which new insights and awareness emerge. For Senge (1990), team learning is vital because the complexity of the contemporary environment means that an individual's learning can never be enough to keep up with new developments and generate responses. Unless teams can work together effectively and learn, then organizations will not develop the capacity to be responsive.

Challenges for social policy and social work lecturers: commonality and differentiation

The extent to which the worlds of social policy academics and social work academics overlap has been the subject of continuing debate. In the UK, they share an important common history in their development prior to the First Word War at the London School of Economics, where both social administration (the forerunner of the inter-disciplinary field of social policy) and social work were established. The common focus on social welfare has clearly linked the disciplines, although there have been central tensions and debates between the disciplines:

- The professional nature of social work education is contrasted with the more theoretical or 'academic' nature of social policy programmes.
- The focus on personal social services for social work education (in the UK) is contrasted with a wider agenda for social policy, encompassing poverty, housing, education and health.
- Social work, and thus social work education, may be seen as an instrument of state control, whereas social policy has long positioned itself to provide a critique of state intervention.

However, the domains of the two disciplines have perhaps moved closer in recent years, with a new emphasis on transferable skills and employability for social policy, as some courses have returned to their own, more vocational, roots. Similarly, the research agenda may serve as a cohesive influence, especially in universities where the two departments are co-located.

The tensions between the disciplines are played out in the reconstruction of university departments, schools and faculties. Traditionally social policy and social work were co-located within a school, often in conjunction with sociology. Since the transfer of the colleges of nursing into higher education in 1992, there has been a trend for social work to move into an academic unit bearing a title such as 'Health and Social Care'. While co-locating social work with other professional programmes enables opportunities for interprofessional education and research, key links with policy development may be lost. Social policy, on the other hand, is increasingly drawn into new configurations within social science faculties, combining with sociology or urban studies. The advent of programmes such as criminology, early childhood studies and gender studies further complicates the picture, since they may encompass elements of both social policy and social work.

The research on social work and social policy academics undertaken by SWAP (LTSN Subject Centre for Social Work and Social Policy) suggests the shared focus between the disciplines is very much alive. In a survey of academics in departments identified as teaching social policy and/or social work, 24 per cent of respondents defined their teaching focus as both social policy and social work, with 45 per cent defining it as social work, 29 per cent as social policy and 1 per cent other (Waldman, 2002). It is not surprising, therefore, that some of the challenges facing social policy and social work academics are shared, while others are discrete. Both have had difficulties in recruitment in recent years, and both have experienced ambiguity in their status as university subjects.

Recruitment

A range of factors has led to a change in attitudes to the public sector, both as an area of study and a source of employment. These include widespread government and media criticism of the pubic sector, challenges to professional autonomy and falling relative pay levels. There has also been a shift in cultural values, with increasing celebration of the individual over the social, consumer spending and the accumulation of wealth over civic duty, which has contributed to a view of social policy and social work as unattractive. A loss of political idealism and many young people's disengagement from conventional politics have also led to a decrease in interest in welfare issues (Heron and McManus, 2003).

As a result of these and other factors, social policy and social work have experienced difficulties in recruitment. In social work, recruitment to qualifying courses is clearly an essential component of workforce planning. The twenty-first century began with a workforce crisis in social care (Social Services Inspectorate/Department of Health (SSI/DH), 2001), so government bodies across the UK have worked to augment entry to social work. Measures have included recruitment campaigns, a dedicated website, a 'fast-track' route in Scotland for postgraduates and the introduction of bursaries and payment of fees for social work students. These measures appear to have paid dividends; data from the General Social Care Council (GSCC) for entry into social work education show a 10 per cent increase in the number of students enrolled on the Diploma in Social Work (DipSW) in England in the year 2002–3, compared with 2001–2 (General Social Care Council (GSCC), 2003a). Introduced from 2003, the new degree in social work is long-awaited good news for social work, but may be another draw away from social policy in the future.

Recent years have seen a decrease in the numbers of students applying for undergraduate courses in social policy. This trend is cause for serious concern and has led to the closure of some programmes. There is evidence, however, that social policy continues to be taught in higher education. The Social Policy Association reports increases in the sales of social policy books (verbal feedback from committee member) and suggests that, although there are fewer students on single honours programmes, social policy remains popular as a subject within joint degree provision and at postgraduate level. It is also the case that changes in fashion can be short-lived. There are a number of factors that could have a positive effect in the future:

- Social policy is an increasingly important activity in society, as the government sets ambitious targets across the public sector and generates social policy legislation at a rate unequalled since the Second World War.
- There are moves to increase funding of the public sector and to attract people into careers in welfare and education.
- The emphasis on evaluation and evidence-based policy and practice has increased research opportunities in social policy.
- There is a process of 'modernization' of services across the sector and increasing community and user-involvement.
- Citizenship has become part of the national curriculum for schools and social policy is recognized in postgraduate teacher training.
- The Social Policy Association, the Learning and Teaching Support Network Subject Centre for Social Policy and Social Work and the Joint Universities Council Social Policy Committee have agreed to collaborate to promote social policy as an undergraduate subject.

Disciplinary status

Social policy has a long history of interdisciplinarity and inter-relationships with other social science courses, and remains closely linked with other social science subjects such as sociology, economics, history, politics and urban studies. There is some disagreement as to whether social policy is itself a discipline or a 'field of study'. Erskine (2003: 12) presents his view that it is a 'multidisciplinary field of study rather than a discipline'. Although the benchmarking statement for social policy has been influential in clarifying the identity of the subject there continue to be ambiguities in the relationship between social policy and other disciplines and with the vocational areas of social administration and social work.

In both social policy and social work, debate over boundaries and core content continues. The traditional concern of social policy was with 'five giant evils' identified in the Beveridge Report (1942) – want (poverty); squalor (poor living environments); ignorance (lack of education); idleness (unemployment); disease (ill health) – and the welfare services relating to these issues – social security; housing; education; employment services and health services. To this list can be added the personal social services. More recently, some academics have developed views of the subject which seek to include wider areas such as environmental issues, on the basis that they are relevant to welfare (Clarke, 2002). In 1994, Michael Cahill wrote a ground-breaking book *The New Social Policy,* which offered a radical re-think of the subject, arguing that social policy analysis could be widened to take in key aspects of everyday life with chapter titles covering 'Shopping', 'Working' and 'Playing'. Evidence of the re-framing of the subject is also found in new variations in nomenclature with the inclusion of terms such as 'social exclusion' and 'social justice' in course titles.

Social work has also had a contested history as an academic discipline, with a lack of clarity about its nature, content, methodology and boundaries (Lyons, 1999a: 82, drawing on Becher, 1989). The Economic and Social Research Council (ESRC) does not yet consider social work as a discipline. Traditionally, social work education has drawn on social policy, sociology, psychology and law. These subjects may be offered as discrete modules (shared with students from other courses) or adapted specifically for the social work context. The requirements for the new degree in social work emphasize the need for 'academic learning supporting practice, rather than the other way round' (Department of Health, 2002b: 1).

The ambiguous status of social work education is also attributable to its professional orientation, which was not, until recently, widely recognized to be part of the university remit (despite the longstanding tradition of medical education). Many early social work courses were located in extra-mural studies departments at the periphery of universities. The confusion over the level of the professional award has not helped. From 1970 to 1990, there were two awards: the Certificate in Social Services (a two-year programme outside higher education, based in employment) and an HE-based Certificate of Qualification in Social Work (which could be taken at four different academic levels). In 1990, the Diploma in Social Work was established using a common curriculum framework (Central Council for Education and Training in Social Work (CCETSW), 1989), set at diploma in higher education level, although it could also be offered as a postgraduate diploma. Only from 2003 has social work gained the status of an honours degree as the minimum award across the UK, equal to other professional qualifications.

Another contested issue has been that of employer influence. The DipSW was established with the requirement for programmes to run in partnership with social work agencies, and the professional qualification was awarded by the former Central Council for Education and Training in Social Work (CCETSW), separately from the academic award. However, from 2003, universities are accredited by the Care Councils to award the degree. The programme partnerships have been replaced with a requirement for universities to engage with a range of stakeholders (including user groups) in course design, monitoring and review.

A rapidly changing feature has been the role of research. Prior to 1980 the research tradition in social work was somewhat thin, and many academics were former practitioners with little research experience. The priority given to social work research in UK universities has shifted dramatically, fuelled by the RAE, the extension of the ESRC programmes to encompass social work, and the recognition that research must build the knowledge base of social work, to enhance the quality of practice and outcomes for users. Social work educators, therefore, have a remit to introduce research-mindedness among qualifying students, and to work with post-qualifying students to doctoral level, as well as being active researchers themselves. This in turn has impacted on the profile of newly appointed academics. Slowly but surely, social work has gained a more secure footing as an academic discipline.

Accommodating change

Taylor (1999) is one of the few writers on higher education to acknowledge the loss often experienced by professional staff working in times of great upheaval. His recommendation of six principles for academics' self-management of change reflects the themes developed in this chapter. He suggests that academics are best positioned to manage change where they are able to:

- develop a knowledge base for key roles, including an awareness of the beliefs and attitudes underlying everyday practices, and the values and purposes that these practices serve;
- expect roles to change and to engage with opportunities for change primarily in terms of consideration of values and purposes;
- expect to experience grief during any change in role and distinguish between grief and doubt. Doubt grows out of a questioning of practice and is a productive basis for the improvement of practice. Grief grows out of emotional attachment to things that are threatened by change. Grief provides a basis for moving on;
- develop an awareness of the basis of academic identities in terms of both their context specificity and their underlying values and purposes. That awareness allows a distancing from experience which might otherwise be personally destabilizing;
- extend capacity for self-interested activism, including collective engagement with colleagues in support of shared values and purposes;
- develop strategies that allow continuing professional support and growth outside the immediate place of employment. Academic careers will increasingly be built through extra-institutional networks.

Adapted from Taylor (1999: 157)

These principles offer a way in which academics in social policy and social work may reconceptualize their approach to managing the continuing onslaught of change, and successfully dance on the moving carpet.

2

Designing the curriculum: complexity, coherence and innovation

Hilary Burgess and Zoë Irving

Introduction

Curriculum design should be the cornerstone of effective learning and teaching. However, balancing the demands of the discipline with students' learning needs and the resources, skills and different approaches of staff is no easy task. In the past, curriculum design has perhaps not received sufficient attention from academics; institutional conventions, tradition and basic notions of content and coverage may have shaped practice. More recent conceptions of curriculum design have taken into account research and models about the nature of learning, the need to respond to national and institutional requirements, practical considerations about students and staff time and resources, contextual factors and the need for imagination and creativity. The different ways in which students learn are explored in Chapter 5. In this chapter the focus is on the way the curriculum is constructed, beginning with a map or visual representation of what this task entails, followed by an exploration of the issues identified. Overall, the task facing curriculum planners is one of managing a complex array of factors which impinge on the design, to produce a programme that is coherent but is also flexible and open to innovation.

Mapping curriculum design

The use of conceptual imagery and visual representation in curriculum design is a developing area for educational practitioners (Jackson, 2002a). With this in mind, the design process is shown diagrammatically in Figure 2.1. Each feature is subsequently elaborated. While the diagram is shown to be sequential, it is not suggested that a linear design process would or should prevail, since some elements will need to be reviewed as others are decided.

Contexts

Shaw (2002) draws attention to the impact of contextual forces on curriculum design. He identifies epistemological and ideological drivers, which translate into cultural, political, vocational, social or humanist issues. These in turn are implemented through agencies such as the Quality Assurance Agency (QAA), regulatory and professional bodies, employers and universities themselves. Many of these issues were identified in Chapter 1.

In social work, recent contextual forces include the reform of qualifying and post-qualifying education, the workforce crisis, concerns about the quality of practice and thus education, the establishment of the social care councils and the development of interprofessional work, linked to a corresponding drive for interprofessional education. Epistemological concerns have included the use of evidence-based practice, critical thinking and reflective practice. Ideologically, education for anti-oppressive and inclusive practice and the incorporation of user and carer involvement have been significant. In social policy, the curriculum must take account of rapid change in policy, legislation and organizational practice. Furthermore, the problem of recruitment to traditional social policy courses sits alongside an expansion of programmes in related domains such as social studies, social welfare, early childhood studies and criminal justice, so courses must be constructed and marketed to compete for students. The benchmarking statement for social policy drew attention to the full range of areas encompassed by social policy, and many programmes have placed growing emphasis on areas such as comparative international work, including globalization.

Time

The dimension of time is clearly central to curriculum design. A distinction can be drawn between wholesale curriculum reform and incremental change. Where curricula are re-designed (e.g. in response to external requirements such as benchmarking) time is a valuable commodity, essential to negotiate competing demands and the university annual cycle of course validation. Major changes must be planned well in advance to enable coherent and smooth implementation. In the recent reform of social work education across the UK, such coherence may have been compromised by the short time between publication of regulations and requirements and the date for submissions for approval

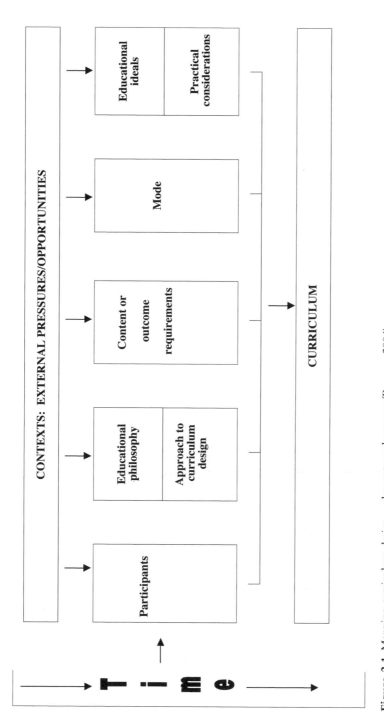

Figure 2.1 Mapping curriculum design – elements and process (Burgess, 2004)

by the Care Councils (Burgess, 2004). When time is tight there are dangers that participation may be restricted and there may be pressure to convert or adapt existing modules.

For incremental change, the annual academic procedure also imposes constraints and opportunities. New modules, re-designation of what is 'core' as opposed to optional and the re-working of core modules are considered on an annual cycle. Young and Irving (2003) found change in most social policy programmes to be incremental, with new course construction being rare. In many institutions there was little time for academics to discuss teaching development. On the other hand, time was found to enable the 'repackaging' of social policy programmes in response to recruitment problems. Here, a balance must be sought between leaping onto the bandwagons of apparent 'youth culture' and recognizing that some developments in social policy must be incorporated in teaching content. Some academics felt such repackaging was both inevitable and refreshing.

Participation

Participation in curriculum design and review reflects ownership, power and the development of pedagogic practice. For new academics, understanding and participating in such processes can be quite baffling unless the process is made explicit. While incremental review might be undertaken by a small group or the whole team at the end of each year, wholesale curriculum re-design brings the opportunity to involve a wider group. Vital debates may then take place about educational practice, different value bases and conceptions of the discipline, the weighting of perspectives or topics and the balance between theory and practice.

The literature on educational innovation suggests that for change to be sustained, staff participation must be characterized by integrative working. This would include sharing and developing vision, values and ownership of the new curriculum, with leadership that fosters teamwork, collaboration and indigenous leadership (Mathias and Rutherford, 1983; Fullan, 1993). On the other hand good management and organizational skills are clearly required to manage the process and meet deadlines for approval or validation. Even if a small group is charged with detailed planning, the engagement of the whole staff team (however that is defined) is essential for ownership. This might be achieved through small groups working on different aspects of design, or by regular consultations with the broader team. Achieving an explicit consensus on the educational approach underpinning the curriculum (see below) may be hard to achieve; it may be that the final curriculum represents a compromise between quite different views.

In social policy and other primarily academic programmes, the whole staff team may be relatively easy to define, although there will be cross-departmental consultation for joint honours programmes. Potentially, key local and regional bodies may also contribute (see Chapter 3).

For UK social work education there has been a requirement since 1990 to involve social work agencies in programme management. The extent to which this translated into working partnerships has varied; while some were productive, others worked less well, with tensions about the cost inputs. The uncertain legal standing of such bodies also caused concern in terms of accountability. For the new degree, introduced from 2003, the requirement for partnerships as such has been dropped, though universities must undertake to involve stakeholders in curriculum planning, delivery and review; for the first time this includes users and carers as well as agencies. Academics face both opportunities and challenges in working with new partners to deliver effective social work education. If user participation is to be meaningful, it is likely that systems and partnerships will need to be developed over time (see Chapter 3). Where interprofessional education is planned, there are yet more complexities in terms of participation (see Chapter 10).

Student involvement in curriculum design for both social policy and social work should be a natural corollary of an effective review process, with student feedback and evaluation contributing to planning. With wholesale curriculum change, there is an opportunity for more sustained student engagement. While staff may be wary of current students helping to shape a programme that they themselves will not experience, such participation gives academics the opportunity to hear how a programme is received (rather than how it was taught) and students an important learning opportunity in itself. With user and consumer participation being taken more seriously in social welfare agencies, this must surely be reflected in the academic world.

Another question raised is the extent to which module conveners have autonomy in the detail of curriculum design once the overall plan is established. On a programme requiring close articulation across modules, such as a problem-based learning course (see pp. 72–4), tight planning is needed to ensure pedagogic integrity. Elsewhere, collaborative work to prevent duplication or gaps may have to be balanced with the desire for and tradition of academic freedom.

Choice of educational approach

Ideally, an educational approach to underpin the programme design should be agreed. Wholesale curriculum reform may bring the opportunity to debate philosophies and expectations. Reaching a consensus may be hard, since there are likely to be different views. In some institutions the underlying philosophy may never have been spelt out (so the new academic must somehow deduce it), although the development of programme specifications as required by the QAA has encouraged such articulation.

Toohey (1999) suggests that, broadly, five different philosophical approaches to curriculum can be found in higher education:

1 *traditional or discipline-based*, in which the design follows the structure of knowledge in the discipline;
2 *performance or systems based,* in which learning objectives or goals are defined, study methods devised to enable students to meet these, and assignments set to determine if these have been met. Competency-based education provides an example of this approach;
3 *cognitive*, in which the university sets out to help students learn how to learn, and develop their critical thinking and problem-solving skills;
4 *personal relevance/experiential*, in which the curriculum is shaped jointly by staff and students to meet individual needs, with a value placed on learning from experience. Learning contracts may also be used;
5 *socially critical*, in which the programme seeks to develop a critical consciousness of social institutions and of major questions confronting the discipline taught.

Many programmes would subscribe to more than one of these approaches. For example, courses using problem-based learning would place a high value on both cognitive and experiential approaches.

In social work the demands of the profession and employers have led to a performance approach, emphasized in the UK by linking curriculum requirements to the National Occupational Standards for Social Work (TOPSS (Training Organisation for Personal Services) England, 2002), but also reflected in the benchmarking statement. Taking account of personal experience is central to developing professional social work practice, and experiential approaches are commonly used to enable students to comprehend and reflect on their experiences, and to develop their skills and value base. This is the discourse of reflective learning for practice (Gould and Taylor, 1996). Academics are likely to stress cognitive aspects of curriculum design, for example through evidence-based practice, critical thinking skills and problem-solving. Arguments have been made for social work education to adopt a more socially critical approach, encouraging students to question links between social work and state, and to make connections with wider social interventions at both neighbourhood and national level. Indeed the modality of social work education in some other countries (particularly developing or 'third' world countries) focuses strongly on this approach.

In social policy, research by Young (2003) suggests the traditional or discipline-based approach still predominates. However, it would be hard to envisage a social policy course that did not also subscribe to the socially critical approach, and the benchmarking statement for social policy encourages other approaches. Analysis of the role of 'content' in social policy teaching (Irving and Young, forthcoming) suggests that attempting to grapple with the vastness of the social policy curriculum area can be a frustrating and unsatisfactory experience for both lecturers and students. The volume of 'core' knowledge potentially transmissible from lecturers to students is immense, and many staff appear compelled to engage in information overload. Where the focus has shifted to learning outcomes such as developing skills for analysis and knowledge of debates, programmes combine cognitive, personal relevance and socially critical approaches. These include thematic, case-study and problem-based approaches. Irving and Young (forthcoming) suggest that a more selective and focused approach to content, both across courses and within units of study, could better accommodate staff teaching, practice and research interests and the dynamism of social policy as an area of study.

Constructive alignment

The concept of constructive alignment, as developed by Biggs (1999), provides a useful framework to conceptualize the process of learning and teaching and to plan courses. The framework holds, regardless of the educational philosophy adopted. Biggs' view is that the design in itself should ensure that 'learners should not be able to escape without learning or developing', and that this learning should relate closely to what the planners intended. He considers that the learner *constructs* his or her own learning through learning activities and assessment procedures which connect new learning with existing knowledge and understanding. He argues that we need to work towards *alignment* of the components of teaching and learning so that they address the same agenda and support each other. The key components include:

- the curriculum that we teach;
- the teaching methods or learning activities employed;
- the assessment procedures;
- the climate we create in our interactions with students;
- the institutional climate, rules and procedures.

In an aligned curriculum, the curriculum is stated in clear objectives, at both programme and module level. These indicate the level of understanding required, rather than being a list of topics to be covered. Teaching methods or learning activities are selected to realize those objectives. Finally, assessment tasks are designed to test whether students have learned what the objectives state they should have. While this may sound straightforward, it is hard to achieve in practice. Writing clear, concise, appropriate and achievable learning outcomes is not easy; the teaching or learning activity may not successfully deliver these outcomes (but may deliver others!), and academic conventions about assessment may mean the assignments test rather different outcomes, resulting in 'assessment backwash'!

Content or outcome requirements

In the UK, the national reference points for curriculum design at under-graduate level are the QAA subject benchmark statements (BMS):

> broad statements which represent general expectations about standards for the award of an honours degree in particular subject areas . . . [describing] the intellectual capability and understanding that should be developed through the study of that discipline to honours degree; the techniques and skills which are associated with developing understanding in that discipline, and the level of intellectual demand and challenge that is appropriate to honours degree study in that discipline.
>
> (QAA, 2000)

While concern has been expressed about how the statements were developed in some disciplines, and the variability between disciplines in the product, they are accepted as key curriculum planning documents. From 2003, a QAA advisory board will oversee reviews of benchmark statements when the subject community deems these necessary. Benchmark statements may also be produced for new subject areas; these might include, for example, criminology, early years' studies and gender studies.

Other national requirements relevant for curriculum design include the QAA guidelines for programme specifications and the QAA codes of practice. Of the latter, the following may be relevant for curriculum design: postgrad-uate research programmes, collaborative provision, students with disabilities, assessment of students, programme approval, monitoring and review, and placement learning.

National: social policy

Jackson's review of the first set of BMS (Jackson, 2001) shows the social policy statement to be not untypical. Twenty-eight intended learning outcomes are specified, about half of which relate to knowledge and understanding and about half to skills. Overall, Jackson considered the learning outcomes to have been written in an explicit format, thus providing a basis for measurement.

Social policy lecturers interviewed by Young and Irving (2004) were familiar with the contents of the BMS, although some more familiar than others if curriculum review had recently taken place. While some lecturers were critical of benchmarking as a process, most were content with the outcomes and felt the statement was a fair reflection of what 'actually existing' social policy teaching is (as opposed to what it could or should be). Thus the statement was largely regarded as a welcome impetus to reflection on what is taught, and a help to course planning and revalidation. Other benefits mentioned were that so-called 'marginal' or 'threshold' teachers would be forced to rethink their teaching, and that there would be a shift in the balance from what lecturers wanted to provide (based on their research interests) to what students needed to learn. The arguments surrounding the shift from producer to consumer interests are well rehearsed in social policy writing so it comes as no surprise that they are being played out in relation to curriculum content in higher education.

One concern about the social policy statement was that the focus on 'content' might lead to its treatment as a prescriptive *checklist* rather than an *indicative* list as intended. This has created problems, particularly for smaller course teams and those who teach only on joint awards, who have a sense of heightened vulnerability in institutional terms where they are not able to demonstrate delivery outcomes on all the points listed in the statement (the checklist approach). In one case this has led to the (probably unnecessary) closure of a single award course in social policy. Other lecturers reported that the benchmarking statement was a close fit to the pattern of provision already existing on their course(s) and had little impact on criteria for redesign. However, it is reasonable to expect that even in larger departments it is unlikely that all the areas of social policy listed could be covered at more than a superficial level. Course teams have therefore to take both a pragmatic and creative approach to the use of the benchmarking statement in curriculum design, treading a fine line between maintaining integrity in delivery, while responding to institutional interpretations as well as the national expectations within which course design is situated.

National: social work

The requirements for social work at a national level are complicated by two factors: the need for articulation of academic and professional requirements and the emerging differentiation of requirements following devolution in the UK. A new award for social work was introduced following devolution, so government bodies and social care councils in England, Wales, Northern Ireland and Scotland have worked with higher education institutions (HEIs), employers and users in their planning, resulting in variable requirements across the UK.

Jackson's analysis of the QAA subject benchmarking statements indicates the social work statement to be one of the most complex, with 80 intended learning outcomes (Jackson, 2001). These must be blended with the National Occupational Standards (NOS) (TOPSS England, 2002), which comprise 6 key roles, 21 units and 77 elements. Together, the two documents must form the basis of curriculum design in social work. In Scotland, Wales and Northern Ireland the NOS and BMS have been combined into one document. Similar links between academic and professional requirements are being progressed by the QAA, for example in the benchmarking for healthcare professions, which explicitly articulated academic and practitioner standards in eleven subjects (including nursing, occupational therapy and physiotherapy).

Other variations have emerged in terms of curriculum requirements for the new award. In Northern Ireland (NI) additional requirements include a statement of expectations by users and carers, and a list of areas of knowledge specific to NI (including the sectarian conflict, the political context and specific issues of social policy and practice). In Wales the NOS and BMS are supplemented by requirements to equip students to work in the context of the Welsh language and culture, and the NOS have been mapped across the three levels of the degree. In England there are requirements for study in five areas:

1   human growth, development, mental health and disability;
2   assessment, planning, intervention and review;
3   communication skills with children, adults and those with particular communication needs;
4   law;
5   partnership working and information sharing across professional disciplines and agencies.

In all four countries 200 days of practice learning in a practice setting are required, but there are variations in how this should be used and whether prior experience can be credited. Placements and practice learning are discussed in Chapter 9, but here it should be noted that the impact of these arrangements on curriculum planning is substantive. First, the timing of agency-based practice learning must be negotiated with a gamut of organizations, and what might be educationally desirable may not be feasible for agencies. Moreover, practice learning may clash with plans for inter-professional learning (see Chapter 10). It may also be hard to ensure alignment, as advocated by Biggs, when there are so many learning environments in which students are placed.

Recently, an international dimension to requirements and quality assurance for social work education has emerged with the development of Global Qualifying Standards through a joint committee of the International Association of Schools of Social Work (IASSW) and the International Federation of Social Workers (IASSW, 2004).

For post-qualifying programmes in social work, the parameters were set by the former Central Council for Education and Training in Social Work, through the post-qualifying framework established in 1990. This framework is under review at the time of writing.

Modes of delivery

The changing ways in which higher education is delivered, such as part-time routes, distance learning and e-learning were discussed in Chapter 1. Clearly, the mode selected has a big impact on curriculum planning. Increasingly, institutions offer programmes that may be accessed on a part-time as well as a full-time basis. A major consideration here may be the time at which modules are offered; when modules are available to students studying on both routes, there may be a conflict of interest. When open learning or distance learning is available, the proportion of time spent by student groups in the classroom with an educator decreases, and the time spent on independent or asynchronous study increases. Curriculum planning for such a programme entails far greater 'front-loading' of resources to enable independent study to be fruitful. Similar shifts may take place by introducing e-learning into the curriculum; this is explored in Chapter 8.

Balancing educational, institutional and practical considerations

In the detail of curriculum planning a compromise may have to be reached between what might be educationally desirable and what is possible in practice. Central to this are the policies, guidance and norms of the university. The institutional teaching and learning strategy will set broad parameters, and may also be translated into faculty, school or departmental level. In some universities, the policy has resulted in institution-wide curriculum features, such as a common level one study skills or information technology (IT) module, a common framework for core and optional modules or in some cases university-wide educational approaches. Validation procedures, a mechanism for assuring quality and consistency within the university, may sometimes delay progress, or, where validation for a new programme is required a whole year in advance of that programme being mounted, may considerably foreshorten the available time for planning.

Universities may also have parameters for module type, design, assessment, semesterization, student choice and key skills. An HEI that requires all modules to be 30 credit points, with a faculty pattern of two 'short fat' modules in the first semester, followed by two in the second, will give a different experience of learning to the HEI where modules are 'long and thin' across the year. In other institutions units may be smaller, of 10 or 20 credit points. There are different views about whether learning takes place most effectively over time, with space for reflection, development of ideas and consolidation of learning, or is more effective in shorter more intensive blocks (see Deliberations Forum, 2003). In some universities, once a module outline has been included in the prospectus or the website, it must run; in others, modules may only run if at least 15 students register; these rules all impinge on curriculum design. The nature and timing of assessment points may also be significant. Most faculties require set numbers of papers or assignments to be undertaken in particular ways, which mould the process of curriculum planning. It is worth pointing out that such requirements may be worth contesting if educationally sound arguments can be put forward.

An increasingly complex issue in curriculum design emerges from inter-disciplinary programmes or modules, whether this be interprofessional education (see Chapter 10) or joint honours programmes (such as social policy with politics or sociology), where there must be co-ordination over core units, prerequisite modules and availability of options. Within a modular system when many units are 'open' to other students, the task is further complicated by teaching cohorts of students with different learning needs. For example students on a professional social work course may be in a classroom with students on an academic social sciences route, whose starting point and perspective on the topic will differ significantly. If the different learning needs conflict, this can be addressed by holding separate seminar groups; in other cases the cross-fertilization of ideas engendered by inter-disciplinary debate may outweigh the disadvantages.

Other significant practical or resource constraints often impinge on curriculum planning. These include the availability of rooms of appropriate size for teaching, timetabling considerations, staff availability, links to other programmes and the size of the student cohort.

As pressures in HE have increased, so has pressure on resources; thus some aspects of the intended curriculum may be compromised if it is not possible to locate rooms of the right size, at the right time to deliver the planned learning activity. Interactive teaching may be difficult to implement if the majority of large teaching rooms have fixed seating. IT facilities may be limited, so that the facility may be used only by the lecturer, or only by students working alone.

Fundamentally, the curriculum must be manageable for both staff and students. Students need sufficient space for reflection, accessing the library or Internet and independent study. With increasing numbers of mature students with caring responsibilities, and students who travel some distance to the university, it may be better to avoid 9 am starts, and days with only one or two hours of required attendance. Curriculum planners may work towards ensuring one or two days without timetabled commitments to allow for independent study (or employment). On the other hand, staff–student contact hours on some courses may shrink to such an extent that students feel isolated. The timing of module requirements for assessment should be planned to avoid student and staff overload. Curriculum planning from the perspective of staff is essential to ensure academics are available to teach across the different years of a programme and manage other activities, including course administration, planning and their own research.

The size of the student cohort may be important when linked to the availability of staff and rooms. For example, planning small-group work for a cohort of 250 (as may be found in some level one social policy undergraduate courses or in interprofessional learning) may require 20 groups and staff working together. Larger cohorts may be an advantage when it comes to offering choice of modules.

Finally, the curriculum must build on the strengths and teaching experience of the staff. Their skills, research, interests and preferences are vital ingredients of curriculum planning, though some core teaching must shape all programmes. It is often the differing nature of staff expertise that lends each programme its distinctive character, and is an ingredient in terms of the competition for students. While some social policy courses may be strong in relation to comparative study and globalization, others may put a stronger emphasis on criminology. In social work, some may have a tradition of inter-professional education, or expertise in child care, mental health, disability or adult care teaching.

Once the ingredients of a programme have been specified in terms of learning outcomes, decisions will be made about how to combine these into modules to make up the programme. The way this is done will reflect the degree of linkage between different subject strands, between theory and its application, and the degree of specialism to be introduced. In social work the interplay between knowledge, skills, values, practice and theory must also be explored. While some topics might lend themselves to discrete modules, others might need to be built in throughout the course on a 'permeation' model (e.g. anti-oppressive practice or international perspectives).

Imagination, creativity and innovation

Notions of creativity and imagination in curriculum design have been promoted. Jackson (2002a) suggests that creative curriculum construction is likely to entail personal innovation (new to that academic) and creative working at and across the boundary of acceptability within the institution (that is, norms and expectations must be tested and risks taken). This will involve making sense of complexity, working with multiple, often conflicting factors, pressures, interests and constraints. Meanwhile, enabling students to be creative (that is, to be comfortable in complex and unpredictable situations) requires educators to engender a belief that obstacles can be overcome (Jackson, 2002a). Students need to learn in ways that develop their self-confidence and self-esteem, and encourage them to take risks in safe environments. Dewulf and Baillie (1999) argue that fostering student creativity and the ability to manage complexity entails enabling them to visualize ideas (holistically, spatially and metaphorically), helping them to make effective use of memory and connections, and both convergent and divergent thinking strategies. Thus, a curriculum that promotes creative and complex learning must involve mastering four categories of aptitudes and behaviours, namely:

- a well-organized and accessible domain-specific knowledge base;
- heuristic strategies for problem analysis and transformation;
- metacognitive knowledge and self-regulating skills;
- positive beliefs, attitudes and emotions.

Creativity in social policy programmes can be found in the construction of new modules that anticipate emergent national developments (e.g. citizenship), learning activities that enable students to understand the reality of welfare issues, and where students are treated as practitioners, who, in a structured way, research and produce evidence of their own. In social work literature there are many examples of creative teaching and learning, fuelled by the interplay of theory and practice, and knowledge, skills and values; however, there is a risk that the burden of requirements for the new degree may lead to some conformity.

Consistency, flexibility, renewal and complexity

Achieving a programme that is coherent and consistent is hard to achieve. In some ways modularization may have made this harder, given the fragmentation and isolation of curriculum areas. Staff have a role in helping students understand the map of the course, and the links between modules. However, we should remember that the curriculum is seldom fixed: there must be flexibility and room for innovation.

It has also been argued that curriculum design is too complex to be controlled or described using a linear model. Tosey (2002) and others have worked on the application of complexity theory to this field. They highlight features such as emergence (behaviour and qualities emerge from local, at times unco-ordinated interactions), paradox, self-organization, connectivity (the quality of relationships between agents in the system) and the 'edge of chaos' (a point where the components of the system do not lock into place, yet never quite dissolve into turbulence) as aspects of complexity theory relevant to curriculum design.

In conclusion, we would suggest some key suggestions for curriculum design:

- sufficient time and resources should be devoted to this activity;
- wide participation should be encouraged to share ownership;
- the contexts within which the activity takes place should be mapped;
- we need to encourage creativity by both staff and students;
- the curriculum will always be more than the sum of all the parts (for both students and staff);
- we should listen to the curriculum 'as lived' by students to develop our practice.

3

Participation in social policy and social work learning

Peter Beresford

Introduction

There is an important point that needs to be made early in this discussion. The focus of this book and this chapter is learning, teaching and training. But social work and social policy education and training cannot be considered in isolation from social work and social policy practice and provision. This is not only because much learning goes on in practice and in policy settings rather than in academic and training institutions – and thus learning needs to be seen as a continuing lifelong activity; it is also important because citizen engagement and involvement are important in both learning *and* practice settings. Social work and social policy education cannot be considered in isolation. In recent years particularly, social work and social policy have become heavily politicized areas of public activity. Social work, for example, has been dominated by political and managerialist influences. (Jordan and Jordan, 2000; Parton and O'Byrne, 2000) A participative process of social work and social policy education and learning that culminated in non-participative social work and social policy provision and practice would be pointless. The two must be considered together and in relation to each other.

The policy background

Social policy and social work are interrelated disciplines and areas of public policy concerned with the state processing of people. Both have had major impacts on people and considerable powers over them historically, particularly people who are poor, with little power and devalued identities. Historically, neither has prioritized involving or 'engaging with' the people most associated with their services. Instead, they were associated either with a paternalistic approach based on the idea of 'doing good' to people through a top-down process, or of addressing broader state and societal concerns relating to demands for conformity, social cohesion and economic effectiveness. Both social policy and social work have always been concerned with both social control *and* social and personal support or assistance.

It was only in 1970 that the first major social work text concerned with service users' views and perspectives, *The Client Speaks*, was published (Meyer and Timms, 1970). This has often been seen as a milestone in social work interest in what service users say. It can also be understood more narrowly as a marker for the development of a new domain of social work research, 'client studies' (Beresford and Croft, 1987). Social policy as an academic discipline has been even slower to involve the subjects of policy. The dominant approach to social policy, fabianism, was strongly based on state-driven paternalism. Social policy service users were perceived as beneficiaries of, rather than partners in the policy process. It was only with the undermining of fabianism following the emergence of the new political right at the end of the 1970s that this tradition began to be challenged (Holman, 1993).

Social policy as a policy area does have a track record around citizen involvement in some specific contexts, notably in community development and statutory provisions for public participation in land use planning established in the 1960s. It is still open to question, though, how enthusiastically social policy as an *academic discipline* has embraced ideas of user and citizen involvement. Old habits die hard and even the demise of fabianism has not meant that paternalistic traditions have disappeared too. The 1994 QAA Subject Review Overview Statement for social policy, for example, found that 'there was considerable scope for improving local links' on most courses (QAA, 1995). While this may have improved subsequently, links with local service users and community organizations are generally very limited. Public participation and user involvement still have to be identified as priorities by social policy's professional association and its core publications still do not feature them centrally (Alcock *et al.*, 2002a and 2002b). Social work, on the other hand, as part of a broader social care project, does seem to have sought to address user involvement more determinedly and coherently (Braye and Preston Shoot, 1995). Social care has become one of the policy areas where discussions and developments have been particularly advanced.

The new context of involvement

There has, however, been a more significant development over the last fifteen years or so, which has affected the relation of both policies to 'the people'.

For a complex range of reasons, ideas of involvement, empowerment and partnership have come to be at the core of government and political rhetoric about public policy and services. Whatever the preferences of social work and social policy might be, it is no longer possible to avoid acknowledging and addressing these issues. Some policy-makers, managers and practitioners are now engaging with them with enthusiasm, seeing this as a way of improving the nature and quality of services and meeting service users' rights and needs more effectively and economically. Others, less persuaded, prefer the old unequal balance of power and respond to the demands for partnership and participation as far as they have to. It is important to recognize and under-stand these different responses. They are, perhaps, not surprising, given the radical culture change that citizen and service user involvement can represent. Health and social care service users and their organizations are already keenly aware of the range of responses to their participation and talk of 'box ticking exercises' and 'consultation fatigue' arising where there is no real commitment to involvement and engagement. The present discussion seeks to offer support to educators and service providers who want to engage with and involve their 'end users', as well as recognizing the importance of practical help and broader cultural change if this is to be possible.

Awareness: a pre-requirement for involvement

If the aim is to involve people in social work and social policy as members of communities and 'the public', then the first essential must be that they have some awareness and understanding of such policies. The signs are not encour-aging, however important such awareness might be seen to be. The findings from a random sample survey of people's views about decentralized social services carried out in an urban area in the 1980s highlighted that:

- Most people showed little or no understanding of what social services did (although a significant minority had had some contact with them).
- Most people had negative, equivocal or mixed opinions about social services.
- Few people saw social services as for them, but rather related them to other marginalized groups.

(Beresford and Croft, 1986: 29–48)

Similar findings also emerged more than 17 years later in a study of specialist palliative care social work. Again, people had little understanding of main-stream social work. While attitudes to palliative care social work were very positive, views of mainstream social work were frequently very negative (Croft et al., 2005).

It is unlikely that many people will want to get involved in an area of policy which they know little about, do not relate to themselves and have negative attitudes towards. Media attitudes towards social work continue to be at least sceptical, at worst hostile. The government's recruitment campaign for social workers may help raise public understanding about what social workers do, although resource constraints continue to restrict social workers' capacity to provide the needs-led service portrayed. There is limited public support for funding and valuing social work generally. This is a major barrier to be overcome if broader involvement in social work and social work education are to be realistic goals.

We cannot assume, however, that interest and awareness are any greater in relation to social policy more generally. Significantly, media/public debate about welfare in recent years has focused on groups and issues like:

- asylum seekers and refugees;
- lone parents;
- 'dependency culture', 'benefit scroungers' and benefit fraud.

These have all highlighted and encouraged hostility, division, scapegoating, stereotyping and 'them and us' attitudes towards social policy and the subjects of social policy. We might wonder how much public interest in such a media focus there would be if people had a better understanding of the realities of social policy. However, developments in recent times may have been pulling in the opposite direction. Since the late 1970s, particularly in the UK, but also increasingly internationally, the emphasis has been on taking individual responsibility for personal welfare. Social policy has increasingly been privatized, with a shift to public private partnerships (PPP) and private finance initiatives (PFI). Citizens are increasingly encouraged to make their own arrangements, particularly for health, housing and income maintenance. This has continued under New Labour and its 'third way' (Critical Social Policy, 2001). 'Welfare' has increasingly been presented as something for a marginalized (and questionable) minority for whom safety net provision may be required. Again, interest in policies which people do not identify with and are discouraged from relying on is likely to be limited and narrowly focused.

Engaging 'the community' in social work and social policy at any serious and substantial level may therefore need to be seen as a difficult and long-term task that may be opposed by other trends. The first step to raise knowledge and awareness is likely to be ensuring that understanding of these policy areas is encouraged from an early age. This should be included in the new components of the national curriculum concerned with citizenship and being a citizen. There is, however, much that can be done at a more immediate and local level, although this will demand a much more proactive and outreach approach from both local and national educational and policy-making agencies.

In the early 1990s when discrimination against people living with HIV/AIDS was still at its strongest, locally based social services in Fulham, London, set up a stall in the local street market to provide information and advice to local people in an informal and accessible way. The stall was a regular feature of the popular market and provided an approachable contact point locally. People could meet social work and social services staff informally on their own ground and find out more. This initiative was linked with other outreach activities undertaken in the area. Community workers and community social workers were involved. There was also a local forum made up of people living with HIV/AIDS which had an input into local policy and practice.

(Walton, 1993)

Engaging whom?

There are many approaches to and understandings of participation and involvement. These have most often been framed in terms of the degree of involvement people have – from zero to control; from tokenism to a primary say – in decision-making (Arnstein, 1969). There is, however, another way in which it may be helpful to consider involvement. This is in terms of *who* is to be involved. Bearing in mind the wide range of constituencies that social policy and social work are concerned with, it is important to address this issue. At least three different approaches to structuring the focus for involvement can be identified currently (as well as historically) in policy. These different approaches seem to be related to different policy areas – all of which are of concern to social policy and social policy education and training. Thus participation in social work and social care has tended to be framed in terms of the involvement of 'service users and carers'. Participation in the National Health Service has been presented in terms of 'public and patient' participation. Participation in areas of policy like area-based initiatives/regeneration and housing and community development has tended to be discussed in terms of 'community' (and sometimes 'local') involvement. Each of these approaches has its strengths and weaknesses.

It is important to be clear here that we may not be talking about involving 'different people', but certainly what is happening is that these approaches are being conceived and constructed differently. First we need to consider some of the internal issues and problems raised by each of these conceptualizations. Service users and their organizations have long been critical of the coupling of 'users and carers' in social care. These are seen as two different (if sometimes overlapping) categories that need to be uncoupled and considered separately. Many service users reject the idea of 'carer' as unhelpful. They see it as perpetuating traditional hierarchies of 'carers' speaking and acting on their behalf. They see it as institutionalizing and formalizing the imposition of responsibilities on the loved ones of service users for want of the provision of appropriate formal support. There are also concerns about the term 'service users' itself. Many people dislike being identified primarily in terms of services which are stigmatic, which they dislike and which they feel confirm them in a passive identity.

The government has appointed a 'Participation Czar' for the NHS and established a range of formal structures from local to national level framed in terms of 'patient and public involvement'. Concerns have been raised about the distinction drawn in NHS thinking between 'patients' and 'public'. This implies that 'patients' are a group separate from the 'public', rather than part of it. This not only means that they may be considered in isolation from the 'public' and without consideration of their rights and role as members of the public, like anyone else; it has the potential for setting the interests of one against the other and of prioritizing them differently. This has happened notably in the context of current mental health policy, where 'patients' have been presented increasingly as a danger to the 'public', rather than part of it. There is now a political commitment in England to extend restrictions on mental health service users' rights through the extension of compulsory 'treatment' beyond hospital in the interests of 'public safety' – a central priority in current policy thinking. This essentially sets the 'public's' rights against those of 'patients' and prioritizes the former over the latter – a worrying development.

'Community-based' approaches to involvement that highlight locality, 'local people' and neighbourhood raise another problem. While the concept of 'community' is sometimes presented in reassuring and cosy terms, it has often been concerned more with *conformity* and *exclusion* than inclusion and the acceptance of difference. Women have been confined to the 'community' rather than ensured equal access to the workplace. Many groups facing discrimination, particularly in relation to sexuality, race and ethnicity, have traditionally been marginalized both in dominant conceptions of community and in local arrangements for living (Bornat, 1997; Williams, 1997).

Community-based approaches to involvement have a long track record of seeking to involve local, often disempowered and impoverished people. It is arguable, however, whether they have generally been successful in developing inclusive approaches to involvement. Groups which are more broadly devalued in society, like disabled people, mental health service users, people with learning difficulties and people living with HIV/AIDs, have often not been adequately represented in such 'community action'. Indeed sometimes they have been the target of it. 'Nimbyism' (not in my back yard) – the desire to exclude people perceived as 'different', like people with learning difficulties or users of mental health services – is a powerful expression of this.

What this discussion highlights is that each of the conceptual bases for who to involve in social work and social policy (education) – service user, public, patient or community – has limitations and weaknesses. Whichever of these concepts is employed, it needs to be related to the others and it needs to be considered in terms of its capacity to include *and* exclude. Any attempt to involve people more generally in social work and social policy education and learning must work hard to challenge the very real problem of reinforcing exclusion and not leave it unconsidered.

If the idea of community is adopted as the basis for approaches to involve people, then it must be based on an inclusive rather than an exclusive concept of community. This must be one which acknowledges the wide range of expressions that community may have, going beyond communities of place to communities of interest, identity and expression, and taking account of more recent electronic and virtual 'communities'. It must also avoid reinforcing the role of women in the community by using them as a low or unpaid pool of labour to assist in the construction and development of social work and social policy learning. It must challenge social divisions based on gender, sexuality, age, 'race', culture, class and disability.

Challenging exclusion

The equal inclusion of people in participatory developments has so far been a major and unresolved problem in all areas of public policy, regardless of which conceptual framework has been used to take it forward – 'public', 'community' or 'service user'. Service user organizations and movements, however – for example, those of disabled and older people, mental health service users and people with learning difficulties – have been particularly effective in challenging exclusions. They have developed considerable skills and experience in enabling people to take part, supporting their access requirements, however complex and varied these might be, and seeking to enable service users to speak and act for themselves. This has, perhaps, been the special contribution of developments for participation in the field of social care. However, it may have as much to do with the difficulties encountered by such groups in broader initiatives and developments for involvement as with the disempowering nature of specific social care services themselves. Because the barriers to participation which social care service users face have been so comprehensive, it has not been possible to take their involvement for granted. Instead, it has had to be systematically supported. This has often not happened in other areas of policy and participation.

Principles for engagement and involvement

Addressing diversity is perhaps the first principle for engaging with people in social work and social policy learning and education. Existing experience points to the importance of a series of such principles, which offer the possibility of systematic and coherent involvement in teaching and learning from the widest range of participants.

Health and social care service users and their organizations have identified a number of such principles for effective involvement in recent years. These include:

- involving people from the earliest stage;
- resourcing involvement adequately;
- meeting potential participants' access requirements in full;
- enabling equality and diversity in involvement;
- prioritizing the involvement of people's own independent self-organized groups and organizations;
- involving people in all aspects of learning;
- involving people in all roles relating to learning;
- involving people in research and evaluation;
- developing ongoing structures for involvement;
- ensuring that there are positive outcomes for service users in both the process and product of involvement;
- monitoring and evaluating involvement.

Involving people from the earliest stage

If the involvement of service users is to be effective, meaningful and avoid tokenism, then it needs to be built in right from the beginning of any initiative. This is crucial in developing training and learning so that service users are not invited to become involved when (non-user) agendas have already

> In 2000, Shaping Our Lives – the independent national user-controlled organization including and working across different groups of health and social care service users – organized the first national seminar for service users focusing on user involvement in social care education and training. A diverse range of service users took part in the event. They highlighted the wide range of activities in social work and social care education that service users were already involved in, for example, recruiting staff and students, providing placements, developing course materials and student assessment. Their key concern was the big continuing problem that, while many good things were going on, progress was very patchy and there were very few, if any, examples of training and education programmes and courses where service user involvement was systematically built into learning. This was identified as the key challenge and goal for the future.

been set and their capacity to influence developments is already significantly restricted.

Resourcing involvement adequately

Good-quality user involvement has resource implications. It requires funding to pay participants' costs (travel, support, etc). There is now also increasing recognition of the importance of paying service users (like any other consultants) for their expertise and experience. Not all resources required are directly financial – for example, meeting places, information and capacity building may not be – but all ultimately have a price ticket. Experience highlights that effective user involvement needs to be properly budgeted for. It cannot be done on the cheap.

Meeting potential participants' access requirements in full

In recent years, with the implementation of the Disability Discrimination Act, there has been increasing recognition of the importance of addressing people's 'access requirements' if everybody is to be involved on equal terms. But these are still often thought about in narrow terms of physical access, for example, for wheelchair users. This is important, but only a start. Access needs to be understood more fully to include the requirements of a wider range of groups, including people with small children, people who communicate differently and need information available in a range of accessible formats, and people who need support to be involved, for instance, people with learning difficulties or aphasia. Some access requirements may be inconsistent with others. People with one access requirement are no more likely to be familiar with somebody else's requirement than anyone else is. Ways of working which are inclusive will ultimately benefit everyone, but they are likely to demand that people work in new and different ways. Educators and trainers need to develop access policies which include the provision of fully accessible information technology. All this has big implications for learning.

Enabling equality and diversity in involvement

Service providers and policy-makers often question the 'representativeness' of people who get involved. There are concerns that it is 'only the usual suspects' or 'professional service users' who get involved. Partly this relates to anxieties about more experienced participants being clearer about their goals and more determined to achieve them, but there is also a real issue about ensuring that the widest range of potential participants is able to get involved. Proper resourcing and access policies for participation are essential here. So also is a proactive approach that seeks to address diversity in involvement strategically, by reaching out to groups and individuals who have sometimes been described as 'hard to reach' and by experimenting with creative forms of involvement that may encourage their participation. The experience of Shaping Our Lives, the national user-controlled organization, is that groups that have tended not to get involved, including black people and members of minority ethnic communities, are much more likely to if they are properly remunerated, feel their rights and interests are respected and if there are effective outcomes for them from 'getting involved'. It is particularly important to address issues of race equality in efforts to involve people. Older people have also tended to be under-represented in participatory developments.

Prioritizing the involvement of people's own independent self-organized groups and organizations

One way of ensuring the involvement of as wide a range of participants as possible is to enable people who are not affiliated to groups or organizations to get involved. This is important because such affiliations are still not the norm for many people in western societies like the UK. However, it is no less important to ensure that people who are involved in self-run, self-organized service-user, community and citizen organizations are fully and equally involved. Such organizations are frequently democratically structured and can claim to involve and represent wider constituencies. It is important to distinguish between these organizations, which people control themselves, and those established and controlled by others. Such self-organizations have an important role in supporting people's empowerment, developing their assertiveness, self-confidence and self-esteem. They support people to gain new skills and expertise and familiarize them with collective working and engaging in the policy process. Arrangements for involvement in learning need to connect and engage with them. They should be seen as an early port of call capable of helping trainers and educators to link up with most effect with the widest range of people (Beresford, 1994).

Involving people in all aspects of learning

User and community involvement in social work and social policy training and education has so far been patchy and limited. It has often extended no further than service users being brought in to talk about their experience. If involvement is to be effective, then it must extend to all aspects of the learning process, from designing the curriculum to assessing learners and teachers. This should also include the involvement of service users as practice teachers, having placements in user-controlled organizations and making use of the large and growing body of learning materials produced by service users. The new social work degree calls for the involvement of service users in all aspects of professional education and this is a model which can helpfully be extended to other health and welfare professions and education and training courses.

Involving people in all roles relating to learning

It is not enough that service users and broader communities are involved in all stages of learning. They also need to have equal access to all *roles* relating to it. This is particularly relevant to health and social care service users, where barriers have traditionally reduced the access of disabled people to professional social work education and training. A measure of effective involvement is that service users have equal access as learners and educators and that longstanding 'glass ceilings' in the way of career development are removed. This has far reaching implications, especially if serious efforts are made to access people with learning difficulties and mental health service users on equal terms (Snow, 2002). The Special Educational Needs and Disability Act 2001 (SENDA) and the extended provisions of the Disability Discrimination Act can offer strong supports to this. The increasing involvement of service user trainers will have an important role to play in changing cultures in the shorter term. Equal access in such education and training will also demand systematic policies and provisions for access and for accessible information technology. Such policies need to be effectively implemented and monitored.

There are, of course, already students and educators with experience as service users of, for example, the benefits system, child care, fostering and adoption, disability services and so on. This can greatly add to their own and other people's experience of learning. But it can also raise complex ethical issues. These relate, for instance, to self-disclosure, the availability of support and the nature of learning paradigms. Mental health service users, for example, can find themselves on courses which internalize medical models of madness and distress which they may find oppressive and pathologizing, and which they are reluctant to sign up to, but may feel under some pressure to accept.

Involving people in research and evaluation

Education and training in social work and social policy are not only about learning and teaching. They must also develop understanding and skills in research and evaluation. With an increasing emphasis on evidence- and knowledge-based policy and practice and with academic institutions encouraged more and more to be 'research-led', interest in research is only likely to increase. It is important, therefore, that communities, and particularly service users, are fully and equally involved in research and research learning. Learning will need to address new paradigm, participatory and emancipatory research approaches, as well as approaching traditional positivist approaches to, and values in research more critically. Emancipatory disability research, particularly, has produced a significant and innovative body of work which needs to be included routinely in both social work and social policy research training (Mercer, 2002; Beresford, 2003).

Developing ongoing structures for involvement

Longstanding experience in all areas of policy and practice suggests that if involvement is to be effective, then it needs to be ongoing and based on formal structures and arrangements for participation. Ad hoc, short-term initiatives tend to be of limited and short-lived value. In itself, the establishment of formal structures is not necessarily a solution. They can become bureaucratic, procedural and tokenistic – a rubber stamp for decisions that are still made elsewhere. For this reason they must be carefully integrated with other decision-making systems. However, so long as such formal arrangements are transparent and participants have support to be involved in them, they have an important part to play, to maintain interest and enthusiasm in involvement, to become a resource of skills and experience to take them forward and to provide a basis for wider input as and when needed.

Ensuring that there are positive outcomes for service users and other people in both the process and product of involvement

Terms like 'involvement' and 'empowerment' are often used as if they are synonymous. But as anybody with significant experience of 'getting involved'

In 2001, as a special session at their annual conference, the Irish and British Social Policy Associations supported a debate to explore service user involvement in social policy research. This provided a rare opportunity for public discussion of the pros and cons of involving health and social care service users in such research. Methodological and ethical issues were raised, as well as the practicalities of involving people. The panel included a range of service users (who supported the idea of involvement!) as well as an academic who was prepared to express his own reservations about it publicly, with a large audience to take discussion forward. This was in helpful contrast to a more common situation of researchers and academics expressing public support for participation, but privately often being wary or positively unwilling to take it forward. The session highlighted the importance of open and inclusive discussion if the idea of involvement is to be taken forward effectively in learning and research.

knows, much involvement feels the opposite of empowering. If the aim is to make involvement a positive experience, then efforts must be made to ensure first that its process is positive, for example, by providing good conditions for involvement, including rapid payment of expenses and fees, good-quality food and accessible meeting places. The best route to achieving this is to seek advice (and involvement) from a local user or community organization (if one cannot be found, then a national organization should be consulted). Second, the most positive outcome from involvement is that it leads to change in line with what participants want. This may not always be possible and competing interests often have to be negotiated. But user involvement that does not or cannot lead to change and improvement has little to commend it and little point. People who get involved are generally realistic and understanding about the constraints that may be operating. But it is important to remember that people do not just get involved to be heard, but to be *listened* to. The whole point is for things to change and get better.

Monitoring and evaluating involvement

Participation and participatory initiatives do not have a strong record of achievement in UK public policy. While there has continued to be a wide interest in user, community and public involvement, hopes and expectations have frequently been dashed. There has been a frequent tendency to 'reinvent the wheel', starting again from the beginning, without drawing on the considerable body of knowledge and expertise that has been accumulated over the last 30–40 years. This failure cannot just be laid at the door of bad intentions or a desire to tokenize. Indeed, we need to know much more about why the gains from participation seem to have been so limited. A key requirement for the future development of policy and practice generally – and specifically in the context of social work and social policy learning – is for involvement and schemes for involvement to be evaluated systematically and rigorously. Such evaluations are still the exception rather than the rule. This pattern needs to change. It is only when such evaluation is routinely undertaken and built into the growing number of participation initiatives – to explore what works and what does not, what gains and problems there may be – that any real progress is likely to be made. Participants, as service users, members of communities and the public, need to be centrally involved in this process of evaluation. There is a key role here for 'user controlled evaluation'. Participation demands participatory approaches to its evaluation.

Conclusion

If participation is to progress helpfully and effectively in social work and social policy learning and research, then safe and open debate about it needs to be

---

Improving practice on user involvement in social work education

In 2004 the Social Care Institute for Excellence [SCIE] published a guide to user involvement in the new social work qualification based on a survey of existing practice in English universities. It subsequently supported a national consultation with service users, organized by Shaping Our Lives, to comment on a draft. At this event, concerns were expressed about how patchy user involvement was in different colleges, with some having done little or nothing and others developing strong links and involvement with service users and user-controlled organisations. Service users also thought that it was important to see such a report as part of a broader continuing process to monitor user involvement in social work education. They felt it was essential to provide ongoing funding to make this possible and to involve service users and their organisations centrally and equally in evaluating progress on user involvement in social work education and training.

With a small grant allocated to each programme in England by the Department of Health to develop user involvement, the report shows patchy practice. Some colleges have handed over all or part of the funding to develop user involvement in the new social work qualification to democratically constituted user-controlled organisations. This has made it possible for effective and truly independent involvement and partnerships to develop, which service users can have confidence in and feel there is much less likelihood of tokenism or a 'tick box' approach to involvement.

(Levin, 2004)

---

encouraged to develop. Such debate needs to include *all* stakeholders, notably the 'end users' of these policies, however they are conceptualized – whether as public, service users or community. This is a massive challenge, but without it, progress is likely at best to be limited, at worst tokenistic. What is under consideration here is a fundamental culture change – from provider-led to service-user-led policy, practice and learning. This is an exciting possibility, but the difficulties should not be underestimated. It is essential, nonetheless, to confront them. There is limited public understanding of both social policy and social work. Until this is developed, there is likely to be little public support for either, and policy proposals are likely to be overshadowed by the kind of reactionary and populist agendas which have had a disproportionate and divisive influence in modern times. Effective involvement in learning offers a modest but important starting point for breaking this vicious circle.

4

Promoting equality and inclusion

Bill Beaumont and Sarah Cemlyn

Introduction

This chapter focuses on how social work and social policy educators can respond to diversity among their students and promote equality and inclusion in learning and teaching. The profile of students studying social work has for many years included a relatively high proportion of those euphemistically termed 'non-traditional learners' (that is, mature students, disabled students, students from minority ethnic groups and those from educationally and financially disadvantaged backgrounds). More recently, the profile of entrants to social policy courses has become more diverse, with more mature entrants (including some with experience of issues featured on their courses, such as poverty and homelessness) and, in some institutions, more minority ethnic students. For educators, such diversity generates issues of inclusion, but a sharp focus on equality is also demanded by the content of both disciplines. Any serious analysis of the impact of social policy measures or social work practices must recognize their record of (and continuing potential for) oppressive effects as well as beneficial outcomes.

In this chapter we have drawn on the literature, discussions with colleagues at Bristol University and elsewhere, and our own teaching experience. Our primary subject area is social work but we have also taught on social policy programmes and researched questions of policy. While there is a body of literature on social work teaching, including equalities issues, there is little on teaching social policy (Young, 2003). Our ideas are therefore largely drawn from social work sources but we will seek to apply them to social policy teaching.

Promoting equality and inclusion should incorporate several dimensions, including national policy, institutional strategy and culture, access to and support for participation in higher education (HE) and the characteristics of student engagement. This multi-level framework for analysis reflects frameworks for study developed within the two disciplines (Williams, 1989; Thompson, 2001). Links between subject content and the experiences of students, including those as service users (Chapter 3), add particular significance to this discussion.

The extent to which these issues can be explored is limited here, so we refer readers to fuller discussions elsewhere. We start by considering the interplay between policy contexts and institutional responses, then analyse some barriers to, and resources for widening participation, including issues related to admissions and induction, student support and retention, and assessment. Finally, we base further discussion of curriculum design and delivery around a case example.

Policy and response

At national level, there is now a series of policy initiatives and legislative frameworks enjoining higher education institutions (HEIs) to promote equal access (see Chapter 1). The government aims to increase to 50 per cent the proportion of younger people (18–30) entering HE by 2010. It has prioritized widening participation among those currently under-represented (lower socio-economic groups, minority ethnic groups, disabled people and mature students). A new framework of equalities legislation (Race Relations Amendment Act 2000, Disability Discrimination Act 1995 and SENDA, the Special Educational Needs and Disability Act 2001) impacts on HEIs.

The institutional response of HEIs to these initiatives directly affects their social work and social policy courses. While these developments provide an enabling context for improvement, they have not been supported by adequate funding and compete for priority with other demands (e.g. pressures to improve research ratings). In addition to the benchmarking criteria which affect both disciplines, social work programmes must fulfil a series of external requirements relating to programme management, admissions, curriculum, occupational standards and practice learning. For example, the new requirement for social work students to be health checked raises potential new areas of discrimination and reflects a heightened focus on risk awareness (Manthorpe and Stanley, 1999). Other issues posed by this regulatory framework include its competence focus, its employer-driven 'technicist' content and the reduced focus on anti-oppressive practice in the General Social Care Council (GSCC) Code of Practice (GSCC, 2002a), in contrast to earlier Central Council for Education and Training in Social Work (CCETSW) iterations and international codes.

Barriers and resources

Barriers to participation in HE operate at all levels of oppression (structural, cultural, institutional and personal) and take various forms for different disadvantaged groups. The relative success of social work programmes in attracting a higher proportion of learners from such groups has been hard won over many years, potentially providing universities with an example of how to meet widening participation targets. However, this should be seen as 'work in progress' and courses continue to face challenges in moving towards more inclusive practices.

Admission is only the first stage in attempting to provide equal access to learning and adequate support in overcoming institutional and personal barriers. 'Inclusion' is itself problematic if it simply means pressure to assimilate to the dominant institution, instead of HE modelling a mutual process of change as 'an exemplar to society' (Cropper, 2000). Opening the doors but perpetuating exclusionary practices does not promote equality and may set people up to fail. Learning strategies and assessment processes for the whole student group need review, as does course content (Kirk, 2002b; Worcester University College/QAA, 2003). In social policy and social work, where curriculum topics can relate directly to students' life experiences of disadvantage, it is particularly important to challenge dominant discourses.

What resources can be drawn upon to promote equality? Until recently 'there was no formal literature concerning the teaching of social policy in higher education' (Young, 2003) and correspondingly little advice on issues of inclusion. However, the content-focused literature contains much that students will find relevant to their experiences. The social work education literature provides more direct access to a range of research, experience, ideas and reflection about teaching on equality issues (e.g. Thompson, 2001; Dominelli, 2002). These discussions partly arise from the professional character of social work education, involving both academic and practice learning. They include the importance of linking personal and political understanding, and the need for learning strategies to support this. Such strategies involve: the provision of safety and challenge; the application of adult learning and emancipatory education principles; validation of prior experience; shared approaches to learning; enabling oppressed groups to take power; and the centrality of critical reflection on practice. There is potential for these to be employed in social policy teaching, linking to developments in social policy theory, such as the growing recognition of the importance of emotional issues in social policy (Hoggett, 2001).

Admission and induction

For disadvantaged groups, many barriers arise early to put universities beyond reach. These include the educational segregation of disabled children (Oliver,

1996) and the under-achievement in school of many black students (Cropper, 2000). More immediate barriers include poor knowledge of HE provision, finance, geography and lack of confidence arising from negative experiences. The culture of universities may seem alien and exclusive. Barriers for specific groups include physical access for disabled people and child care provision for parents (Crawshaw, 2002; Lister, 2003).

While the government's widening participation strategy legitimizes a challenge to entrenched inequalities in access, active institutional policies are needed to dismantle these many-layered barriers. A Higher Education Funding Council for England (HEFCE) study found that examples of improved practice are driven by use of research, student feedback and individual champions of change (HEFCE, 2002). In social policy and social work programmes, some developments pre-date recent policy concerns about widening participation. Social work attracts significant numbers of mature applicants, predominantly women, often with caring responsibilities, and frequently from working-class backgrounds. Some programmes, particularly in ethnically diverse urban areas, have made specific efforts to attract local minority ethnic students. Access courses have played an important role. Persistence is required to generate confidence among local target groups. Social policy courses have also been proactive in seeking applicants from less advantaged schools and colleges. Some have set up links with Access courses or pre-entry programmes.

Disabled students remain under-represented in both disciplines. Despite flaws in the disability rights legislation (Gooding, 1996), SENDA has now positively raised the institutional profile of disability discrimination. Institutional audits and development plans provide valuable tools for chipping away at barriers (Crawshaw, 2002). In our department, the disability policy developed by the social work programme has been extended to social policy (and other degree) programmes. Admissions tutors and teaching staff now have clear guidance about working with disabled applicants and students at different stages. Learning contracts, prepared in early tutorials, promote attention to the requirements of individual disabled students.

Having attracted applicants, courses' commitments to equality need to be reflected in the material sent to candidates. Important practical steps include offering materials in different formats, site visits to allow disabled applicants to self-assess the institution's accessibility, and demonstration of inclusivity in open days and interviews. Between acceptance and registration, courses can actively anticipate students' needs. Early engagement with assessing disabled students' requirements may avoid the problems often experienced in getting support arrangements established on time.

During induction a commitment to inclusion requires accessible handbooks and course materials, and efforts to make sure that all students can develop the study and computing skills needed for work at HE level (Kirk, 2002b). Early teaching on issues of inequality should signal that they are taken seriously.

Support and retention

Mechanisms for supporting and retaining students must be clearly framed within an institutional approach and link the different levels of oppression. Students from oppressed groups have often had to take the lead in ensuring their own needs are met and in pushing for institutional change. While the student voice remains crucial to the process of developing inclusion, the responsibility for dismantling barriers rests elsewhere.

As on many social work courses, peer support groups and mentoring have been running for some years at Bristol for black, disabled, gay and lesbian students and, more recently, for carers. Support groups facilitate mutual support and empowerment in responding to institutional discrimination. Cropper (2000) refers to internal barriers for black students once in HE, culmi-nating in experiences of racism and difficulties maintaining a positive racial identity. She discusses mentoring as an 'inclusive device', building on self-help and consciousness-raising principles, to assist in overcoming such barriers.

Lister (2003) describes a part-time route specifically geared to the needs of mature women carers. The barriers they face could be reduced by improved finance, transport and child-care arrangements, but these are largely national issues. Local strategies include outreach and improved information about learning opportunities (important for all excluded groups), flexibility in programme design, open and distance learning, and teaching strategies based on adult learning principles. Such students find themselves pulled between HE, employment and family demands, and left to juggle competing priorities. Institutional commitment to their needs reduces role conflict and makes them 'feel more liberated to learn' (Lister, 2003: 133). Many disabled students also prefer part-time courses because they ease practical difficulties such as fluctu-ating energy levels, transport needs and making time to use support effectively.

Class and poverty have been implicit themes in this discussion, since 'non-traditional learners' are overwhelmingly from poorer backgrounds. Students from working-class communities can experience strong feelings of marginal-ization in a middle-class dominated university environment. Lesbians, gay men and bisexual people can be invisible as an oppressed group; they face not only a constant barrage of heterosexist attitudes but the personal risks of 'coming out' or not. Lesbian and gay issues are of considerable importance in social work, particularly for young people, yet within social policy and social work these issues remain inadequately researched and theorized (Logan, 2001). Any discussion of oppression runs the risk of fragmenting experiences, setting up false dualisms, appearing to prioritize some oppressions over others and ignoring the uniqueness of individual experience and of simultaneous oppres-sion (McDonald and Coleman, 1999). Support arrangements for students need to be sensitive to the full range of potentially excluding factors and interactions between them.

Assessment

A key element in retention strategies is an approach to assessment which does not leave students from disadvantaged groups facing a series of failed assignments to re-sit. One common consequence of success in recruiting students from disadvantaged groups on to social work courses has been a 'tail' of students taking longer to complete (some of whom end up withdrawing); this often contains disproportionate numbers of minority ethnic and disabled students.

One positive response, with benefits for learning outcomes generally, is to develop a varied diet of assessment tasks which does not place over-reliance on traditional academic skills such as essay writing and exam technique (Burgess, 1992). The practice component of social work training allows students who are not so strong in these skills to demonstrate their knowledge and understanding through analysis of their practice. Some college-based tasks (e.g. applying knowledge to case studies, work-related tasks such as report writing, assessment of contributions to group learning, skills assessment through video) can also achieve this. Marking criteria for each assignment should include coverage of equalities issues, and marking frames can give weight to a student's reflection on their experience.

Assessment strategies should be reviewed to ascertain potentially discriminatory elements (e.g. assuming all students can see or hear). A key component in ensuring equality of opportunity in assessment is flexibility in the way students are allowed to demonstrate that they have met the learning outcomes. Most universities now make arrangements for disabled students that allow, for instance, extra time and the use of computers in exams, though practical arrangements often fall short of being satisfactory or inclusive. Careful pacing of formal assessment tasks can help students with caring responsibilities or impairments. One persistently difficult area is the weight placed on students' ability to write formal, academic English. Academics may experience uncertainty between defending 'academic standards' and making allowances for diverse English usage. A positive response might be to try to devise methods of assessment which can discern the difference between good levels of understanding and the ability to express that understanding in academic English (e.g. tests requiring short and specific answers may be better at this than long essays).

Curriculum design and delivery

Learning and teaching strategies to promote inclusion should be integrated across the curriculum. The central importance of enabling students to 'learn how to learn' and to feel supported in this is explored in Chapter 5. Adult learning principles reaching back to Freire (1972) emphasize the importance of:

- valuing students' own experience;
- student involvement in identifying learning needs and designing learning experiences;
- reflection on learning.

Lister (2003) discusses the importance of facilitating initial engagement, of participatory strategies which make use of experience in new learning situations and of discussion, feedback and modelling. Even traditional mixes of lectures and seminars can include elements of such approaches by using relevant material, buzz groups and question-and-answer sessions in lectures, and by varying the approach to facilitating seminars (see Chapter 6).

The placements or practice learning opportunities that are a requirement in social work education, and a feature of some social policy programmes (see Chapter 9), provide a framework for experience-based and collaborative learning. Practice learning poses challenges in promoting links between theory and practice, and reinforces the importance of learning strategies that reflect the dynamic nature of social work practice. In the context of anti-racism, Butler et al. (2003) discuss a collaborative approach between tutors, practice teachers and students, grounded in a dynamic power analysis and a shared adult learning approach, focusing on the analysis of oppressive structures and attitudes. Support for ethnic minority practice teachers is another key element in holistic strategies (Singh, 2000). Attention should also be given to ensuring accessibility to practice learning for disabled students (Sapey and Turner, 2004).

The central importance of theory that clarifies the structural nature of oppression is emphasized by Lister (2003), who found a clear theoretical framework helped students integrate their learning. Trotter and Leech (2003), in analysing theory–practice integration, discuss an approach to facilitating development of students' personal theories for practice, strengthening the links between personal experience and theoretical learning. Maidment and Cooper (2002) also found that an overall theoretical perspective helps students address issues of oppression thoroughly.

Many social work courses tackle issues of oppression by combining a specific module early in the course with a commitment to ensuring these issues permeate subsequent learning. This dual approach is less common on social policy courses, which tend to rely mainly upon permeation. In our experience, this can leave social policy students seeing these issues as having little relevance to their 'mainstream' learning.

Understanding oppression – a case study

Our case study outlines one example of an early and specific social work unit, from which we draw further lessons about course design and delivery.

The 'Inequality, Power and Anti-Oppressive Practice' (IPAOP) module on the Bristol DipSW course has run since 1996 and is, we believe, a relatively successful learning experience for most students.

Format and content of IPAOP module

- 10-credit-point module in year 1 taught in seven weekly (short) day sessions during the first term.
- A theoretical framework drawn from a systematic analysis and synthesis of a wide range of social work sources (e.g. Ahmad, 1990; Phillipson, 1992; Oliver, 1996; Dominelli, 1997; Cosis Brown, 1998; Thompson, 2001), outlined in an initial lecture.
- Each session starts with a lecture conveying established knowledge, or a panel of visiting staff speak about their experiences of oppression.
- Work in small groups (2 x 1.5 hours) combining exercises (e.g. 'statements', sculpts, reflections on experience, case studies) with group discussion.
- The middle five sessions focus on anti-sexism, anti-racism, class and poverty, countering heterosexism, and disability equality.
- A final lecture addresses simultaneous oppression and relates learning to placements.
- Comprehensive handouts cover law, terminology, book and journal resources, and a 'resource box' contains more ephemeral material.
- A follow-up sequence (two half-days) follows each placement.
- Assessment is by a 2,000-word essay on one area of oppression and its impact on one area of social work and a student self-assessment of learning.

Context

Despite efforts to widen participation, Bristol University's intake continues to be predominantly white. Links with a local Access course enabled the social work course to make progress, but minority ethnic students remain a smallish proportion of the intake (ranging from 5 to 20 per cent in different years). There is a richer mix of class backgrounds, a majority of women students, some disabled students and some 'out' lesbian and gay students. This profile is not dissimilar to many social work programmes, but some others have much higher minority ethnic representation.

Prior to 1996, the course developed one-day workshops on anti-racism, anti-sexism, countering heterosexism and disability equality. Since 1991, Enquiry and Action Learning (EAL), a version of problem-based learning, had been the predominant pedagogical approach (Burgess and Jackson, 1990). Established preferences for small-group work, and active styles of learning, influenced the approach taken to these workshops. Visiting staff were employed to extend the limited diversity of the staff group. In planning the IPAOP unit, it helped us that the university had already accommodated the additional staffing and rooming resources needed for such learning. However, the discrete workshops meant lost opportunities for emphasizing common themes. Modularization and the redesign of the programme in 1996 provided the opportunity to devise a more coherent unit.

Impact

Like most teaching, the impact on students' learning has not been formally researched. Our claim to be 'relatively successful' rests on a range of available indicators; these include student evaluations and course feedback; student self-assessments; feedback from visiting staff, practice teachers and staff who teach students subsequently.

Students have made some constructive criticisms of the unit, but generally it has been highly rated. Typical of the positive comments made in formal evaluations have been:

... the most enjoyable part of the course ...

... made me think more deeply than I had ever done before ...

Facilitators who had experienced the oppression themselves were very useful ... generally gentle and unthreatening, allowed people to open up.

Everyone should be offered a unit like this, not just social work students ... in schools, other courses ...

Student self-assessments add further depth. While some are formulaic, many are convincing accounts of personal learning. These are two common reactions:

- Some students acknowledge they knew little about some areas of oppression and have learnt a lot.
- Some say they have been encouraged to think more deeply about issues where they thought they were already free from prejudice.

Suggestions for improvement have broadly been that more time should be spent on these issues.

Practice teachers generally comment favourably on how the unit prepares students for placement. Visiting staff are very positive and committed to the unit. Some course staff are concerned that some students settle for a form of tokenism in their later writing. However, the unit is only a foundation, which needs actively to be built on throughout the course.

We do not claim more than relative success for the unit. There is clearly a limit to what can be achieved in the time available and many improvements would be possible. More could be done to ensure the impact is fully followed up as the course continues. Coleman *et al.* (1999) identify three types of student response to anti-oppressive practice teaching:

- a majority who show some 'heightened awareness';
- a minority for whom it is a 'key point of life discovery', enabling them to make connections between self-awareness and cognitive learning;
- a minority who remain 'closed and resistant' to this learning.

We see all these responses, and are particularly concerned about the minority of students who remain only superficially engaged with equalities issues. However, overall we think the IPAOP unit has produced major learning gains for many students.

Key lessons

The following factors have, in our opinion, contributed to the effectiveness of the unit:

1 *The personal is political.* This is not an area where a purely intellectual understanding shifts the way issues are approached; a 'hearts and minds' commitment is required to view questions and sift evidence differently. We encourage students to think about their own starting points, how their subjectivity affects their views and how others view problems and solutions, and to make connections between various levels of understanding (personal, institutional, cultural and structural).

2 *Good adult learning approaches.* Nervousness about teaching in this area seems sometimes to lead staff to take an unusually dogmatic, didactic and/or challenging stance. We have tried to apply the course's general principles to this learning. We draw on students' existing knowledge and experience (which includes, for some, more profound experiences of oppression than most staff can draw upon). Willingness to exchange views and debate issues is a recognition that staff, too, are still learning. Small-group teaching, and the pace and spacing of learning, allow opportunities for active and mutual learning, and personal reflection. Students are encouraged to set both short- and longer-term goals. Some students experience sharp conflicts between the ideas encountered and the contexts in which they live, and so take these challenges forward personally as well as professionally.

3 *Use of a common theoretical framework.* There has been concern in the social work education literature that the more generic approach to anti-oppressive practice favoured by some (e.g. Macey and Moxon, 1996) may dilute the attention given to specific issues and, in particular, racism (e.g. Williams, 1999). Our review of social work writing on anti-oppressive practice, much of which focused on a single area of oppression, identified considerable common ground relating to both understanding and proposals for improved practice; this facilitated the common framework that informs the unit's delivery. Time is devoted to particular oppressions but contributors and students are encouraged to consider links. Integration into one unit encourages students to carry forward learning between weeks and understand oppression more holistically.

4 *Providing a foundation.* Coleman *et al.* (1999) argue that 'a *substantial* AOP [anti-oppressive practice] sequence at the *beginning* of the DipSW course' is a necessary basis for subsequent teaching in which anti-oppressive practice permeates all other learning. It has been helpful to regard the unit as a foundation for other learning. This early teaching anticipates issues which might arise between students and reassures those from minority groups that relevant issues will be tackled (before their invisibility can become a problem between them and other students, or them and staff).

5 *Normalization and reassurance.* While there remain some differences in teaching arrangements, we have adopted a strategy of normalization. This learning is presented as no more difficult than other learning expected of students, with progress likely to be at varied paces and depths. It is better for students (and staff) to avoid, as far as possible, any 'hype'. We encourage mutual support rather than 'political correctness' competitions, and an atmosphere in which students believe it is better to engage with issues than keep quiet to avoid 'making mistakes'.

6 *Staff commitment.* As in other subject areas, the quality of staff input matters. It helps if staff are confident and relaxed in how they facilitate learning, open and encouraging in how they respond to questions. In this area, it is easy to present a relentlessly grim picture and play into feelings of helplessness. Contributors to the unit, particularly in panel sessions, taught us a valuable lesson by demonstrating that a light touch facilitates, rather than inhibits, learning. Panellists have made serious points by recounting their experiences of racism, homophobia and disability with wit and warmth. They have amply demonstrated the strength oppressed groups can generate by mutual support and collective organization. The unit is permeated by humour, with sessions shifting rapidly from being good fun to being deeply moving. Anti-oppressive education should not be experienced as oppressive.

7 *Promotion of core values*. We encourage students to approach this learning with certain core values:

- Step outside your 'normal' space and view the world as others experience it.
- Respond to any challenge by taking a step back from your established view, listening carefully and considering properly what has been said.
- Value the experiences of those with direct experience of discrimination and resisting oppression.
- Guilt is not a productive reaction to injustice; oppressed people prefer a more active orientation, welcoming allies in their efforts to achieve greater equality.

While not underestimating the problems still to be tackled, we encourage students to think progress can be made, to which they can contribute.

8 *Valuing experiences of oppression*. Although it is possible to lead learning about oppression without personal experience of each discrimination, such experience lends authenticity. For each focus, we have worked with and progressively passed the lead role to people who have experienced the particular oppression addressed. Given the limited diversity in the staff group this has usually meant hiring in some visiting staff – disability equality trainers, additional gay/lesbian and minority ethnic professionals. There are gains and losses in having such a range of people involved in this teaching, but some loss of coherence is more than compensated for by the authenticity achieved. We worked hard initially to plan sessions jointly with visiting staff, to ensure support for them and consistency of approach. Over time, our role has shifted to some shared planning and looking after our visitors. As an important signal, one of us sits in on each plenary session to indicate the course's continuing commitment, and to refresh our own learning.

9 *Prioritizing the needs of students from oppressed groups*. In forming groups for this sequence, it would be simplest to keep the same groups throughout. We do use familiar EAL groups for the introductory, middle and final sessions. However, we ensure that students with direct experience of particular oppressions can meet together. Thus when we focus on sexism, women meet in all-female groups and the minority of men have the (still unusual) experience of working in an all-male group. Minority ethnic students meet together so they can focus on their own learning needs related to racism rather than being a learning resource for white students. In relation to heterosexism and disability, minority group preferences and other reasons require a variant of this approach, with some joint and some separate working.

10 *Staffing and practicalities*. Successful teaching in this area may depend partly on overcoming practical difficulties, such as lack of diversity in the available

teaching staff, or the pressure to teach large groups. On staff diversity, IPAOP provides one solution through use of visiting staff. Even where there is more diversity among core staff, it is not appropriate to assume that those with direct experiences of discrimination should lead teaching on oppression. They may not be willing to draw upon that experience so directly, may have other priorities, and could find lead involvement in this teaching complicates other roles (Chand *et al.*, 2002). These writers also describe a unit delivered in a group of 60 students, but identify the lack of small-group work as a weakness inhibiting learning. We were able to draw upon a course tradition of small group teaching. Staff working in institutions less used to such provision may want to argue for some small-group work as a prerequisite for effective education in the fields of diversity and equality.

Our case example is drawn from social work, but we think many of these key lessons could be usefully adapted by social policy colleagues. Heron and McManus (2003) identify difficulty engaging first-year social policy students in course content because of their limited 'political awareness'. We have found that second- and third-year social policy students have a rather distanced understanding of racism and sexism as theoretical issues of concern to their left-leaning lecturers. The level of student engagement found in EAL groups contrasts sharply with the detachment often found in the more traditional lecture/seminar diet. Social policy colleagues are concerned about the poor level of involvement in seminars achieved with young 'traditional' students, and increasing diversity of entry can only strengthen the case for using more varied learning opportunities and strategies. A sequence like IPAOP may help first-year social policy students absorb later course content more fully.

In many institutions, social policy is taught to very large groups of under-graduates, drawn from a range of subject disciplines, on open modules and with seminar groups so large they may inhibit many students' contributions. To include some smaller-group sessions for core social policy students may help build group coherence and improve retention rates, as well as promoting deeper learning. Social policy students are also likely to gain from contact with a more diverse range of staff than most departments can provide internally. We hope that this account will provide some ideas to support teaching and learning in this area.

Conclusion

We close this chapter by identifying some issues about building, and general-izing, good practice.

Care must be taken to ensure that 'widening participation' does not descend into an assimilation strategy. This creates challenges for institutions and staff teams, who need to reflect on their culture and expectations. However, change inevitably takes time and, in the meantime, students from disadvantaged groups can find themselves unfairly taking the lead; this can take energy from their own learning. We need to balance specific support for 'non-traditional' students with determined pressure for institutional change.

We should also consider how to match changes in the curriculum and teaching/learning methods with changes in composition of the student group. We would argue that seeking to respond appropriately to the needs of disadvantaged students promotes good practice for all students. However, we all face challenges (of resources, time, institutional and government expecta- tions) which can undermine progressive and locally responsive change. How to sustain innovation and change in teaching and learning within these limi- tations is a further challenge (see Chapter 14).

We have found merit in the teaching and learning approaches explored here, including a greater emphasis on facilitating links between personal and theo- retical understanding. However, we also recognize the importance of balancing the provision of safety for personal exploration and challenge with avoiding over-exposure of students, which can exacerbate oppression. Mechanisms for ensuring safety in very different contexts need wider exploration.

What are the mutual lessons for social work and social policy? Social work teaching has long borrowed heavily from the discipline of social policy and will continue to do so. However, approaches to teaching and learning in social policy in response to diversity could gain some ideas from social work education. How diversity and equality issues enhance the mutual relationship between the two disciplines is therefore a key issue for further exploration.

5

Students learning to learn

Viviene E. Cree

Introduction

There has been extensive interest in recent years in student learning. This is
not surprising given that we live in a rapidly changing world in which
yesterday's knowledge may become quickly overtaken by ideas and practices
which are today largely unimagined. The need for learning has become
an imperative, and academics across disciplines have devoted attention to
attempting to explain the process of learning, and how it might be facilitated.
This chapter will examine what is known about learning, and about learning
to learn in higher education. There is considerable evidence to suggest that
much can be done to facilitate students learning to learn, and that the development of critical thinking remains a central part of this. I will review the key
findings, while considering the lessons for learning to learn in the context of
social policy and social work programmes. This is especially as National
Occupational Standards, benchmarking statements and, of course, the new
social work degrees in the UK come together and at times compete with one
another to set parameters for learning in social work and social policy. But
first, a word about my own path in and through learning.

'Have ye no' finished with the learnin' yet?'

This was the question my grandfather greeted me with when I embarked on
a PhD at 31 years of age, after three years as a full-time undergraduate student,
six years as a part-time Open University (OU) student, and a further two years
spent in professional social work training. His question forced me to address

not only his ideas and values – which presupposed that there was an 'end-point' in learning (which I should have reached by now) – but also my own deep-seated thirst for learning. What was it about me that meant that I needed to continually put myself in the role of learner? Who or what was I competing against in this process?

I suspect that the answer lies, in part, in my position as the middle daughter in a family of three girls. But there is also, I believe, a more immediate answer. I went to university aged 18, the first child in my family to do so. Here I faced a wholly alien environment in which I was totally out of my depth, intellectually and socially. I went quickly from being a bright, successful state-school pupil to being a 'failing student', and it was not until my third and final year that I began to put the pieces back together again. I left university with what was then called an 'Ordinary' MA degree, and with a huge feeling that somehow I had missed an opportunity. Enrolling with the OU three years later began the process in which I have been engaged ever since, a process of lifelong learning which I have shared with subsequent generations of students with whom I have worked as a social work practice teacher, tutor and lecturer.

My experience has taught me much about my own learning, and about the factors that may hinder as well as encourage learning. I have learnt first-hand that good school grades do not necessarily translate into attainment at university and that the study skills employed for examinations at school may not transfer readily into the university context. I have learnt that the impact of social class and cultural background can lead a Scottish student to feel out of place at an ancient Scottish university.

What is learning?

Over the last 150 years or so, educationalists and psychologists have sought to understand the process of learning by studying and categorizing it. In spite of much effort on their part, it remains something of a mystery or, as Collins (1989) suggests, it is a 'black box':

> We do not know how we manage to learn. There are various ideas such as positive and negative reinforcement, ostensive definition, the building of new concepts from old by logical extension, hard wiring of the brain for certain aspects of knowledge (such as linguistic structures, the ability to recognise elementary orientations and movements, and so forth) but these are all inadequate and insecure. One might say that the science of learning was still in the pre- or multi-paradigmatic stage. The evidence for this is that brand-new speculative 'theories' of learning can still grow out of nothing and yet not be completely implausible.
>
> (1989: 207)

Academics have different ideas not only about how we learn, but also about how learning might best be applied in practice. This can make for a bewildering set of choices for those of us charged with the task of facilitating learning. Should we focus on methods which allow for staged learning (in a behaviourist tradition), problem-based learning (a commonly used approach which draws on cognitive principles) or switch our emphasis to the learning environment (as social and phenomenological theorists might encourage)? I believe that the most helpful answer is a pragmatic one. Teachers and learners are eclectic: we draw on different ideas and methods in different situations at different times (Hartley, 1998). This implies that all these approaches may have a useful place in enabling students to learn, and in facilitating learning to learn.

What is learning to learn?

The notion of learning to learn (sometimes referred to as metacognition, 'thinking about one's thinking' or 'monitoring one's learning') has become a central plank of educational ideology in recent years, demonstrated in subjects as diverse as social science and artificial intelligence. The assumption is that students (and indeed machines) can be taught to recognize and so amend their own learning strategies, goals and objectives so that they can become more effective learners. As their learning progresses, they will then assume more and more responsibility for regulating their learning (Hartley, 1998).

Learning to learn is thus underpinned by four key ideas, which will each be explored in turn:

- that individuals (not learning tasks) are central to learning – hence the importance of taking account of previous experience, motivation, fear of change etc;
- that students have distinct learning styles and strategies which can be identified and modified;
- that the social environment in which learning takes place can facilitate or inhibit individuals' capacity for learning;
- that learning to learn can be taught, and that, once learnt, it can be carried forward into new learning situations.

Individuals as learners

Learning to learn assumes that while the nature and management of learning tasks have an inevitable impact on the learning process, it is the learner her/himself who determines whether or not learning will take place. Psychologists assert that the motivation to learn is intrinsic: individuals have an innate propensity to seek knowledge about the world (Piaget, 1972).

Learning is consequently an active process in which 'learners strive for under-standing and competence on the basis of their personal experience . . . old knowledge is always revised, reorganised and even reinterpreted in order to reconcile it with new input' (Cust, 1995: 280).

The concept of the centrality of the learner is basic to all models of adult education, and can be seen in the work of Knowles (1983), Mezirow (1983) and Freire (1983). In this context, an acknowledgement of the experience the learner brings to the educational arena is vital in developing programmes which are relevant to their needs (Macaulay and Cree, 1999). Students entering higher education bring their own unique personality and family biography, as well as their social and cultural background, based on class, 'race'/ethnicity, gender, sexuality, etc. They also bring ideas and attitudes towards learning which have been built up over years, as children and as adults. If their previous experiences of learning have been positive, encouraging and successful, then students are likely to bring an open and optimistic attitude to a new learning situation. If their experiences have been discouraging, this 'baggage' can get in the way of them settling into learning (Harris, 1985). Learning is thus both active and indi-vidual: knowledge and experience are constructed and represented in ways determined by personal dispositions and by personal and cultural histories (Boud and Miller, 1996).

Motivation is a key factor in learning, but learning can be scary, even when someone wishes to learn. Entwistle and Ramsden's (1983) research on student teachers indicates that it is not the learning situation per se which is frightening as much as the student's perception of that situation as anxiety provoking. Green Lister demonstrates this in more recent research on students on a social work programme designed to meet the needs of mature students with caring responsibilities. She quotes a student who said: 'It's hard – before you move on there are certain things you have to undo, you know' (2000: 166).

This suggests that students will benefit from the opportunity to reflect on their own learning in the past, in order to bring into sharper focus the conscious and unconscious processes that are at work in their current learning situation.

Learning styles and strategies

Learning to learn presupposes that students have different approaches to learning, and that these approaches lead to different outcomes in terms of learning. In other words, *what* we learn is determined to a large degree by *how* we learn (Entwistle, 1988). Some students see learning as mainly about the acquisition of 'facts', and believe that they are expected to simply reproduce information and ideas presented by teaching staff. Others believe that learning is about making sense of what is presented in a meaningful way. This has been described as the difference between a 'surface' and a 'deep' approach to

Practice example 1: begin with the past

Ask students to discuss in small groups the last time they learnt something new: perhaps it was learning to drive a car, or taking an evening class in salsa dancing or Italian for beginners. Ask them to identify:

- What were your feelings at the outset?
- How did you go about learning? (e.g. by panicking, by reading as many books as you could lay your hands on, or by methodically working your way through the course materials?)
- Was there a turning-point at which you began to relax and enjoy the learning process? If so, what else was going on at this time?
- Alternatively, what got in the way of the learning process?
- What were the outcomes for you of the learning experience, in the short and longer term?

Moving on from this, what about the students' previous educational experiences – at university, college or school? Ask them to consider whether there are some general lessons to be learnt from their experiences:

- Do you tend to approach each new situation with the same kind of feelings?
- What do you think are the origins of these feelings?
- What will need to happen in your life for you to begin to approach a new situation differently?

The results of this small-group discussion may be fed back by students to the whole class in a plenary session. Students will then be able to see their own learning processes alongside those of others, thus broadening their perspectives and allowing them to see similarities and differences in approach. This exercise may be taken forward and reviewed at key stages throughout the degree programme.

learning. A third group of students uses a 'strategic' approach, which leads them to organize time and distribute effort to the greatest effect in order to achieve the best possible grades.

Research on learning approaches has led to the creation of typologies of students' learning styles. Two frequently used models are those of Kolb (1976) and Honey and Mumford (1986). Cree *et al.* (1998) comment that the concepts and techniques of learning styles have become a routine part of the landscape of learning in social work. Students are frequently asked to complete learning styles inventories and questionnaires at the outset of programmes or in practice placements, and these are often used as a kind of diagnostic tool, to assess where a student is in terms of their learning and to encourage them to move on to a different approach. However, there has been sustained criticism in recent years about the deterministic way in which learning styles approaches have been employed in some settings. Shardlow and Doel (1996) express concern that use of learning styles inventories has led some students and teachers to believe (wrongly) that learning styles are somehow fixed.

There is, in addition, a more fundamental issue here. Educationalists have pointed out that the learning styles which students adopt are related not only to their personal preferences or individual personalities; they are symptomatic of the learning and assessment tasks with which learners are presented (Entwistle, 1988). This suggests that if we wish students to adopt a more holistic approach to learning, then a tightly managed competency framework will not provide the best opportunity to achieve this. Similarly, an assessment diet made up of a series of short examination-type assessments is unlikely to lead to deep learning, or to improve a student's capacity for reflective observation.

Kolb proposes that 'Learning, the creation of knowledge and meaning, occurs through the active extension and grounding of ideas and experiences in the external world and through internal reflection about the attributes of these experiences and ideas' (1984: 52). He depicts this process as a continuous learning cycle in which the relationship between concrete experience and conceptualization of this experience is constantly re-defined through:

- concrete experience;
- observation and reflections;
- formation of abstract concepts and generalizations;
- testing implications of concepts in new situations;
- returning to concrete experience.

Schön (1983, 1987) explores similar ideas in his work on professional education. He argues that professional practice is more than simply the application of theory to practice; instead, learning may begin with practice, since each new situation is likely to have novel and unexpected aspects which require the professional to 'think on their feet'. Taken together, the insights of Kolb and Schon indicate that traditional modes of course organization (where practice is frequently preceded by academic input) may not provide the ideal sequencing for students learning to learn. Instead, we need to find a way of managing teaching and learning which accepts that learning is going on all the time, and is constantly being refined on the basis of new information and experience. By actively reflecting on this process, we can become clearer about where our ideas are coming from, and make more refined choices about what we think and believe.

Practice example 2: explore learning approaches

Students should first be encouraged to reflect on the ways that they have learnt in the past, as introduced in Practice example 1. They can then take this further by considering the following questions:

- Is there a time of day when you work best? (e.g. first thing in the morning, or late at night?)
- Is there a place where you work best? (e.g. in the library, in your bedroom at home, at the kitchen table?)
- Do you prefer working alone or in a group?
- How big or difficult is the learning task in hand? Do you need to break it down into manageable chunks and create a study plan?
- What else competes for your attention? Do you need to prioritize?
- What outcomes do you wish from this learning situation?
- How will you reward yourself when you have completed the task in hand?
- Who will you seek help from if you need it?

Thereafter, the following tools may be used, either to help modify a student's existing learning style, or to build on what is already a strength in their approach to learning:

- Learning logs, diaries or journals may be used so that students can note on a daily (or more occasional) basis their thoughts and feelings about what they are learning (see Tait, 2000).
- Some students may find it helpful to paint a picture or produce a poster which expresses their feelings about their learning.
- Some students may be usefully directed to websites or textbooks on learning to learn.
- Use of case studies and problem-based learning will encourage self-directed and group learning (see Burgess, 1992; Taylor, 1996; Cree and Davidson, 2000).
- Students undertaking practice learning may be asked to write a critical incident analysis or a process recording to 'unpack' their thoughts and feelings about a specific event or situation (see Davies and Kinloch, 2000; Napier and Fook, 2000; Clapton, 2000.)
- Tutorials should periodically take a step out of any planned programme to reflect on the learning process.
- Students could be asked to build portfolios of their work throughout their course, containing examples of critical learning that have taken place. At the end of the course, this will provide a useful tool for reviewing the learning experience as a whole, and for identifying future learning needs (see Taylor *et al.*, 1999).

The influence of the learning environment

Although individuals are central to learning, the social context within which learning is located must also be favourable for students to learn to learn. This suggests that attention must be given to factors at institutional and course level as well to the individual learner. This is considered further in Chapter 2 and discussion of constructive alignment of the curriculum.

One of the biggest shifts which has taken place in higher education in the UK over the last 30 years has been the change in the arrangements for funding students and institutions. While students are entering higher education in greater numbers, so the introduction of student fees and loans has forced many undergraduate and postgraduate students to take on significant amounts of paid work during the time of their studies (Callendar and Kemp, 2000). It would be clearly unwise to make over-inflated claims about the impact of this on students' capacity to learn. Nevertheless, it is plainly evident that a student who has worked late into the night stacking shelves in a supermarket may be less receptive to a lecture at 9 am. Similarly, mature people with caring responsibilities are becoming students in ever-greater numbers. This has clear implications for the management of teaching, suggesting the need for a more flexible approach to course organization to take account of individuals' situations, and for an approach to learning which acknowledges and values the experience adult learners bring.

What is proposed here is far from the reality for many students currently in higher education. Working-class students, disabled students, mature students and those without 'standard' entrance requirements may feel that they do not 'fit' in their university. Worse still, they may feel that they do not have an 'entitlement' to be in higher education. The same may also be true for black and Asian students. Channer (2000) argues that black students on social work courses can be totally alienated by a Eurocentric knowledge base and world view which ignores their experience. She writes: 'The experience of being a Black student in a largely White educational institution is potentially, and often in reality one of being a powerless, vulnerable observer' (Channer, 2000: 184). Issues of diversity in learning are further discussed in Chapter 4.

Institutional oppression can only be transformed by structural change. Individual students may need reassurance, particularly in the early stages of their degree programmes, to trust that they are wanted and that they have legitimate 'voices' which deserve to be heard in the classroom and in the institution more broadly. But they will only believe that they are equal when courses and institutions themselves change.

Practice example 3: re-think course organization and structure

The following suggestions may be useful here:

- more acknowledgement of prior learning (through formal APEL – Accreditation of Prior Learning – schemes and other more informal arrangements);
- better student support systems (including mentoring schemes where students in their senior years befriend beginning students);
- more flexible delivery of teaching (e.g. through greater use of online materials, evening classes, weekend courses);
- more open course organization, including part-time courses and courses managed over a longer period to take account of caring responsibilities;
- a teaching curriculum which reflects a broader range of histories, theoretical ideas and experiences;
- a course structure which builds in more opportunities for students to learn from each other in a collaborative atmosphere, in contrast to the highly individualized, competitive environment which currently characterizes much of higher education;
- more opportunities for group learning, where students can learn from each other and at the same time provide much needed support to one another.

Teaching learning to learn

The fourth assumption which underpins learning to learn is that this is a skill which can be taught, and that once taught, it can be taken forward into new learning situations, in both academic and workplace settings through continuing professional development (CPD).

In a classic text on adult learning, Rogers (1989) makes a distinction between 'teaching' and 'learning', arguing that the one does not necessarily lead to the other. She recounts the story of the lecturer who prepared well for class, but whose students were bored to tears and did crosswords during her lessons. Her message is that for learning to 'stick', it must be internalized: 'you have to make it your own' (1989: 41). Helping students to make learning their own is an entirely different enterprise to traditional, didactic teaching. We must capture and seek to maintain students' interest by providing a mix of learning tasks which will introduce them to different possibilities in their learning. We must give them opportunities to try out their learning in practice, through the use of case studies, exercises and role-plays. And, most fundamentally, we must enable students to build from their personal knowledge and experience.

Hobson urges that we slow down the 'usual rapid-fire stream of thoughts and opinions' to allow students the time and intellectual space required to analyse, synthesise and evaluate their efforts (1996: 46). 'Critical thinking' has become a popular buzzword in recent years, most notably in the United States, where it has frequently been held up as the solution to all the ills of the education system and of society as a whole (Barnett, 1997). While some of this may be rightly regarded as over-inflated 'hype', nevertheless in teaching students to think more critically (that is, to stop and reflect, to challenge their everyday assumptions and those of others, to explore alternatives and compare and contrast evidence before reaching a considered judgement), we will come some way towards teaching them to learn to learn. We must therefore find ways of encouraging critical thinking, by allowing them to challenge their settled ways of thinking and by helping them to make explicit connections which might otherwise be unconscious or unplanned.

Critical thinking does not come easily; students need to practise it, and they need to be supported in it. The shift which is being outlined here is one from teacher as 'instructor' to teacher as 'facilitator', 'coach' (Schön, 1983) or 'animator' (Boud and Miller, 1996). When teaching becomes centred on facilitation or 'animation', it becomes clear that the educators in the learning situation are not only the paid teachers. Instead, students, lecturers, tutors and practice teachers are all part of the shared enterprise of learning about social work or social policy. This suggests that there must be ample opportunities for students to be able to reflect on what they are learning, and to learn from each other. Social work and social policy programmes have traditionally made good use of group activities to encourage learning, as outlined by Taylor (1997). But this must be taken further. Educators have much to learn from students who bring a wealth of different experiences of background, culture and ideas. Students should be encouraged to pass on ideas and resources, while at the same time challenging and contributing to the development of the intellectual life of their programmes. Similarly, lecturers should be honest enough to acknowledge areas where others may have greater expertise.

There is one final observation here. Just as teachers are not the only educators, so classrooms are not the only sites in which learning takes place. Learning takes place across all settings: the informal, everyday learning in which we are all engaged (at home, in the café, on the bus) may be more significant in terms of self-development than the learning which goes on in classrooms or tutorial groups. This again means that the curriculum needs to have gaps to allow 'social transmission' to occur (Ehrenberg, 1983).

Conclusion

Learning to learn is a considerable challenge to higher education. It is much more than simply a matter of developing study skills, of students being able

Practice example 4: teaching a sequence on homelessness and social exclusion

This practice example offers teaching methods which may be used separately or together to encourage students to learn to learn:

- Begin by finding out what students know and do not know about the subject. For example, has anyone prior experience of working in this area, as a volunteer or paid worker?
- Introduce an exercise which encourages students to explore their values in relation to homeless people. For example, ask them to write a story or poem based on a 'day in the life' of a homeless person.
- Give students access to information on the topic. For example, direct them to websites of government and voluntary agencies which work in the area of homelessness and social exclusion. Ask them to work together in pairs/threes to collate fact sheets with up-to-date statistics on homelessness and social exclusion. Alternatively, ask students to read and take notes on key government publications, then present their work to each other in small groups facilitated by a teacher or tutor.
- Give a lecture or series of seminars in which key concepts and debates in relation to homelessness and social exclusion are presented. Ensure there is sufficient time for questions and discussion.
- Introduce a case study of a homeless person or family. Ask students in small groups to identify the range of issues which need to be addressed, as well as the legal context and the agencies which may be able to help. Alternatively, ask them to make a poster presentation displaying the agencies likely to be involved in working with this person or family, outlining their remit and function.
- Invite an agency representative to come into the classroom to discuss the case and the work of the agency. Alternatively, make arrangements for students to go out to visit agencies in the field, such as voluntary organizations, a social security office, the local housing department.
- Role-play the members of a case conference called to discuss the case of a woman who has fled the marital home with her two small children after a serious assault by her husband.
- Set a range of appropriate assessment tasks which encourage students to develop their insight and learning. For example, ask students to write an essay which reviews the causes of homelessness; invite students to assess each other's work (peer assessment).
- Give thoughtful, encouraging feedback to students throughout the learning process in the classroom and on their written work.
- Finally, ask students to reflect on their learning on this subject and identify gaps in their knowledge and how these might be addressed in the future.

to take 'good' lecture notes or write a 'good' examination paper. Instead, learning to learn is based on 'knowing about one's knowing'. It is about students understanding the ways by which and through which they learn; it is about encouraging them to become active and creative learners who will always be prepared to make the best out of each new learning situation in which they find themselves. And it is about giving them space, time and encouragement to reflect on what they are learning in a critical, constructive and open atmosphere. None of this will come about automatically; it requires support and guidance (Bridges, 1994). It also demands a shake-up in the way that courses and higher education institutions are organized so that students, not learning tasks, become central to the learning process.

Further resources

United States Foundation for Critical Thinking: www.criticalthinking.org

6

Promoting interactive
learning and teaching

Hilary Burgess and Pat Young

Introduction

The preceding chapter on learning to learn has demonstrated the importance
of engaging students as active learners in both social policy and social work.
To achieve this, educators must develop a range of approaches to promote
learning, which are reviewed in this chapter. We begin with the lecture
(which, despite its limitations, has retained a central place in higher education),
looking specifically at strategies for enhancing interaction. We move on to
seminars, group work and project work, and outline the central facets of
problem-based learning. Experiential learning features strongly in education
for social work, and may also play a part in social policy programmes: the use
of role-play, simulations and observational tasks are reviewed. Educators in
both social policy and social work are concerned to develop students' ability
to critically analyse theory; case studies illustrating two ways of approaching
this using interactive methods are outlined. Finally, there is discussion of how
student learning can be supported over the whole programme through the
tutorial and the wider process of personal development planning. Overall, the
focus in this chapter is on enhancing the quality of the learning experience
through interaction.

Lectures

Despite the persuasive arguments that lectures are not the most effective
form of teaching (Gibbs, 1982), there is evidence (Edwards *et al.*, 2001) that
they continue to play a key role in higher education. A number of factors

constrain radical changes in teaching methods. The geography of the university, with its lecture halls, together with the economics of higher education which demand increasingly large numbers of students are taught in the most cost-effective ways, deter innovation. Cultural expectations of students as well as staff are expressed in the language of higher education: we are employed as lecturers, and students' timetables show the lectures taking place in lecture theatres. With these powerful factors operating against radical departures, it is not surprising that the lecture remains at the centre of university teaching.

Biggs' (1999: 99) argument on the limitations of lectures is essentially that 'sustained and unchanging low-level activity lowers concentration', while it requires 'concentrated effort to follow lecture content'. The argument is not that lectures inherently prohibit active learning, just that the format is very demanding and makes active learning more difficult for the majority of students. The traditional lecture gives the lecturer maximum control over teaching, but minimal control over learning with no means of assessing the extent or quality of learning. However, as is argued by Edwards *et al.* (2001), the lecture format can be adapted to incorporate current understanding of effective learning and used flexibly in ways that preserve its advantages, while minimizing the limitations. Introduction of a framework at the beginning of the lecture will help students to organize more detailed information, while a conclusion reinforces key points students should take away. Increasingly, lecturers in social policy and social work provide information in multiple forms, using hand-outs to free students from note-taking and overhead projectors (OHPs) or Powerpoint as visual aids. Placing material on a virtual learning environment (VLE) such as Blackboard or Web-CT allows students who miss lectures to access material, frees the lecturer from handling paper copies, and provides a means for students to check out their understanding at a later point. The medium also allows follow-up questions from students.

While lectures offer the opportunity to communicate a large body of information, they are problematic in terms of effective learning. Goodyear (2002) suggests that 'good learning' must be active learning, in so far as the learner needs to carry out a variety of cognitive operations on new information, in order to make it personally meaningful. Biggs' critique of lectures (1999) suggests that, although some students will engage with lecture material in ways that enable effective learning, the lecture does not require or facilitate students' engagement. The passive role of the students and lack of guided learning makes active engagement a challenging task, which defeats many students less skilled in learning. These students will engage at surface levels only, catching snippets of information and missing the overall picture.

There are a number of ways in which lecturers can encourage students to make the cognitive operations that result in material becoming meaningful for each individual student. Some of these encourage mental activity alone; some involve the students more actively in interaction with each other and with the lecturer. By posing questions for students at the beginning or throughout the lecture, the lecturer encourages mental involvement. By asking students to note their decisions at the end, the lecturer can take a step further in requiring rather than just offering this opportunity for active learning.

Breaking up the lecture with short activities that can be carried out individually, in pairs or in small groups encourages active learning and overcomes the difficulty of maintaining concentration with changes of activity. Activities can include completion of question sheets, brainstorming of existing knowledge, ranking opinions, relating theories to areas of practice, providing examples, or summarizing key points of the lecture. These can be fed back orally, on overheads, or in writing to the lecturer, or placed on a VLE by students or the lecturer. Although involving students in interaction is easier with smaller groups, it is possible, and perhaps more essential in very large lectures, where the impersonal nature of the communication makes concentration harder to maintain.

Examples: interactive teaching in social policy and social work lectures

A lecture on issues in implementation of social policies starts with a game of Chinese Whispers in which the lecturer whispers a sentence (of relevant material) to students at the end of each row who pass the message along. After the message is passed on through perhaps 10 students, it is fed back, usually in distorted and shortened forms. Students are then asked how the game relates to the process of implementation of social policy, and why the message is not accurately reproduced. Their responses can be referred to throughout the lecture.

A lecture on the relation of politics to social work begins with a sounding of students' views. Students rank their responses on a scale of 0–5 to the following statements:

Social work and politics are related:	Not at all (0) . . . Closely related (5).
Social workers should engage with political processes:	Not at all (0) . . . In all their work (5).

A show of hands gives a sense of students' opinions at the start of the lecture and the exercise is repeated at the end to assess any changes in thinking.

Learning groups: seminars, group learning and projects

Learning in small groups is another long-established component of higher education, in the shape of the seminar. Other forms of group learning activities have been introduced more recently. Group work has a number of advantages as a form of learning. These include the development of meta-cognitive awareness, in which students learn what they know, and do not know, as a result of having to explain their thinking and knowledge to a group. This process also consolidates learning. Learning groups offer the opportunity to develop subject-specific and transferable skills, increasingly recognized as vital for new graduates. The benchmarking statements for both social policy and social work cite problem-solving skills, evaluative and analytical skills, sensitivity to the values and interests of others, communication skills, interpersonal and teamwork skills, making presentations, self-awareness and an ability to self-manage their learning (QAA, 2000); all these can be developed through group learning. In order to run group learning effectively, academics must themselves become skilled as facilitators of learning, paying attention to both task and process.

Seminars

Seminars can be the best, or the worst, of teaching and learning experiences. In the best of worlds, seminars provide space for students to develop their confidence, their own ideas and their intellectual and presentational skills. They can learn from each other as well as the tutor; reflect on the sources of ideas, and the most effective kinds of learning. For the tutor too, seminars provide unique opportunities for insights into student perspectives, and informal assessment of the effectiveness of teaching approaches. In the worst of worlds, students may feel unable to express their ideas, attendance may be poor and students who do attend come unprepared and unwilling to participate.

The changes in higher education examined in Chapter 1 have impacted on seminars. Higher student numbers, with falling unit finances, have increased group sizes in most institutions. Many students are now juggling paid employment with study and, in some cases, also have family responsibilities. Students have become more instrumental in prioritizing activities and increasingly look to assessment requirements to motivate their study. Expectations of students' seminar work have to take account of their changing lifestyles.

To run a seminar effectively, academics need to be aware of some basic techniques to enable students to feel confident and engaged, as shown in the box at the top of p. 71.

The traditional university seminar, in which students read prepared papers, has mostly been replaced by a structured use of the time that more effectively involves all students. One format is to use seminar time for students to discuss

---

Techniques to enable student participation in groups

1 Take time at the beginning of the module to discuss the purpose of the seminars and their relationship to learning; this can help students understand their importance and how they can benefit from active participation.
2 Build strong personal relationships and a sense of belonging through ice-breakers which help students relax and participate without feeling intimidated.
3 Establish shared ground-rules, which may improve attendance, participation and help deal with any later conflicts.

---

critically, and thus integrate, their learning from a previously given lecture. Students may start by working in pairs to identify key learning points or questions to start the dialogue. Where students are expected to prepare for seminars through reading a key text, structures are needed to ensure central questions are addressed and all students participate. Pairs of students may be asked to present differing views of a topic to initiate a discussion. Feedback on presentations should develop students' confidence with an initial focus on strengths, before identifying areas for improvement.

Where no advance preparation is required, tasks may be given in the seminar. Large groups can be split and allocated activities, with feedback to the larger group. Groups can be provided with worksheets, case studies or sets of questions to discuss, drawing on material from the Internet, newspapers and professional journals. In social work education, seminar groups can experiment with the use of techniques such as ecomaps, genograms, culturagrams, flow diagrams and life road maps (Parker and Bradley, 2003). Seminar groups provide ideal opportunities for discussing ethics and values in both social policy and social work.

Example: seminar activity: decision-making within welfare organizations

A large seminar group splits to work on two case studies involving welfare decisions (e.g. a care package for a disabled person, education for a child with learning disabilities). The group identifies the 'stake-holders' in the situation, then students work in pairs representing one stakeholder and prepare to argue:

● why they should have a say in the decision;
● the effects, costs and risks of them not having a say.

Working on group projects and activities

Most programmes now include modules in which students learn and are assessed in small groups, working outside the formal timetable. Students pool their ideas and information, learning from each other and generating new ideas through discussion. Virtual learning environments, such as Blackboard and Web-CT, which facilitate online group work can help overcome barriers of geography and time for meetings.

In designing such activities, academics should specify the intended learning outcomes not only in terms of content, but also in terms of process skills. The skills and benefits should be made explicit to students; this may help them deal with the frustration that can arise when group work seems inefficient and time-consuming, or when group dynamics become difficult. Potential problems can be made more manageable by the creation of shared and agreed ground rules at the beginning of an exercise. Tasks need to be structured with feedback and monitoring built into the process of the work. Groups can present their work in a variety of ways, including presentations, posters, videos and online and written documents. Additionally, students can be asked to provide individual or group reflection on the process of the work.

Example group project: construction of a community or agency profile

Small groups of students (from 4 to 8) work together to draw up a profile of a particular locality or agency. Each student has responsibility for one aspect of the project, but their learning is pooled and debated before presenting back to the class as a whole.

Problem-based learning

Problem-based learning (PBL) is an approach entailing a high degree of interactive learning and teaching. Developed for use in medical schools in North America, it has been applied in many disciplines, both professionally based (engineering, health sciences, law) and academic, such as English, history and religious studies (Boud and Feletti, 1997). PBL is the term most commonly used, but others such as enquiry-based learning (EBL) or enquiry and action learning (EAL) are synonymous. PBL is usually introduced to enhance students' motivation by using 'real' problems, to engage them as active learners, to build on existing knowledge, and to increase application of theory to practice or integration of domains of study within a discipline. Since much course content dates quickly, PBL can be argued to offer a means to equip students with skills for problem-solving and lifelong learning.

The process of PBL can be summarized as follows: the learning starts from a problem, question or scenario, with a number of potential dimensions for learning. With the assistance of a facilitator, students work in groups, using the scenarios as a basis for study. They share existing relevant knowledge, agree what they need to learn and how they will do this (drawing on a range of resources), and reconvene to discuss progress, evaluate their work and decide next steps. The scenarios often run over several weeks, during which the group may meet 4–6 times. The key dimensions of PBL are:

- self-directed or negotiated learning;
- group-based learning;
- linking theory and practice;
- learning that builds on students' existing experience and knowledge;
- collaborative learning;
- teamwork and/or professional development;
- reflective learning, self evaluation and assessment.

PBL courses vary. PBL may be introduced for the whole programme, or for single modules. The aim may be holistic learning across modules, or PBL may be used within existing modules. Lectures may be used to complement group learning, or excluded from the curriculum. There are also variations in the degree of direction, for example: whether learning outcomes are set or negotiable; the extent to which learning resources are provided; the role of the facilitator; and whether students run some of their own meetings. The presentation and format of scenarios also varies. While group size might ideally be about eight, resource constraints may result in larger groups. Finally, some or all of the learning may take place using virtual learning environments. The task of facilitating such learning is explored by Savin-Baden (2003).

There have been many attempts to research the value of PBL, culminating in the ESRC Project on the Effectiveness of Problem Based Learning (PEPBL). The initial findings highlight the difficulties in generalizing, given the variation in forms of PBL and the lack of agreement on outcome measures (Newman, 2003). However, a meta-analysis of research on medical education concluded that students who had studied using PBL rated this learning higher than traditional teaching, performed as well or better clinically, used higher-level strategies for understanding and self-directed study, but might perform less well in examinations of basic science knowledge (Albanese and Mitchell, 1993).

The applied nature of social work education, together with the pace of change in social needs, legislation and agency configuration, provide a sound rationale for the use of PBL. The group learning context provides opportunities for professional development, exploration of values, and critical and reflective practice. Many social work courses use some version of PBL in their teaching and learning, but it has been most extensively developed in the UK at the University of Bristol (Burgess, 1992; Taylor, 1997), Goldsmiths College (University of London), York University, Edinburgh (Cree and Davidson, 2000) and Glasgow/Strathclyde. A programme at the University of the West of England links PBL with interprofessional education for all health and social care students, who take one joint module per year. The third-year module is studied online (thus combining problem-based learning, interprofessional learning and e-learning, see pp. 132–4). An enquiry-based approach has been developed for learning knowledge and skills for social work law (Braye *et al.*, 2003) and joint PBL scenarios have been designed for use by social work and nursing students at Staffordshire (Moss, 2003).

In social policy, PBL is more commonly used within a single module than throughout the programme, as shown below.

Example: use of PBL: a comparative social policy module at APU

Students work in small groups to consider and compare the welfare systems of two countries. They prepare a presentation and produce a booklet comparing their welfare systems; each team member writes a chapter. Students learn from one another, organizing meetings and dividing up the tasks.

The perceived benefits were that students took more responsibility for their own learning, reflected on the process of knowledge acquisition, and improved communication and teamwork skills. The role transition for lecturers from instructor to facilitator was also seen to be positive: 'The most beneficial thing that I learned was that student learning is not as dependent on my "wonderful" lectures as I thought it was.'

For details see www.swap.ac.uk/links/casestudy.asp?casefind=csB Wendon

---

Experiential learning

The term 'experiential learning' is used to cover a wide range of activities in higher education, from work-based learning or practice learning, to learning through observation and action. Learning beyond the campus is addressed in Chapter 9; here we concentrate on experiential learning managed by the HEI outside the workplace. The work of Kolb (1984) referred to on p. 59

(Chapter 5) suggests learning requires a cyclical process of experience, reflection, conceptualization and experimentation. These ideas have been extended by Boud et al. (1993) who argue that experiential learning represents active engagement with the environment of which the learner is an important part, in terms of their unique past. It is influenced, among other factors, by the socio-economic context for learning and social and cultural constructions of learning (Boud et al., 1993: 6).

The term is used here to encompass forms of learning used to develop skills, self-awareness and reflection. Role-play, sculpting, simulations and observation activities are used extensively in social work education to develop skills in communication, interviewing, assessment and interventions. Within social policy programmes, experiential learning can be used to enliven teaching of social issues. In all cases, these activities need careful planning to ensure accessibility for all students, including those with disabilities; alternatively, equivalent activities with the same learning outcomes should be constructed.

Role-play

Role-play is primarily used to practise micro-skills of communication, such as listening, clarifying, questioning and summarizing. It is a powerful tool for understanding other people's needs and perspectives, such as experiences of powerlessness, and for self-reflection. While role-play can be valued highly by students, it may be a source of concern. Beyond the natural worry of being 'put on the spot' or observed by others, exploration of particular user roles may be stressful if relating closely to personal experience, such as abuse, prejudice or mental distress. Some key points for effective use are shown in the box on p. 76. Further ideas on developing students' feedback skills are explored by Koprovska et al. (1999).

A variation on role-play is 'user simulation' by actors. This approach is little developed in social work education in the UK, but is used in social work education in the US and as 'patient simulation' in medical education (Badger and MacNeil, 2002). 'Simulated' patients or clients use a set scenario, but respond to questions from and actions by the student. At Leeds Medical School, former patients and people from community groups have been trained and employed alongside actors, an approach that has potential for adaptation to social work education.

The use of video and one-way screens enables more students to learn through observation, while preserving the privacy of a face-to-face encounter. With video, the student role-players can themselves observe the encounter, and stop the tape at key points for discussion. One-way screens allow observers to discuss the progress of the encounter while it is taking place.

Sculpting is another experiential technique, in which participants take up positions in a room to represent their relationships in a family network or

Making effective use of role-play

Ethical practice	While students can be encouraged to explore different roles, no one should be forced to take on a role. Anyone can ask for the role-play to stop if it becomes stressful. It is not reasonable to expect students to role-play to a large group if they have not practised in small group settings.
Preparing students	The parameters of what will be expected should be carefully explained. A demonstration role-play by staff may provide useful modelling of the technique.
Setting and keeping boundaries	Time should be allowed for de-briefing and feedback. While students may work in small groups, staff should be available for consultation and support. Usually one or two students act as observers. At the end of the role-play students should 'de-role', stating who they are in real life. It is better to start with five-minute role-plays, building up to longer exercises as students become more familiar with the approach.
Establishing rules for feedback	Before the observer/s comment, the role-players themselves should indicate the strengths of the 'interview' and aspects that could be approached differently. A focus on feelings and observed behaviours is helpful; students should be discouraged from making generalized critical observations.

organization. Participants describe their feelings, and may then be asked to move in response to some changed circumstance, or to adopt a preferred position.

In assessing experiential skills work there is a tension between written critiques and direct assessment of skills (e.g. by video). Assessment of the student's skills by service users is a component of practice learning being developed in many social work programmes. At Nottingham Trent University, students present their own life history to a panel of users; assessment criteria include the student's ability to communicate with people with diverse impairments.

In social work education, research to identify effective and innovative practice in learning and teaching skills will hopefully be given an impetus by the SCIE studies on assessment (Crisp *et al.*, 2003) and communication skills (Trevithick *et al.*, 2004; Diggins, 2004). The reports establish a baseline of understanding and practice, but indicate the need for further research and development.

Simulations

Simulations involve role-plays of real and more complex events, and are used in other fields such as legal and human rights education. In some approaches, the focus is on procedures and policies, rather than micro-skills, but experiential feedback is still central. In social policy and social work simulations enable understanding and analysis of complex organizational contexts, such as:

- tribunals: welfare rights, employment, mental health (University of Bristol);
- select committees;
- court proceedings (Brunel University, University of Bristol);
- case conferences;
- communities (e.g. Moss, 2000).

Observation

Learning to observe the behaviour of others is a recognized tool for understanding human interaction in the social and natural sciences. It has an established place in social work education (where the observations are usually of individuals or small groups), but is also used in social policy courses to observe groups of people charged with policy development or implementation. Observation activities not only develop skills of factual recording and analysis, but also contribute to students' capacity for reflection as they process their reactions. Observational study may be undertaken within a scientific, positivist framework (to record, understand and evaluate events), a narrative model (which emphasizes subjectivity and the search for meaning, diversity and complexity) or within a framework of power relations (Le Riche and Tanner, 1998).

The traditional focus of observational learning in social work education has been child observation. It is often linked to the study of child development to encourage critical debate of topics such as developmental 'norms', attachment, and cultural and ecological perspectives. Despite encouragement for all students to undertake an observation as part of their qualifying training (CCETSW, 1991a), not all programmes have arranged this (Barnes, 2002).

Fawcett (1996) outlines the range of techniques for observation:

- naturalistic observation (contemporaneous running record);
- target child method (pre-coded system to record activity and language);

- Tavistock method (recording after visits, focusing on emotional development);
- time sampling (recording the frequency of specified behaviours);
- event sampling (recording the detail of a specified activity);
- checklist method (recording the observation of a list of behaviours).

Observations also vary in setting, length and number of visits. Although arranging such work can be time-consuming for staff and students, the benefits are immense. Alternatively, some programmes make use of videos produced for this purpose.

The potential for observation tasks to be used in a range of other settings in social work is explored by Le Riche and Tanner (1998). Observation can be also built into practice learning settings as a precursor to active involvement (e.g. team meetings). The requirement for students to 'shadow' social workers for the degree in social work in England may lead to more extensive use of such techniques.

In both social policy and social work, observation activities can be arranged in agencies and organizations to further understanding of policy development and implementation. Potential venues include committee meetings of local authorities, board meetings of NHS bodies (both of which are open to the public), public consultation meetings and court proceedings. In all these activities, class discussion will significantly enhance the learning, both in preparation for the visit and in subsequent analysis.

Critical analysis of theory

One important and potentially difficult area for both students and educators in social policy and social work is finding effective ways of enabling students to understand, critically analyse and apply a range of theories. Interactive learning approaches are clearly of value in this respect, as students are enabled to articulate their understanding. Examples of two approaches are given in the box on p. 79. The first is small-scale, used within a single class at the start of a module; the other took place over a whole module.

Supporting student learning: tutorials and personal development planning

Traditionally, universities arranged tutorial support in three ways: academic tutors (to support student learning on specific discipline areas), progress tutors (often referred to as year tutors or convenors) and personal tutors. Increasingly, the key relationship is with the personal tutor who provides academic and

---

Examples: developing understanding and critical analysis of theory

1   University of Bristol: Hilary Burgess

Context: a second-year module on 'Family Support' for students on degrees in social policy, early childhood studies and social work.

In the first session, 'Family Stress', the following question was posed: What theories might help us to understand domestic violence? Students worked in pairs for 15 minutes, then reported their ideas to the large group. Suggestions were recorded, more or less verbatim, on the whiteboard by the lecturer who grouped similar ideas (e.g. structural inequalities on one side, individualistic formulations on another; interpersonal explanations at the top, biological or genetic explanations to the bottom). The lecturer prompted for further ideas. Different ways of expressing the ideas were developed, links made to relevant theories, and the strengths and limitations of different theories were debated.

2   University of Glasgow: Pam Green Lister

Context: a second-year postgraduate module in social work practice, which aims to provide knowledge and understanding of theoretical frameworks of social work intervention.

Students constructed a Critical Analysis Framework, which they subsequently used as groups presented different theories of social work. The framework was reviewed and developed throughout the module. The following term, when the students were on placement, they introduced the framework to practice teachers in a university-based workshop. It was also used during practice discussion group meetings held throughout the placement. In assignments for both the module and the practice placement, students made use of the framework.

A full account and evaluation of the approach can be found at www.swap.ac.uk/swap/miniproject2.asp

---

pastoral support throughout the programme. A student's relationship with his or her tutor may play a key role in student satisfaction and retention. In an era of increasing class sizes, this personal contact is crucial. However, tutorial work increasingly takes place in small groups, with opportunities for personal contact limited to times of crisis.

A suggested framework for effective tutoring

- Continuity of tutor is preferable.
- Students (and tutors) should have the opportunity to ask for a change if the relationship breaks down.
- Tutors need to be mindful of the impact of power differentials in the tutorial relationship, in terms of authority, gender, ethnicity and class.
- A framework of clear expectations and mutual respect should be established, with roles and boundaries clarified.
- The availability of other sources of support should be stated.
- As far as possible equity of access should be agreed within each programme.
- Clear planning and recording should underpin tutorial work.

The framework for learning support has been strengthened by the introduction of personal development planning (PDP), which, along with a transcript to record student achievement, makes up the HE Progress File. This was proposed in the Dearing Report (1997), and plans have been taken forward by Universities UK, the Standing Conference of Principals (SCoP) and the QAA. Progress Files will be implemented for all HE awards by 2005–6. PDP has been defined as 'a structured and supported process undertaken by an individual to reflect upon their own learning, performance and/or achievement and to plan for their personal, educational and career development' (QAA, 2001a). Key features include the opportunity for students to reflect on learning throughout their university career, enabling an integrated and holistic view (particularly important in the context of modularization and potential fragmentation of learning). When expressed as a set of actions, PDP processes contain a set of interconnected activities namely:

- planning (how to achieve objectives or general change);
- doing (learning through the experience of doing with greater self-awareness);
- recording (thoughts, ideas, experiences, both to understand better and to evidence the process and results of learning);
- reviewing (reflections on what has happened, making sense of it all);
- evaluating (making judgements about self and own work and determining what needs to be done to develop/improve/move on)

(Learning and Teaching Support Network (LTSN)
Generic Centre, 2002)

Implementation of PDP varies significantly between universities. While some have adopted an institution-wide approach, others have devolved implementation to departments or faculties. Tutors closely supervise some schemes; others rely more on self-assessment. Information technology may be used to support PDPs; others are portfolio-based. In social work, the PDP has potential to bring together feedback and learning from practice and university-based learning. It can contribute directly to students' future professional development as areas of strength and areas to develop are highlighted. Concerns have been expressed about some issues, in particular the ownership of PDPs, which may at times touch on personal areas. In some disciplines, questions have been raised about whether academic staff have the skills to implement this system. Overall, however, there is a growing body of evidence that 'the processes and actions that underlie PDP do have a positive impact on student attainment and approaches to learning' (Gough *et al.*, 2003: 6).

Conclusion

In this chapter a number of ways in which students' learning may be effectively promoted in both social policy and social work have been outlined. The implications for educators are that we must adopt sound strategies to plan our teaching, co-ordinate and communicate well with other staff, be open to trying new approaches, and above all be committed to supporting students in a framework of equity, transparency and respect.

7

Walking the assessment tightrope

Beth R. Crisp and Pam Green Lister

Introduction

For many people, one of the thrills of going to the circus is the spectacle of the tightrope walker who aims to walk a considerable distance on nothing more than a thin wire, with the ground many metres below. Considerable skill is required, as there is a very fine line between remaining balanced and falling off. As educators, we have over the years come to view our roles in overseeing the assessment process as requiring the exacting skills and knowledge of the tightrope walker, balancing differing functions and forms of assessment with demands on time.

In this chapter, we will explore some of the key issues around assessment which we as educators of social work and social policy students find ourselves grappling with. These issues are:

- What is the purpose of assessment?
- What is an assessment strategy and how do we develop one?
- What are some forms of assessment which we might consider?
- What is the place of peer assessment and self-assessment in our courses?
- The importance of feedback to students.
- Implementation issues.

The purpose of assessment

Sometimes in jest, our students suggest to us that we set them assessment tasks because we do not believe they have enough to do in their already busy lives.

Similarly, around the corridors of higher education institutions, academics feeling weighed down by piles of marking are sometimes heard to complain about how much time they must devote to assessment processes. Given the amount of time devoted to assessment by both students and academics, we need first to consider the purposes of assessment.

The assessment of students in higher education performs a number of functions, which may not always be compatible. As teachers we would like to think that the assessment tasks we set are also learning tasks, so that learning and assessment become aligned, rather than being somewhat independent of each other (Biggs, 2003). The notion of alignment is not only pedagogically sound but likely to have resonance with students who, when faced with demands beyond their courses (e.g. financial survival), and, given a choice between learning and assessment tasks, tend to devote their time to the latter. The reality is that assessment tasks provide an incentive for students to engage with some aspects of course content and enable them to demonstrate their acquired knowledge and understanding of particular subject matter or mastery of certain skills.

The role of the assessor involves determining the level of competence displayed in undertaking the task and, ideally, offering feedback on future learning needs (Rowntree, 1987). Assessment also provides grading for students' work, allowing comparison of performance across a class, and across the curriculum for individual students. The subsequent gaining of a degree or professional qualification depends on students successfully completing a set of specified assessment tasks across the curriculum. As such, there may be stakeholders beyond the higher education institution, such as employers, regulatory bodies or clients, who see the assessment process as being akin to certification or professional gatekeeping (Younes, 1998). In professional courses such as social work, assessment will be associated with notions such as fitness to practice and eligibility for professional registration as a social worker with the new social care councils in England, Northern Ireland, Scotland and Wales.

In terms of gatekeeping, assessment tasks may not only restrict who gains certification on exiting an educational programme but also who is admitted. Requirements by some care councils that students admitted to social work programmes have achieved specified levels of literacy and numeracy require appropriate assessment tasks to determine equivalence for those entrants who have not achieved formal qualifications in these areas.

In addition to gatekeeping, assessment clearly has a vital role to play in the ongoing development of learning and teaching strategies. It can be crucial in determining what, why and how students learn (Brown *et al.*, 1997). Furthermore, in an era when evaluation of teaching is often reduced to student satisfaction surveys, critical reflection on work submitted for assessment can serve as an alternative method of evaluating the success of teaching.

Building an assessment strategy

In an ideal world, an assessment strategy would outline the types of assessment to be used and provide a rationale for every component of a course. However, the use of shared modules across courses in higher education institutions or numerous combinations of electives can place limits on the ability of a course team to develop a comprehensive assessment strategy (Knight, 2000). Shared modules, whether compulsory or elective, may be established for pragmatic reasons (e.g. it is more economical to have one unit taught to students from several courses than repeated to small groups) or ideological reasons (e.g. to facilitate interdisciplinary learning). Thus it may only be possible for a teaching team to control the assessment strategy for the units that they themselves teach and assess.

There are other constraints on the development of an assessment strategy. Institutions or faculties may have established principles and policies around assessment, to which programmes and modules contained therein must conform (Mutch and Brown, 2001; Yorke, 2001). For example, institutional requirements that all work be joint marked potentially limits use of class presentations as a formal assessment task unless a panel of assessors can attend all presentations. In relation to peer assessment by students, a case might have to be made for this to be accepted as equivalent to a second marker.

Institutional requirements undoubtedly underpin the suggestion that 'British students are probably the most assessed in Europe' (Mutch and Brown, 2001: 10). Therefore, before considering the assignments for individual modules, the question should be addressed as to what is feasible for students to do in a year. Having too many assessment tasks and not enough time to do each one are not uncommon problems. In developing a programme-wide strategy, a further question is whether each module needs its own separate piece of assessment or whether some assessment tasks can be developed which can simultaneously assess student learning in multiple parts of their courses.

Accrediting bodies may also place constraints on an overall assessment strategy, by requiring that specific knowledge and/or skills be assessed within programmes. Yet even without such external demands, it is worth considering whether a range of skills is being tested across a programme or if students are always asked to do the same tasks, e.g. writing essays. In the United Kingdom, the benchmarking statements for both social policy and social work (QAA, 2000) suggest that students should undertake assessment tasks that demonstrate a range of abilities and skills. This is consistent with the expectations of employers (and other stakeholders) who expect graduates in these disciplines to have a range of skills.

Assessment strategies may also disadvantage some students. For example, if all the assignments are written tasks, a student with dyslexia may be disadvantaged; a strong emphasis on examinations may disadvantage students who are victims of trauma or who for some other reason are unable to think as quickly as may be required in a three-hour unseen examination. In contrast, it has been suggested that some computer-based assessments may enable visually impaired students to be assessed in the same room as the rest of the class, rather than separately, which is the typical experience of such students (Wiles, 2002). Taking account of the needs of students with specific learning needs can be an opportunity to review the assessment procedures not just for particular students but for all students in a course (McCarthy and Hurst, 2001). The underlying issues of diversity, inclusion and equality are addressed in Chapter 4.

Having considered the core elements necessary to develop an overall assessment strategy, we will now review the issues in developing an assessment strategy for individual modules (although in practice this order is often inverted). Assessment methods play a large part in determining what students learn:

> If we test students for factual recall, then they will memorize a set of facts. If we test them for their ability to analyze relationships, then they will begin to learn to think critically. If we assess how well they can apply classroom material to concrete problems, then they will learn to do that.
>
> (Wergin, 1988: 5)

Obviously, the content of modules and the learning objectives should guide the development of the assessment tasks, so the fit of the assessment tasks to the learning outcomes is essential. Summative assessment, which usually takes place at the end of a module, ostensibly has the objective of grading students; formative assessment, which occurs during a course, places greater emphasis on facilitating student learning (Cree, 2000). These divergent aims may conflict:

> An emphasis on outcomes, for example, may be at odds with the idea of incremental learning and process-based assessment . . . If the learning objectives are to open students' minds and broaden their experience, then the chosen assessment methods will be very different from those that set out to assess a specific piece of knowledge or skill.
>
> (Cree, 2000: 30)

The stage at which the assessment task is set within the overall programme is also important. For example, the role of the first piece of written work in a course may be as much about assessing general skills (e.g. library use, writing style, referencing) as about content or knowledge. Furthermore, it could be more appropriate to offer new undergraduate students several short pieces of assessment, whereas a single longer piece of work may be appropriate for honours or postgraduate students. For students whose course involves a placement, this experience can be utilized in subsequent assessment tasks.

In both individual assignments and the overall assessment strategy, it is important that criteria for assessment are made explicit and provided to both students and co-markers prior to beginning work on the tasks. While the need to make criteria explicit may be obvious when peer or self-assessment is to be utilized, all students should know how they are to be assessed. Information about assessment criteria should also include details as to what students may expect by way of feedback (see the section on feedback later in the chapter).

The mode of teaching may also influence assessment possibilities. Indeed, as we have mentioned earlier, learning and assessment activities should be aligned (Biggs, 2003). Thus for example, if our objectives are for students to learn a set of facts, then both learning and assessment modes need to reflect this. This is likely to involve a different set of learning and assessment tasks than might be used if our objective is to develop students' understanding and ability to critique theories or policies.

There also needs to be alignment between the mode of teaching and assessment tasks. For example, group projects may be more easily facilitated for students who attend classes together than for distance students. Some distance education students may be required to complete more written assessment tasks than their on-campus colleagues, although students at a distance have arguably as much, if not more, need to develop their presentation skills. However, it is possible for most distance learners to produce a presentation on audio or video-tape (Crisp, 1999) or via a telephone conference.

Whatever methods are chosen, these must, prior to the task being set, be deemed appropriate in respect of the skills, knowledge etc. to be assessed, and take into account the known needs of students, including disabilities or family commitments (if a course has been particularly designed for students for whom this is an issue). Finally, an assessment strategy should include an evaluation component, including scrutiny of completed assignments to determine whether they were effective in assessing the learning outcomes specified. While external examiners undoubtedly have an important role in respect of scrutinizing assessment, this does not absolve individual assessors from the responsibility of undertaking their own evaluations.

Different forms of assessment

It has been estimated that essays or reports marked by tutors or unseen timed exams form at least 90 per cent of the assessment tasks on a typical degree programme in the United Kingdom (Brown and Glasner, 1999). After reviewing some of the issues raised by these forms of assessment, we consider some of the alternatives.

Essays

In some higher education settings assessment and essays are almost synonymous, so the question 'Have you set the assessment?' is taken to mean 'Have you set the essay questions?' Educators of social science students regularly set essay questions and, for some students, essays are a familiar task, involving searching for information and developing a coherent written argument that demonstrates their understanding of the issue under discussion. A typical essay does not require students to find time to collaborate with others, nor to access sources of information beyond the university library. As such, an essay can be done at a time to suit busy students. Able students may use the essay structure somewhat creatively as a means of expression.

Essays also have a number of shortcomings as an assessment method. A common criticism is that this is not a form of writing for which there is much demand beyond educational institutions. A more critical question is whether the skills of writing an essay help one write reports, position papers or other documents which social work or social policy graduates might be expected to produce in their working life. Furthermore, while plagiarism has long been an issue in higher education, the ease with which unscrupulous social science students, at least in the US (and probably in the UK), are able to purchase essays over the Internet (Gibelman et al., 1999) is further grounds for actively considering whether an essay is the most appropriate form of assessment. Even without the possibility of purchasing essays, various forms of cheating are common in written work submitted for assessment (Franklyn-Stokes and Newstead, 1995; Ashworth et al., 1997). While there are now a growing number of services to detect plagiarism (e.g. the Joint Information Systems Committee Plagiarism Advisory Service), this undoubtedly adds to the assessment workload.

Examinations

Examinations are perceived by students to offer fewer opportunities for cheating (Franklyn-Stokes and Newstead, 1995), and cheating in exams is considered to be a far more serious offence than cheating in written assignments (Ashworth et al., 1997). However, some critical reflection on the potential and limitations of examinations as a method of assessment is required.

Written examinations may take a number of formats. They may involve students writing a number of short essays, answering several short-answer questions, or numerous multiple-choice questions. Typically, there is a finite time for students to produce their answers, and they may or may not have access to other resources (e.g. notes or books). One variant which more closely simulates the future employment of both social policy and social work graduates is the 'take home' exam, in which students are provided with one or more questions at a given time and required to submit their answers within a few days. This format is based on the assumption that the ability to access resources and produce timely written responses is more important than being able to regurgitate facts and scribble down as much as one can in a set time.

Although not uncommon in social policy courses, many social work academics are reluctant to use written exams to assess core social work theory and knowledge. Written exams are most likely to be reserved for assessing acquisition of knowledge in psychology (Dillenberger *et al.*, 1997), law (Henderson *et al.*, 2002) or research methods (e.g. Sieppert and Krysik, 1996; Petracchi and Patchner, 2001). Yet social workers often have to make decisions rapidly, and exams can arguably simulate this aspect of professional life. There may be an argument for exams in particular aspects of social work courses, e.g. to assess crisis intervention or assessment skills. 'Clients' could be presented to students live in the examination room or on video, or a written summary of the client's presenting problems could be made available. Students could then be asked a series of short-answer questions as to how they would deal with the client on the basis of the information provided to them, or be asked to conduct an interview with a 'client' (Petracchi, 1999).

A focus on the ability to present an argument to experts or colleagues (Butler and Coleman, 1997) has resulted in proposals for students to be assessed on their oral presentation rather than their writing skills. While oral exams or vivas feature in the examination of PhDs in the United Kingdom, they can also be used for assessing coursework for lower qualifications, although this potential is often not realized.

An oral examination of legal knowledge

Students undertaking a training programme to become an Approved Social Worker (mental health officer) in one English higher education institution are assessed on their knowledge of law by means of an oral examination. This lasts between half and three-quarters of an hour during which time students present a case to the assessment panel (two tutors and one practising approved social worker) in which they discuss the legal issues emerging from a case they have been involved in, and answer questions about legislation. All exams are tape-recorded. The rationale is that practising social workers need to be able to recall and discuss legal issues in high pressure situations.

(Henderson *et al.*, 2002)

Portfolios

The development of portfolios has been used to document social work students' developing knowledge and competence over the course in specific subjects such as group work (Marotta *et al.*, 2000) and community organizing (Gutierrez and Alvarez, 2000) and can also be used for assessing educational placements undertaken by both social work and social policy students. This format is particularly suitable for assessing student learning when the evidence of their learning is presented in several and potentially disparate ways. For example, students could present evidence of their involvement in a local campaign, such as background research, briefing papers, press releases and letters they have written. Other evidence might include copies of media coverage, minutes of meetings, and references or testimonials written by others. As some of the materials may originally have been produced for reasons other than the student's assessment, a statement from students in which they introduce the materials and discuss what learning is represented by the contents is likely to be crucial.

While students may choose the contents of their portfolios, this can be prescribed. Most students have no experience of developing portfolios and need clear guidelines to enable them to complete them in a manner which is timely and remains an active method of learning rather than just another task to be completed (Taylor et al., 1999).

Notwithstanding their potential, portfolios can be a problematic method of assessment. Low inter-rater reliability has been found between markers (Black, 1993, in Risler, 1999) and further difficulties arise from lack of verification and the production of unwieldy material not clearly related to predetermined competences, often included if the guidelines are unclear (Edwards and Kinsey, 1999). Moreover, the effort required to both produce and assess portfolios suggests this is a time-consuming activity (Edwards and Kinsey, 1999; Horwath and Shardlow, 2000).

Portfolio with learning contract for distance education students in a practice teacher course

Candidates for the CCETSW Award in Practice Teaching at the University of Sheffield were required to develop a learning agreement with their tutor, detailing how they would meet their learning objectives. There was considerable scope for negotiation as to what the portfolio would comprise. Target dates were set for submission of the various components for formative feedback. Students were allowed to submit all pieces of portfolio work in stages prior to the final assessment for formative assessment, rather than to be graded.

(Horwath and Shardlow, 2000)

Proposals

The development of proposals is often used to assess research methods courses (e.g. Walsh, 1998; Crisp, 1999); this could also be used to assess understanding of the processes and issues in planning and developing interventions which seek to address social problems in the local community (e.g. Moxley and Thrasher,

1996; Hollister and McGee, 2000). Such proposals might be preparation for projects subsequently undertaken, or may be a standalone assignment that enables students to demonstrate their ability to integrate and apply a range of skills and theoretical knowledge in a practical task similar to one that they may have to undertake after graduation. A cohort of students, required to develop a proposal to benefit their local community, reported that this increased their understanding and ability to plan and develop new social programmes, including writing grant applications (Moxley and Thrasher, 1996).

Topics of student proposals which seek to address social problems in local communities

- domestic violence;
- community support of adults with a mental illness;
- homelessness;
- community support for aged persons;
- school retention in minority ethnic communities.

(Moxley and Thrasher, 1996)

Other written tasks

Reports of work undertaken by students are useful in assessing learning in both university-based and placement settings. Carrying out a small-scale piece of research by collecting their own original data or sourcing existing data (e.g. from local authorities or the Office for National Statistics) and preparing a report on the findings may require students to reflect on differences between their findings and what they have read.

While lengthy written tasks enable students to demonstrate their understanding of complex phenomena, the audiences to which graduates in social work and social policy write are often busy people looking for something succinct. An assignment set by one of us required postgraduate students to prepare an abstract of a paper they had read in no more than 250 words. After years of writing lengthy essays, some class members said they found it difficult to write so succinctly.

One problem with the process of writing essays and reports is that often students will just skim over books and articles until they find a point that appears to suit their line of argument. Sometimes this results in quotes being taken out of context and utterly misconstrued. If our aim is to get students to read in depth, then we need to set assessment tasks that encourage this. There may be a key book which takes an interesting or controversial line that may have caught the public imagination through the media. Asking students to write a critical review of such a text not only requires them to have read it from cover to cover, but also to have read more broadly to develop their own critique.

Short written assignment for level 1 social policy students

Level 1 social policy students at the University of Surrey are assessed in a one-hour multiple-choice and short-answer written exam along with two short pieces of written work, each of 800 words. The aim of the written pieces is to encourage students to write clear and concise answers to set questions. The first is set early in the semester; it is hoped that prompt feedback will facilitate growth in student confidence. The timing also enables staff to identify potential problems early on when there may still be time to address them prior to the final exam.

(Driver, undated)

Peer assessment and self-assessment

Peer assessment and self-assessment have been proposed as strategies for enhancing learning; this fits with the development of reflective learning and critical thinking (e.g. Burgess *et al.*, 1999; Baldwin, 2000; Gutierrez and Alvarez, 2000). Proponents claim they develop students' capacities to assess themselves, to make judgements about their learning (and that of their peers) and to evaluate what has been learnt. Further benefits include redressing the balance of power between staff and students, developing anti-oppressive practice and the process of lifelong learning, and facilitating students to take specific responsibility for monitoring and making judgements about their own learning (Burgess *et al.*, 1999).

A common misunderstanding is that peer assessment and self-assessment are necessarily alternative to assessment by staff. In some cases, students complete assessment tasks such as giving presentations or producing reports, and are formally involved in the processes of grading and/or providing feedback in addition to staff. This use of peer assessment and self-assessment can be seen as a 'value-added extra' (Cree, 2000: 30) rather than as an alternative to conventional assessment.

Students typically need considerable guidance to enable them to assess their own work or that completed by their peers, so structured instruments may be used (e.g. Gutierrez and Alvarez, 2000). Alternatively, groups of students may devise their assessment exercises or use less structured reporting mechanisms such as reflective diaries or learning logs (Burgess *et al.*, 1999). As university guidelines generally preclude students assigning their final grade for a unit of study (Burgess *et al.*, 1999), students' self- and peer assessments must be reviewed by their teachers. Interestingly when this does occur, academics often comment that students are much harder on themselves and their peers than their teachers would have been.

Evaluations of self-assessment have primarily been concerned with its use as a method of learning rather than an assessment tool. An evaluation of this method undertaken in three English sites suggests the implementation of self-assessment requires both planning and ongoing monitoring. Prior to implementation, academic staff may require training, including their role as facilitators/tutors/markers, in addition to orienting students to this approach. Consideration must be given to the selection of the self-assessment instruments or tasks, ensuring a balance between complexity and the time required for completion. The extent to which self-assessment is used across the curriculum should also be considered as repeated use may result in self-assessment fatigue (Burgess *et al.*, 1999). Furthermore, it be may be inappropriate to incorporate self-assessment in the early stages of a course as there are likely to be too many unknowns for students to be able to fully engage with the self-assessment activity (Waldman *et al.*, 1999; Baldwin, 2000).

Feedback

Although feedback to students on their assessed work has been described as 'the life-blood of learning' (Rowntree, 1987: 24), insufficient thought may be given as to how and what form this should take. Departmental or programme policies may determine that written feedback is provided within a set time-frame, and there may be proformas which provide a structured format. It is crucial, however, that each assignment is assessed against the specific criteria that are set, rather than students receiving generalized comments.

To build student confidence and assist learning, it is usually recommended that feedback should start with identification of strengths and positive points. Only then should the problems be raised, and it is important to do this in a way which emphasizes that it is the work presented which is problematic rather than the person who submitted it for assessment. Feedback should be constructive, so that if the student was asked to do a similar task again, they would have some ideas as to what they should do differently. The timing is also crucial, especially for formative assessments, if the feedback is to assist students to evaluate their progress and plan for future learning (Cree, 2000).

There are instances when assessors may wonder whether the student who has submitted work has some form of undiagnosed learning disability such as dyslexia. While work submitted should be assessed as it stands, occasionally we would seek advice from the university's specialist learning advisers prior to providing feedback. This may mean the written feedback to the student includes an invitation to discuss their work with the assessor.

Formative assessment using email

Social work students at Liverpool John Moores University are introduced to the concept of social work assessment through the use of an
interactive case study. Students are emailed a task sheet to complete,
which includes questions about the hypotheses they have developed,
and what they perceive to be the issues. Students submit the completed
task sheet by email. Each student is responded to individually, and the
total response of the group is collated and emailed back to all students
with an analysis, commenting on the group performance. This provides
same day feedback to both students and teacher.

(Clifford, 2003)

Unlike written assignments that are generally returned to students with
feedback, many higher education institutions have policies of not returning
examination scripts. While there are many who consider this to be a considerable drawback of exams as an assessment method, there are others who have
no such qualms. For example:

> Recently the notion of returning marked examination scripts to students
> so they can obtain feedback and improve has been discussed. This will be
> a very time-consuming activity. It assumes that students will benefit from
> the feedback and their learning will improve. Before embarking on this
> path, it would be prudent to run a series of well-controlled experiments to
> check costs and benefits of the procedure for lecturers and students.
>
> (Brown, 2001: 17)

Certainly short timelines for marking end-of-year exams can render it difficult for assessors to spend time giving any constructive feedback to students
but, when no other assessment methods are used, this can lead to students
receiving no feedback except for their marks. While this may fulfil the purpose
of assessment as determining level of achievement, the developmental aspects
of the assessment process are lost.

Conclusion

Developing and implementing appropriate processes for assessing student
learning might be likened to walking a tightrope, since many different issues
need to be balanced, such as the different functions of assessment, the need
for rigour and yet clarity, the need for progression during a programme, and
the needs of both students and staff in terms of timing, and it is not hard to

lose one's balance. No single form of assessment is either universally appropriate or without some shortcomings. Furthermore, considerable skill is required to develop the most appropriate set of assessment tasks for a group of students which takes into account the many parameters such as learning outcomes, learning needs, subject matter, stage and type of students, and institutional requirements.

The task of identifying appropriate assessment methods is made more difficult given that rigorous evidence of effectiveness is often scant or non-existent (e.g. Desai, 2000; Hollister and McGee, 2000; Marotta *et al.*, 2000). It is critical that assessment methods can reliably discriminate between students who have met the grade and those who have not (Visvesaran, 2000) but this is not often considered in evaluations of assessment. More commonly, published evaluations of assessment methods report positive feedback from students (e.g. Montalvo, 1999). These say much about the acceptability of the task but not necessarily whether it is an effective or appropriate way of determining if students have acquired particular knowledge or developed specified competencies.

Another issue for further consideration is that many of the more innovative forms of assessment proposed in the literature seem very time intensive for both students and assessors. While we have an ethical duty to our students to ensure that the time required to complete assessable tasks is realistic, our own limits as educators must be recognized (Burgess *et al.*, 1999; Knight, 2000). Many interesting published accounts of assessment methods involved classes no larger than 20 or 25 students in a year (e.g. Butler and Coleman, 1997; Gutierrez and Alvarez, 2000; Marotta *et al.*, 2000). Yet many social policy and social work educators do not have the luxury of such small cohorts of students and must balance assessment of large numbers of students with a myriad of other responsibilities.

It is probably inevitable that the development of assessment strategies for modules and course programmes will involve compromises. Our task as educators is to be informed as to the implications of the various choices available to us, and, when necessary, to have the courage of the tightrope walker and not just stick to traditional, if questionable, approaches to assessment.

8

Towards eLearning: opportunities and challenges

Jackie Rafferty, Melanie Ashford and Sue Orton

Introduction

In this chapter we consider how eLearning contributes to effective social policy and social work education. We begin by clarifying the term 'eLearning', and then contextualize eLearning in relation to the growth of the information society. We go on to explore some of the opportunities and challenges eLearning presents to social policy and social work educators. We end by setting out options for moving forward. First, a word about the term 'eLearning': we have adopted the convention, other than in quotations, of capitalizing the 'L' in 'eLearning' in order to emphasize the 'Learning' rather than the 'Electronic' aspects as emphasized by Lewis.

> The promise of eLearning is that it can deliver a transformational change in the effectiveness of education. . . . In all of this we must not lose sight of the fact that ICT is a means and not an end. But our strategy has to be driven by the needs of the learners and not the mode of delivery.
>
> (Lewis, 2002)

This chapter focuses on the role of eLearning in social policy and social work learning and teaching in higher education and provides a contribution to a continuing revolution that in 2004 is turning out to be more of a slower evolution. Nevertheless 'e' is embedded into our lives in a way that we would not have foreseen even five years ago. Do you buy books online? Do you bank online? Do you check train timetables online? Over 50 per cent of the UK population do. If you do, you are aware of the research and information potential and realities, and the joys and idiosyncrasies of the Internet. There are numerous ways of describing the width and depth of eLearning. Rosenberg (2001) provides a broad but helpful example: 'ELearning refers to the use of Internet technologies to deliver a broad array of solutions that enhance knowledge and performance' (Rosenberg, 2001).

Within this overall definition a study for the Department of Health Steering Group on eLearning developed the framework shown in the box below for social work educators and students, and which, we suggest, is equally applicable to social policy.

'eLearning' may have meanings, including:

1   Formal knowledge and learning resources
    a   a method of learning pre-developed curriculum content;
    b   a means of 'packaging' various learning resources to tailor learning to the student;
    c   access to knowledge and information through databases of research evidence, abstracts, full text journals, web-based information, legislation, law and practice.

2   Learning networks
    a   a means of learning collaboratively: student to student, group to group, student to educator and educator to student;
    b   an ability to learn across and within: courses, organizations and multi- and inter-professionally.

3   Contact, administration and assessment
    a   a mode of formative and summative assessment;
    b   a means of supporting the administration and tracking of learning.

4   Information management skills
    a   ensuring the baseline skills of students and staff include appropriate levels of IT skills to support learning and practice;
    b   development of information literacy, including the critical appraisal skills necessary to make use of online resources;
    c   as a subject in its own right in terms of learning about the effective and ethical use of IT within social care.

(Rafferty and Waldman, 2003)

Some of the different meanings shown in the box on p. 96 will be explored below in the context of the use of eLearning within campus-based learning, as well as learning through practice and workplaces.

We use the terms 'educator', 'academic', 'lecturer', 'teacher', 'student' and 'learner'. This is not a case of inconsistency or carelessness but rather reflects the fluid position of individuals in and out of various roles. An 'educator' may well be an academic but in social work education may also be a practitioner, practice teacher or mentor either within social work practice or a cognate profession or discipline. A social policy student on a work-based placement may equally learn from a professional who is acting as the student's guide or teacher. A professional or academic may himself or herself be pursuing further development through informal or formal learning and in turn become the learner. The advent of eLearning supports the further blurring of the boundaries between the various roles:

> The educators within this process were willing also to be learners, something that does not necessarily come naturally to academics more often considered 'experts'. Boyer asserts 'good teaching means that faculty, as scholars, are also learners' and the outcome of this project affirms this point.
>
> (Skehill, 2003: 188)

Learning in the information society

Parallels to the current state of eLearning can be drawn with the challenge to universities in the late nineteenth century from an earlier revolution in information technology – books.

> The real challenges, however, were not those of space and money. They were organizational and conceptual. How should books be arranged for optimal use? What kind of cataloguing system could be invented to allow rapid access to the huge number of volumes that were now being acquired? . . . How should library books be integrated into the university's programs of instruction . . .
>
> (Neil Rudensteine, quoting Charles Eliot, President of Harvard University in 1876 (Rudensteine, 1996))

Electronic means of communication and information have been with us since the advent of the telephone and the radio. Masuda (1982) and Toffler (1980) mapped the move into the 'information society' as computing and communication came together to form 'information and communication technologies', termed the 'Third Wave' by Toffler, as the post-industrial successor to the agrarian (first wave) and industrial ages (second wave). Debates on continuing challenges such as intellectual property rights, morality, security and privacy started in the first phase of the Third Wave were joined by concerns that a global digital divide was growing between the information rich and the information poor, the haves and have-nots.

Reports by Gore in 1991 and Bangemann in 1994 were key to the advent of eLearning (Ducatel *et al.*, 2000). In the US the Gore Report emphasized the 'call for the creation of a Global Digital Library, so all the world's citizens will have quicker and richer access to all the world's information' (Gore, 1991). In Europe the Bangemann Report included a section on 'Life long learning for a changing society' and promoted extending advanced distance learning techniques into schools and colleges. It also noted the need to: 'engage in a major effort to train the trainers and expand computer literacy among the teaching profession' (Bangemann, 1994: 26).

It was in the 1980s and 1990s that there came the realization that the information society was as much about social policy and social welfare as it was about computing science and globalization because of its actual and potential impact on citizens and nation states (Masuda 1982; Glastonbury and LaMendola, 1992; Castells, 2000). The recommendations of the Gore and Bangemann policy reports are still being played out. We are increasingly a networked society. The UK Government's Office of the e-Envoy (OeE) claims the UK is one of the world's most 'connected' economies. In 1998, less than 10 per cent of UK households had Internet access; by October 2003, that figure stood at 56 per cent. Virtually all schools are 'wired up' and 95 per cent of businesses are online (OeE, 2003). The OeE's role is not just about Internet access but also the delivery of online government services: 'The digital revolution offers huge opportunities to improve public services by better tailoring them to the needs of individual citizens, who increasingly want to be able to choose when, where and how they interact with government' (Electronic Government Services for the 21st Century, 2000).

As indicated above the information society is a subject in its own right, deserving of study within social policy and social work, where issues of digital divides, intellectual property rights, morality, ethics, security, service delivery and policy formation, are still very current concerns. As Toffler says: 'If you don't have a strategy, you will be permanently reactive and part of somebody else's strategy' (Toffler, 1980).

eLearning in social policy and social work

As outlined above, social policy and social work students are living and working in the information age and they will expect their learning modes to increasingly reflect this. We describe below a hierarchy of engagement with eLearning and provide pointers to case studies as examples of practice as well as looking at the challenges to educators and learners, universities and workplaces.

*When should eLearning be used in social
policy and social work curricula?*

The answer is that it depends – on what knowledge and skill learning
outcomes are required; what approach to learning most suits the
module and learner; what eLearning resources are available or could be
developed – and educators need to make informed decisions. There are
various physical scenarios where it can be used effectively. It can most
obviously be used on campus, combined with face-to-face teaching or
giving students the chance to work at a time and place independent of
timetables, and at their own speed. It can be used for learning at a
distance, for example from home; but it can also be accessed from the
workplace, which supports students in practice/workplace settings and
professionals engaging in further learning.

The aim is to use technology to enable learners to engage with the subject
content in a way that will add value. This can be approached through: developing educators' understanding of the learning processes and of the learners
(pedagogic approach); and, through using the technology to support learners
engaging at a different and deeper level with the subject theories, content and
concepts (subject-based approach). We suggest that though the former is ultimately essential, the latter is likely to be a stronger driver to engage academics'
interest and commitment.

Use of email and the web to communicate and find information is now
well established. Ashford and Young (2003: 443) point out that the technical
advances that have enabled computers to become part of everyday equipment
have created the possibilities for electronic forms of communication that are
far reaching in their effects. They argue that traditional power relationships
have the potential to be transformed by the democratization of control and
access to information.

One advantage, which is beneficial to educators and learners alike, is that
educators and learners are on a more equal footing with regard to gaining
access to the emerging conversations, information and/or resources accessible
through communication and information technologies. With required skills,
learners are able to access knowledge and information as quickly as their
teachers; and the subject specialist becomes an adviser to the learner, a prompt
for critical analysis, rather than a knowledge disseminator.

Digital communication has enabled easier access of the one-to-many
concept, in that one email or posting can be written but sent to many students,
thus saving time and resources, and having cost-saving benefits. However, the
downside of this is that the academic may fear his/her easier accessibility to
their students. Traditionally, a student had to seek out support, physically

booking an appointment with their lecturer, ensuring they arrived on time and making the effort to attend. With the ease of email, questions can be sent direct to the lecturer and with a reply perhaps expected immediately. Strategies need to be put in place by academics to ensure that email overload from students does not occur. This is in the hands of the educator concerned to negotiate with the learner population boundaries for timescales for replies and the appropriateness of questions asked. Lecturers adopt different strategies on how to cope with student demand, but the emphasis is on student management.

Three stages of engaging with eLearning

We suggest a hierarchy of three main stages or forms of engaging with eLearning that is developmental in terms of the skills needed by educators and learners. These stages are not only based on access to support or competence in working with the technology but also on the pedagogical aspects of engaging with the learning resources.

Stage 1 – Replacement

Using a different media to do what you probably already do as a lecturer, e.g. using the web as an online depository for students to access handouts, lecture notes, reading lists and/or timetables instead of photocopying and handing out the information. This stage also includes using distribution lists via email to communicate to a group of students or peers, and perhaps as a facility for essays to be emailed and corrected on-screen. This model maintains the lecturer as the controller of the learning.

Stage 2 – Added value

This level incorporates more dynamic interaction and communication, perhaps replacing some face-to-face activity. eLearning at this level may include encouraging learners to work as a group, and develop group discussion.

This level also includes the use of existing, or the development of new, eLearning resources that may or may not pull on real-world sites linked to modules, units or learning objectives, which in turn can be linked to the Quality Assurance Agency benchmark statements (QAA, 2000). This level of development needs a critical mass of resources to be available before becoming an embedded and standard part of a course, just as teachers can choose between a variety of textbooks and writing their own materials. Examples include using a particular eResource for either skill learning or analysis of information to support knowledge and conceptual acquisition, e.g. a subject website or an online journal.

> ### Case study
>
> Brina (2002), in teaching a module on social psychology successfully, used an institutional virtual learning environment (VLE) to encourage group work with her second-year undergraduates. She found that asynchronous interaction (i.e. not real-time) aided group collaborative work and the process of collaboration was made visible to tutors.

Useful resources for social work and social policy students include official government papers that can be accessed from www.official-documents.co.uk, or through individual government departments, for example: The Department of Health, www.dh.gov.uk; The Home Office, www.homeoffice.gov.uk; or Her Majesty's Stationery Office (HMSO) for Acts and other publications, www.hmso.gov.uk. Equally, policy reports and information can be accessed from sources such as lobby groups or the voluntary-sector organizations, e.g. Age Concern, www.ageconcern.org.uk.

Use of these websites requires careful construction of associated learning activities (eActivities) to ensure constructive learning engagement. Timetables and access to computers need to be planned to ensure the learning activity is introduced and the aims of the learning explained, and it must be remembered that teachers need to ensure skills are in place in the student group, as well as the appropriate availability of the technology to gain access to the resource. It is advisable that evidence of using the resource be built into the assessment process in a way that evidences learning occurring.

It is possible to use an individual eLearning resource on its own within a module. An example of this type of resource is *An Introduction to Social Policy* (Spicker, 2000), at www2.rgu.ac.uk/publicpolicy/introduction/index. htm, which offers a brief outline of key topics and issues in social policy. The material is of the kind aimed at a first-year undergraduate. It has a range of content, reading and references, and, although most of the content is from the UK, it is also of international interest.

> ### Case study
>
> A social policy lecturer teaching 'Theories of Welfare' wanted students to be familiar with key original texts to enable greater depth of theoretical understanding. The students were then tested via multiple-choice questions. Although the use of the technology was at times frustrating, students reported they enjoyed reading original sources.
>
> (Heron, 2002)

Other illustrations of resources which fit into Stage 2 are *Research Minded-ness*, which aims to help social work students and practitioners make more effective use of research in their learning and work and *Internet Social Worker*, both available at www.swap.ac.uk/elearning/webpool2.asp.

Stage 3 – Transformation

This more advanced level of eLearning allows engagement in learning activity that would be impossible to orchestrate by other means. eLearning becomes a major element of selected units of a course. At this stage the educator could bring together both pre-developed subject content (maybe with its own content developments) and peer and expert dialogue to transform the learning and teaching approach in a way that it is not possible to achieve without technology. An online learning community can be created that engages students in innovative and collaborative ways, across a course, across universities and workplace settings, even across nation states. An ambitious example of this could be where an international online seminar is held with an invited expert but with additional local resources, learning activities and content built in.

Case study

The transformation stage is employed in Kirk's (2002a) focus on experiential learning, which integrates online material in the curriculum and encourages reflection on theory and practice. The unit entitled 'Communication: Theory and Practice' was designed for foundation year 'welfare practitioners' (undergraduate, postgraduate and employment-based trainee social work students and youth and community students). She found that quality time can be gained in the classroom for experiential learning through the integration of online material in the curriculum and encouraging reflection on theory and practice.

Challenges to educators

At levels 2 and 3 ('added value' and 'transformation') good eLearning facilitation skills are need by the educator – managing the online experience, moderating and encouraging all students to work collaboratively, weaving in responses to other student comments. (For further reading, see Salmon (2000).)

Whatever the stage of engagement with eLearning, the processes involved can support the learning of group work, interpersonal skills, teamwork, presentations, report writing and communication and information technology skills which are all transferable and useful employability skills.

An invitation to an educator to join the technology 'Tour de France' cycle race when you use your bicycle only to collect the Sunday newspapers can seem somewhat daunting. The majority of students now emerging from the secondary education system in the UK will have the skills to engage with the technology and will be expecting to use information and communication technology to support their learning in the same way they use mobile phones to support their social networking.

There are other complexities to face within universities. One of the potential causes of confusion is the exponential expansion of technological systems in so many areas of university life (financial management systems, student tracking systems, online library systems, virtual learning systems) with many 'systems' working independently of one another. For example most universities have a virtual learning environment (VLE) such as Blackboard, First Class and Web-CT for their learning and teaching. This VLE may or may not be part of a managed learning environment (MLE) linking to the administration and student tracking systems within the university.

We focus here on three particular challenges:

1 Technology has the potential to offer greater flexibility and choices for how administration, student tracking and support, resources and learning, teaching and assessment are organized and delivered. However, each 'choice' brings with it changes in personal working practices, local organization of information and administration. Universities and individuals are faced with attempting to make decisions and pragmatic choices within their subject or remit, yet there may be a lack of clarity of support within their institutions about what those choices are and their implications (Boezerooy, 2003). Despite this 'maze', there is increasing evidence that eLearning delivered appropriately allows different types of learning and different types of learners to access education (Higgison and Harris, 2002).

2 Another difficulty is that many educators have limited skills and expertise in eLearning (Kennedy and Duffy, 2000). Anecdotal evidence would suggest that there is a cohort of social science academics for whom extensive use of technology has been seen as a personal preference rather than an essential skill. This situation is compounded by the gender inequality within the IT sector where men are in the majority (Haughton, 2002) and by the fact that technology is not gender neutral. More importantly in this context is the increasing evidence that women may feel less comfortable with computers, or their potential, even when the facilities are made available (Harlow and Webb, 2003). Harlow and Webb argue too that this gender imbalance has had an impact on decision-making with respect to the use and application of technology despite evidence that women are developing good IT skills: 'within the context of social work organizations, the technological experts and senior managers deciding on ICT applications are most likely to be men, while the

practitioners are most likely to be women' (Harlow and Webb, 2003: 17). Transferring this analysis to the university context, it would seem reasonable to suggest that many of the decisions concerning infrastructure, implementation and staff development may be developed from a male perspective. If true, this will impact on the approach to the language, pace and delivery of staff development and the speed of take-up of eLearning opportunities within disciplines such as social work and social policy where women are the majority.

3 Some limited research (Waldman, 2000) would suggest that the IT training available at many universities may be too technically focused and may not be as effective for social sciences colleagues who respond better to a more subject-centred rather than technological approach. Face-to-face email and web-browser management training may not be given priority despite these being the two methods staff use to access information and communicate with colleagues and students. The commercial sector reinforces the message that the take-up of IT systems is not a technical issue but a social one: 'Where implementation has been effective this has been because more attention was put on the human dimension – the social, emotional and relational context' (Gould in Harlow and Webb, 2003: 40).

Social science educators have probably developed expertise in an ad hoc way. It is not surprising therefore that confidence about implementing eLearning may be in short supply. There is also the prospect of technically competent undergraduates arriving at university with greater skills and experience of using technology than their tutors. It may be difficult to admit to being a 'virtual novice' in face of 'virtual experts.'

Options for moving forward

Where does this leave educators wishing to use eLearning with their students? We suggest that there are three areas for consideration. The first is the university support and culture. The second is staff support, training and development, with some examples gathered from case studies and experienced online tutors. The third is the suggestion that both in social policy and social work we should be looking to develop eLearning content and resources not as individuals or even single institutions but collaboratively across the sector.

University support

Unfortunately, there is sometimes a mismatch between the government and university management policies espousing online learning and the actual preparedness or capacity of an institution to support the changes required, though how this plays out will vary from university to university. Kennedy and Duffy (2000) note: 'There are unrealistic notions about the effort involved in developing materials, course programmes, support mechanisms and effective learning, also about the cost-effectiveness of distance learning.' There are the personal and pedagogic aspects of eLearning development too. Thinking about teaching using an eLearning approach should lead to reflecting on how and what you teach, the learning outcomes, forms of assessment and, inevitably, the pedagogy that underpins learning.

Changes you make will impact on your colleagues within the faculty/school who teach related modules and on the tasks related to the administration of the course and challenge the support and infrastructure available. The management of change is a dynamic organizational and personal process. Change is not an inexpensive option: it not only requires investment in new systems but also in training, support, time and development to change the way people work (Bates, 2000).

On the face of it, the types of support needed to develop or embed eLearning seem very similar to traditional forms of teaching. However, to adapt these services to support eLearning requires a different approach, reorganizing and linking of 'systems' and often renegotiating roles and responsibilities. An institution's working practices, and the assumptions about communication, assessment and student attendance which underpin it, may hinder new ways of working. Successful development may therefore only happen when an institution's culture, operations and the assumptions are challenged and changed (Higgison and Harris, 2002).

Some of the issues would include:

- time for curriculum development and gaining relevant skills;
- copyright and intellectual property rights;
- handling of plagiarism;
- network security and secure facilities for summative eAssessment;
- data protection;
- technical support, infrastructure and sustainability.

Staff support, training and development

Although there is no 'right' approach to managing all of the elements above, practitioners have identified factors which may help colleagues embarking on the path of developing eLearning (Higgison and Harris, 2002). Educators in higher education need support for either embedding existing resources into their courses, or developing new eLearning. This needs to extend beyond attending a course on how to use the virtual learning environment.

On a practical level, bringing together a project team or a staff team to develop eLearning resources may prove effective. Project groups can include an administrator, programme co-ordinator, librarian, technical support staff, a

The JISC report (Higgison and Harris, 2000) resulting from the OTiS (online tutoring in Scotland) workshops identified the skills staff need in four broad categories:

- ICT or technical skills;
- management skills, including change agency, team building and the ability to work in multidisciplinary teams;
- educational and pedagogical skills;
- social and communication skills.

member of the senior management team or budget holder, web designer and writers, and academics as appropriate. Kennedy and Duffy (2000) note: 'the key supportive ingredient is the presence of a collaborative team . . . all need each other'.

The current thinking around good practice for student learning and the development of eLearning has focused on ideas of constructivism, social constructivism (communities of practice) and an increased understanding of the different approaches students have to learning and how teachers can respond (Beetham, 2002). Learners learn best when engaged with their peers in activities that value and support them and help them build their knowledge and understanding. This is further enhanced when the subject is delivered in a number of ways to suit different learning styles and outcome requirements (Prosser and Trigwell, 1999). There may also be a difference in the training needs for teachers in subjects that embed critical analysis, qualitative and evaluative discussion and debate and person-centred professional development as these are more challenging to deliver online. It may be reasonable to suggest that educators as learners require similar circumstances and modes of delivery to learn effectively. This is well illustrated by Skehill (2003) who developed and used a peer-group action-learning model with colleagues to facilitate the use and implementation of eLearning in a Masters Diploma in Social Work course. Skehill suggests that: 'in order to enable students to engage actively and constructively with C&IT resources, their educators needed to be familiar with both technical and pedagogical issues involved. . . . a collective and collaborative learning approach seemed most appropriate' (Skehill, 2003).

The social work degree includes a substantial practice learning element and adds the additional challenge of providing eLearning access and support wherever the learner is learning and therefore needs to include practice partners and agencies. The existence of virtual walls (licences, Internet access) between resources available in HEIs and in agency settings also poses major challenges.

Where universities are providing time, support and encouragement for subject-based communities of practice for the development of online learning then the implementation of eLearning will be increased.

A teacher may be aiming to use technology to support the delivery of just one module, but the thinking, planning and design time should not be underestimated whether it is in terms of using existing eLearning materials and resources or developing new ones. A look at the steps a teacher might need to take will illustrate this complexity – see the boxed text below.

Support for educators in all of the areas listed in the box is a crucial question. Investment in time and support, technical infrastructure and opportunities to reflect on the pedagogical context will need to increase for staff to acquire the skills and knowledge to drive and deliver eLearning use and development within social policy and social work. Useful case studies are available on the SWAP website, www.swap.ac.uk.

In preparing to develop eLearning, educators need to:

1 have access to appropriate software and resources – staff may have limited rights to download software on to their computers;
2 know where to look for particular resources and evaluate their fitness for purpose;
3 become familiar with the 'new' technology and consider the range of possibilities that eLearning provides;
4 have time and confidence to experiment with developing resources. Text is relatively easy but other mediums like video, simulations and databases take more support to use confidently;
5 reflect on the subject, the pedagogy and the technology available to develop a 'constructively aligned' module (Biggs, 1999) aligning teaching methods and assessment with learning activities;
6 gather a project team: identify and work with support colleagues from computer services, the school or faculty library and technologist to identify and solve problem issues both on and off campus;
7 collaborate with colleagues to ensure links between modules and courses and clarity of module design and management;
8 pilot new ideas with colleagues and students;
9 review and update the learning approach from a technical, pedagogic and subject perspective;
10 reflect and evaluate the programme and efficacy of eLearning for adding value to student learning and assessing benefits for staff and the institution.

Collaborative development

One approach to overcoming the model of each academic developing his/her own resources and the need for a critical mass of resources could be collaboration on a regional, national or even international scale. These could stand alone, with each teacher using the resources in class (either face to face or online) to fit in with a specific module, or as learning objects, a type of 'bite-size' learning, which can be used as a 'pick and mix' approach, suited to problem-based learning methods and used across modules. These resources could be for all educators to share and use, with appropriate review and quality standards applying. This collaborative approach is the one that was recommended in the Department of Health Scoping Study: *Building capacity to support the social work degree* (Rafferty and Waldman, 2003).

Conclusion

It is recognized that there has been some development and shift of culture in the use of eLearning within the social work and social policy communities. A step change is required in capacity building, however, to enable students, teachers and practitioners to take advantage of appropriate eLearning and eKnowledge skills and opportunities across social policy and social work, in both HE and work-based settings. The step change requires growth in the range and depth of eLearning resources available and effective change management both by individual teachers and within schools and organizations to make effective use of such resources.

e-government and e-society are major planks of government policy, including wired up communities, wired up services and eLearning. The incorporation of eLearning is no longer a choice but an expected part of the student learning experience. eLearning can be used to optimize the student experience and it has both strengths and limitations. The task is to maximize the advantages and minimize the disadvantages for academics to engage in eLearning that enables social work and social policy students to become twenty-first century learners and practitioners.

9

Developing learning beyond the campus: increasing vocationalism and declining pedagogy?

Duncan Scott and Steven M. Shardlow

Introduction

Social policy and social work share an interwoven history of extra-mural curriculum work, i.e. learning that takes place beyond the classroom, is external to the campus and is located in real-world settings that provide students with diverse 'sites for learning'. During the last third of the twentieth century, social policy has increasingly prioritized the establishment of an academic identity and retreated from the field, while social work has embraced 'practice' as a vehicle to achieve professional competence. Developments in both disciplines have been in response to: national demands for increased 'relevance' to real world issues; the widening participation agenda; teaching quality assessments; and research selectivity exercises. Learning beyond the campus has been both a victor and victim of these national trends. In this chapter we begin by considering some practical and conceptual issues common to both social policy and social work, then review the most significant trends in each discipline. While the term 'off-campus' can be taken to mean any form of learning that is not part of the specified curriculum or that is delivered outside formal classes such as distance or e-learning, in this chapter our concern is with practice learning that is part of a formal curriculum.

The process of learning off-campus

There is a series of processes to be negotiated, either positively embraced, lightly skimmed or ignored that are embedded in the purposeful construction of learning experiences off-campus. These are:

- preparation and planning with the agency at a general level to set up the arrangements for student learning (which might, for example, include selection and training of agency-based teachers, agreement about information sharing and so on);
- identification with students of their individual learning needs;
- deciding upon the particular practical experience for each student (this may be fraught if students, academic tutors and agency-based teachers all expect to exercise choice or control over where the individual student is placed);
- determining an individualized agreement or contract that specifies the arrangements for a particular period of learning;
- providing teaching or supervision during the placement to promote the student's acquisition of skills and knowledge (with discussion about the nature and quality of the relationship between the student and the teacher or supervisor);
- managing the experience and implementing quality assurance mechanisms (for example, the frequency of meetings between the various parties to monitor progress);
- examining the student's learning or competence achieved (mechanism and timings for assessment must be determined, and the respective contributions of student and the agency-based staff and tutor);
- evaluation of the placement experience to enable improvement for future use.

What perhaps differentiates off-campus learning in social policy from that in social work is the nature of the response to these processes and events. In many cases, social policy staff feel less constrained than their counterparts in social work, where there are national requirements in force. In social policy different levels of resourcing and departmental commitment to pedagogic integration may be a strong factor. More generic guidance for a wide spectrum of off-campus work is available as codes of conduct produced by national bodies such as the Quality Assurance Agency (QAA, 2001b) or the National Council for Work Experience (NCWE, 2003) or through initiatives such as the Sociologists in Placements project (SIP).

Conceptual and explanatory issues

Social policy and social work have traditionally placed considerable emphasis upon experience gained 'off campus', in different situations such as:

- prior to admission to a formal programme of learning (a prerequisite for professional social work education);
- during the course, through formal periods of practical learning (the primary focus for this chapter), and informal learning away from recognized learning settings (see, for example, Coulshed, 1989);
- protected learning after the academic components (for example, the degree in social work in Northern Ireland is followed by a protected year of practice: see www.niscc.info).

Opportunities may involve either *sponsored* or *unsponsored* experience. Has the student acquired knowledge and understanding as a more or less unconscious by-product, or has she operated within an explicit, purpose-driven institutional framework, attempting to shape both the experience and the understanding?

From unsponsored activities, the student may gain a rudimentary understanding of the 'welfare geography' (how the organizational unit works, how it relates to service users and peer agencies). In addition, she may absorb some inter-personal skills such as running a group, or handling minor conflict. However, most commentators believe that sponsored experience is preferable to the contingencies of general social life.

The dichotomous representation of 'Training' and 'Education' is clearly contestable, yet many higher education institutions have found themselves re-designing the extra-mural elements of their curricula with these distinctions

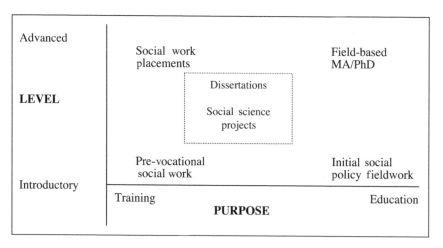

Figure 9.1 Social work placements and social policy fieldwork: a basic typology (Scott and Shenton, 1995:3)

in mind. While a student may construct pathways (from introductory to advanced) which cut across these dichotomies, our critical awareness is helped to the extent that 'Level' and 'Purpose' open up monolithic conceptions of what may be involved in moving beyond the campus.

At a personal level, a typology (Figure 9.1) is potentially helpful where individuals and institutions frequently incorrectly label all or most students as embryonic social workers. Second, this typology can assist an understanding of the shifting importance over time of placements, projects and fieldwork, defined partly in terms of their relative formalization along the training–education continuum.

Learning ethnographies

Formal frameworks, such as Codes of Practice, necessarily emphasize common processes, but students learn within and beyond these in different ways and at different rates. A primary imperative is for the student to 'fit in', to learn their role and place in an organization, to minimize uncertainty, and to maximize personal and professional acceptance. Figure 9.2 provides a four-cell typology as an heuristic framework. This is based on a sociological analysis of organizational roles and behaviour (Burrell and Morgan, 1979, outlined in Coleman, 1991).

One student may fit in: 'I was interested, excited – I felt I would fit in, being black and a Seventh Day Adventist . . . I felt I would get on reasonably well. . .', black female in secondary school run by black Seventh Day Adventists (Scott and Shenton, 1995: 17).

On the other hand, a trio of students in a Romanian orphanage:

found themselves getting frustrated and angry. . . . They concluded that some of the difficulties had been triggered by clashes of personality (including theirs) but that others reflected on the way the orphanages were organised, and the level of social policy provision for children in the society

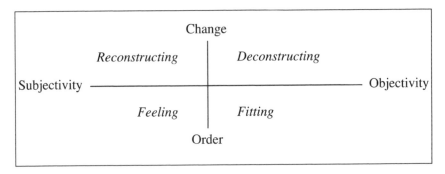

Figure 9.2 Learning ethnographies (Burrell and Morgan, 1979)

as a whole. Instead of fitting in mentally and intellectually . . . they had learnt how to explore both their feelings and their analytic abilities.

(Scott, 2003: 401)

In short, they had made a 'journey' across the typology of Figure 9.2.

Social policy fieldwork

Origins and contemporary tendencies

Historically, there was a strong link between social administration and social work training (see p. 8). However, while critics argued that such links had made social administration too empirical and value-laden (Mishra, 1989), the links were not as close or influential as has been suggested. Even the field-based activities in the early twentieth century were much less social casework oriented than designed to provide:

> experience and opportunity for observation in Charity Organisation Society local offices, labour bureau, Poor Law receptions and other social and civic institutions of the modern state. The purpose of the practical work was imaginative expansion of citizenship rather than vocational training.
>
> (Harris, 1989: 35)

The taken-for-granted merits of fieldwork in social policy, mixed with polite-ness and procedure, are generally seen to be sufficient; most fieldwork guidance has little to say about structured inequalities or who really benefits. The com-mentary by Hall and Hall (1996) on the salience of 'negotiation' begins to address some ethical issues, but the context is that of maintaining inter-institutional collaboration to ensure a flow of fieldwork opportunities. Everitt and Gibson (1994: 230) are less persuaded of the inevitable worth of such placements, because: 'To walk away with knowledge is to walk away with power.' Most social policy students are in effect 'cheap (but welcome) labour'; if their purposes are transparent, then questions about benefit and power are more complex and more contingent.

Despite the citizenship emphasis, it remains the case that social administra-tion/policy fieldwork was closely associated with social work. One of the few studies of this relationship concluded that between 80 per cent and 90 per cent of social administration graduates between 1940 and 1960 subsequently entered social work (Rodgers, 1963: 10–11). Even then, there were signs of a gradual divergence as social administration began to develop distinctness from both sociology and social work. At first, fieldwork was 'regarded as playing an essen-tial and integral part in the teaching of an academic subject, rather than concerned solely with the training of a social worker' (Sainsbury, 1966: 8).

Nevertheless, it was not long before the price of acceptance as a free-standing subject or field of study involved an even greater degree of distancing from what were perceived as the reformist, value-laden activities under the fieldwork umbrella (Mishra, 1989: 75).

Pedagogic and vocational tendencies

Over the last decade, universities have admitted greatly increased numbers of students without comparable resourcing. Thus economic logic may now be added to the pedagogic arguments for 'relevance' and 'employability'.

Several, partially contradictory, responses appear to be connected to those structural changes. First, there has been a move towards work experience, either via placements and projects or (more diffusely) through a mix of Active Citizen initiatives (Student Community Action) and student employment services (portfolio building, as part of personal development planning, see p. 80). At the same time, much of this appears to have been de-coupled from mainstream academic frameworks; the experiences become part of a portfolio but not a critical pedagogy. There is a powerful assumption that the very acts of outreach carry an authenticity all of their own. We can term these responses 'vocational re-integration' and 'pedagogic disintegration' respectively. Examples of outreach programmes that are integrated within a critical literature, that borrow from the best of a discipline, field of study or research approach *and* that are anchored in appropriate classroom discussion are rare.

Some social policy departments have been quick to embrace both responses, particularly if it means that other cost centres now deal with fieldwork. In addition, the most common intellectual justification for this 'retreat from the field' is that it both disassociates them from what they define as the narrow empiricism of field-based work and frees up their time for the further development of a conceptual and theoretical foundation for their inter-disciplinary work. This is a familiar dichotomous perception: practice (without theory) is out there; theory (without practice) is on the campus. Given the strong vocationalizing current flowing through parts of higher education, the retreat from the field could have serious consequences; there is a real danger that the definitions of 'relevance' and 'employability' will become narrowly utilitarian. Considerations of the creative potential of a healthy theory–practice relationship may then be swept away on a tide of vocational rhetoric.

Developing strategies

A national survey of undergraduate courses in 1978 revealed a majority insisting on compulsory fieldwork (38 responses; 30 with fieldwork), but only four used fieldwork reports as part of their formal academic assessment (Collis,

1978). By the late 1980s, a study of 31 social administration/policy courses noted that about one-third had abandoned fieldwork (Shenton, 1987) – a trend which has continued in the 1990s, particularly in those universities aspiring for a high grade in the increasingly prominent Research Assessment Exercise (RAE). Not all social policy departments have turned their backs on learning beyond the campus; some have embraced the new enthusiasms for work experience (WE) (Universities UK, 2002). Significantly, the strongest proponents of WE have tended to come from the post-1992 universities, delivering broader social science courses (Sociologists in Placements (SIP), 2000). Two trends have paralleled this 'retreat from the field':

- First, the promotion of different forms of 'Active Citizenship' such as those advocated by Community Service Volunteers (CSV). For example, even as the Manchester department argued against compulsory fieldwork, the Vice-Chancellor was corresponding with Alec Dickson, the Honorary Director of CSV. Their exchange revealed an uncritical agreement about the need to find ways in which 'students in higher and further education can apply their knowledge to the service of the community as part of the curriculum' (Dickson, 1978). Active Citizenship varies across HE; but only 1 or 2 per cent of FE/HE students are regularly involved in volunteering schemes (Universities UK, 2002: 34).
- A second trend stems from more vocationally oriented subjects (e.g. law, pharmacy and dentistry) promoting 'real life skills'. Underpinning many initiatives was the 'Enterprise in Higher Education' (EHE) programme. Established in 1978, it had recruited over 50 HE institutions within six years, with substantial resources for innovative curriculum developments particularly those linked to increasing real life skills and employer involvement (Scott and Shenton, 1995).

Since the publication of the Dearing Report on Higher Education (1997), there have been increasing attempts to make curriculum content and processes more sensitive to the worlds of work. By the late 1990s it was estimated that over 17 per cent of the UK undergraduate population were involved in some kind of work experience programme (Universities UK, 2002: 33), loosely overseen by the National Council of Work Experience (NCWE) (www.work-experience.org). Two related pedagogic strands, within the broader social science community, have been:

- a critical examination of the extent to which the concept of 'employability' has become explicit in undergraduate education (see Darvill, 2004);
- the production of audio-visual materials to support community-based learning and different models of work experience (COBALT, 1999 (Community-based Learning Teamwork); Hall and Hall, 2002).

Administrative and pedagogic models

It is clear that the size and significance of a fieldwork approach depend at least as much on the interaction of government policies with university economics as on pedagogic justification. Furthermore, the 'survival' of a strong fieldwork presence may also depend on an influential 'champion'. Shifting resources, therefore, underpin the extent to which 'thin' and 'thick' fieldwork administrative systems exist.

Thick systems include dedicated staff and financial resources, close relationships between university and fieldwork agency and the intermediary clearing houses such as student units in councils of voluntary service, university settlements and research exchanges. Thin systems have few or no financial resources, may have devolved administrative responsibility to a retired staff member or a secretary, make no direct contact with field agencies even to the point where the fieldwork becomes a 'do-it-yourself' affair. Although most thin systems are weakly integrated into the curriculum, many institutions try to build on a do-it-yourself approach rather than retreat even further from the field. Figure 9.3 summarizes four ideal types, based upon the degree of pedagogic integration and the level of resourcing.

		Level of resourcing	
		'Thick'	**'Thin'**
Degree of pedagogic integration	High	Fieldwork + Module + Assessed work	DIY fieldwork + previous/present experience
	Low	Work/citizenship experience + Tutorials	Free-standing projects

Figure 9.3 Administrative and pedagogic models (Scott and Shardlow)

Prospects

Social policy fieldwork can be justified to the extent that students learn about the complexities and contradictions of welfare organizations, begin to appreciate how groups make decisions, handle conflict, embrace or deflect change. Finally, they can learn about themselves, not only as beginning field researchers building their first ethnographies, but also as adult learners, working through initial anxieties, coping with fears and prejudices and becoming more sensitive to the strengths and weaknesses of their necessarily marginal roles. All of these processes may be present in the thinnest of pedagogic frameworks, but it is likely that deeper learning will only be achieved when appropriate resources are systematically dedicated to it.

Ironically, the 'real social policy environment' of contemporary fieldwork is very much a function of the increasingly casualized, do-it-yourself field-work regime. Students, left more or less to their own devices, make inroads on the margin of state welfare (e.g. day care, probation hostels, learning diffi-culties) and the Third Sector. Indeed, the dominant emphasis may be more on the lower slopes of unqualified social care than the upper and middle floors of the health, education and town hall bureaucracies. The latter locations are accessible if HEIs can devote time and influence to effect openings. For the moment, much of the outreach is re-visiting territories traditionally occupied by social administration nearly a century ago.

The last ten years have witnessed the rapid arrival of mass higher education at the same time as the RAE has been reconfirming old stratifications within and between the 'old' and 'new' universities. Many of the former cling to elite conceptions of their primary purpose, often ignoring the demands, from even their prizewinners, for a new synthesis between intellectual development and critical employability. Many of the latter are forging new links with extra-mural institutions without having constructed clear conceptual and explanatory

---

Examples of positive practice

University of Liverpool (Department of Sociology)
- 'Voluntary Service Learning' is a first-year undergraduate module, with induction from Student Community Action.
- Students maintain 'reflective logbooks', attend seminars, contribute to presentations and produce mini-essays about their work in a range of voluntary agencies.
- The student work is underpinned by a web-based personal devel-opment planning tool.

University of East London (School of Educational and Community Studies)

- Use of part-time paid work in a second-year undergraduate module.
- Students maintain a reflective log and produce a written report; workshops and tutorials support the work.
- One example was a student working as a street-crossing attendant, who researched child road-safety and gave a presentation in a school.

(Universities UK, 2002: 25)

frameworks within which to educate their students. We have, therefore, on the one hand a 'retreat from the field' and on the other a 'march into the field'; both tendencies have much to learn from each other. But the commitment and the relevant resources need to be in place first. Otherwise, social policy fieldwork will become ever more fragmented and marginal; even where strongly supported the danger of an uncritical vocationalization will also remain.

Practice teaching and learning in social work

Social work education has always been located at the intersection of a perennial tension between the need to establish academic credibility for the discipline (to be and be seen to be rigorous, theoretical and analytic) and the need to provide soundly based, practical applied learning experiences that will enable the social work students to work effectively with people. At the crux of this tension lies the 'placement', the site where learner, teacher, theory and practice confront each other warily across an often misunderstood conceptual territory. While there are many publications about practice learning (e.g. Danbury, 1994; Thompson et al., 1994; Bogo and Vayda, 1998; Doel and Shardlow, 2005; Shardlow and Doel, 2005), there is little empirical research in the UK. The empirical literature can be divided into three types: small-scale qualitative studies of a number of placements (e.g. Gardiner, 1989; Secker, 1993); large-scale studies of placements and placement policy (Thompson and Marsh, 1991; Walker et al., 1995); and studies of social work education of which practice learning forms a part (Marsh and Triseliotis, 1996). A review of practice learning in preparation for the new degree was commissioned and published by the Scottish Executive (Dick et al., 2002).

To impose order on the potential for chaos: five broad strategies have been adopted variously by government, regulators, HEIs and agencies providing 'off-campus' learning:

1   the development of codes of practice;
2   specifications about the kind of person deemed suitable to teach social workers;
3   prescriptions about what may be taught, and the methods to be used while the student is on placement;
4   theoretical constructions about the nature of the relationship between the respective sites for learning (i.e. the agency and the university);
5   strategic mechanisms for the management of the supply of placements.

These strategies interact with each other and remain in a 'shifting state of settlement'. They are explored in more detail below.

Codes of practice

There are generic codes of practice produced by national regulatory bodies such as QAA and NCWE (see p. 118). Typically, they specify the nature of desirable practice in relation to all forms of 'off-campus' learning and, while not mandatory, adoption is encouraged. Other bodies such as the National Organisation for Practice Teaching (NOPT) have also produced codes of practice (NOPT, 2003) as have the Subject Centre for Social Policy and Social Work (SWAP, 2003) and the Scottish Organisation for Practice Teaching (SCOPT, 2003). These all provide useful statements about good practice that can be incorporated into the planning and delivery of 'off-campus' social work learning.

Qualifications of the person to teach on placement

Opinion has varied over the past forty years as to the need for the person who teaches during a placement to have a professional qualification. At one extreme are those who think that 'the only qualification necessary for a supervisor [is] that she should be 'reasonably competent and knowledgeable in her own field of practice; if, in addition, she [holds] a recognised professional qualification, so much the better' (Young, 1967: 12).

This is not a widely held opinion currently. At the opposite extreme is the view that only those who hold a designated qualification should be able to teach. The Central Council for Education and Training in Social Work (CCETSW) introduced such a qualification, the Practice Teachers Award, for the Diploma in Social Work (CCETSW, 1988), expecting that those with this qualification would, at a future date, be the only ones permitted to so teach. A further regulation (CCETSW, 1989, 1991b) stipulated that agencies providing practice placements would also have to be approved. These plans were abandoned as insufficient numbers of practice teachers gained the award (CCETSW, 1995). The successor competent body to CCETSW for England, the General Social Care Council (GSCC),* has taken a different position in respect of the new social work degree. Its focus is not who *teaches* the student but who *assesses* the level of a student's practice competence (GSCC, 2002b). Hence, universities providing social work education in accordance with the national regulations (Department of Health, 2002b) are required to provide 'an assessment by an experienced and qualified social worker of the competence and safety of the student to become a social worker (GSCC, 2002b: 15). A neat solution in a climate of shortage, but not one that will

*   For full details of the respective approaches in each of the countries see: England www.gscc.org.uk/new_degree.htm; Northern Ireland www.niscc.info/; Scotland www.sssc.uk.com/SSSC.Web/index.aspx; Wales www.ccwales.org.uk/. For example, in Wales work is being undertaken to specify different levels of practice learning.

necessarily please all. In theory, this offers the opportunity for a significant expansion of practice learning. It also places greater responsibility upon each university, rather than a national regulatory system to determine who should assess students' competence. Potentially, this arrangement offers considerable flexibility, by allowing other people to play a major role in the delivery of learning, including non-social workers, service users or other professional groups. This also opens the way for the development of an interprofessional context for learning (Bartholomew *et al.*, 1996; Whittington, 2003). A review of the future of the Practice Teaching Award as part of the GSCC review of post-qualifying education will lead to changes. In the interim, a National Vocational Qualification (NVQ) has been introduced for practice supervisors, targeted specifically for those providing early (first periods of practice learning).

Prescriptions about what may be taught as part of practice learning

Here again the 'settlement' is changing. Under the DipSW, there was a national prescribed set of requirements, in six areas: Assess and Plan; Promote and Enable; Communicate and Engage; Intervene and Provide Services; Work in Organizations; Develop Personal Competence (CCETSW, 1996). These constituted a curriculum for practice learning, and shaped the mode of assessment. Guidance for practice learning in the degree is less detailed and prescriptive, but specifies the key roles of the National Occupational Standards for social work:

- Key Role 1: Prepare for and work with individuals, families, carers, groups and communities to assess their needs and circumstances.
- Key Role 2: Plan, carry out, review and evaluate social work practice with individuals, families, carers, groups and communities and other professionals.
- Key Role 3: Support individuals to represent their needs, views and circumstances.
- Key Role 4: Manage risk to individuals, families, carers, groups, communities, self and colleagues.
- Key Role 5: Manage and be accountable with supervision and support, for your own social work practice within your organization.
- Key Role 6: Demonstrate professional competence in social work practice.

(TOPSS, 2002)

Rather more emphasis is given to the generic requirements of practice learning, for example, as found in the QAA Code of Practice (QAA, 2001b). Hence, the current 'settlement' is less concerned with the content of practice than with the mechanisms for ensuring the quality of that practice. This places individual HEIs in a position of much greater freedom to develop their own practice curricula. It may provoke a need for exemplars or materials that construct a curriculum for practice in other ways (see, for example, Doel and Shardlow, 2005). Deregulation in respect of both teachers and curriculum, while simultaneously placing emphasis on quality assurance systems is a bold move. Certainly, it provides a great deal of 'space for innovation' both by programmes and by individuals.

Another area for innovation concerns the assessment of learning. Most programmes used a portfolio of work to assess the student's practice on the DipSW. Portfolios normally contain: reports of direct observations of the student's work; a critical appraisal of the student's performance; evidence supplied by the student to demonstrate that all the required areas of competence have been met; and the student's own reflective and critical commentary. Other material might include video evidence of student practice, formal collection of service user opinion and a *viva voce* examination. For the degree, there are opportunities for experimentation and development of new modes of assessment.

The relationship between the respective sites for learning

The nature of the relationship between learning that occurs in the classroom and learning 'off-campus' has been variously regarded. Claims can be justified about the intellectual primacy of one or other site for learning. Learning in practice environments may be conceptualized as two polar points (and various intermediary positions):

- the site to apply theoretical learning acquired in the classroom (i.e. secondary);
- the primary site for professional learning (i.e. providing the driver for skills and knowledge acquisition – 'practice-led learning').

These two different notions about the nature of the relationship between practice and academic content shape course design both in terms of curriculum content and timing of learning. Similarly, a claim about the nature of the relationship may also be a claim about the contrasting sequencing of the respective sites for learning. Hence, if practice learning is a site to *apply* learning, then it must occur sequentially after the theoretical learning. This is not the case in respect of 'practice-led learning' which would be highly congruent with problem-based learning models (see Chapter 6). The implications for the construction of a practice curriculum are profound depending upon the perceived relationship between the sites for learning.

Resourcing practice learning

A constant feature of practice learning in social work in the UK has been the shortage of learning opportunities within agencies (CCETSW, 2001). In England, several strategies have been adopted to address this, including the development of a Practice Learning Task Force and the development of e-learning strategies, redefining the range of potential sites for practice learning and increasing levels of financial support for practice learning.

An interesting debate that took place during the development of these strategies concerned the nature of practice learning. It seems likely that during a period of professional education there will be at least one traditional placement-type experience. However, some periods of direct practice could evolve to become more like 'off-campus' work in social policy – i.e. learning that is project based, since the regulations allow for experimentation and innovation. This may also enhance the supply of practice learning opportunities.

Reflections on the future

It is difficult to predict with accuracy likely trends for the future of practice learning in social work. There are, perhaps, three features we propose should have an increasingly significant role. The first is the involvement of the consumer in the teaching and learning process. Parsloe and Swift explored how service users might contribute to the assessment of student competence (CCETSW, 1998). Further engagement of users and carers in teaching and learning is only to be welcomed (see Chapter 3). Second, there should be a reappraisal of the contribution made by students to the agencies and communities in which they practise. In the past ten years there has been a concern to emphasize the importance of the learning opportunities for students, with less attention given to the contribution that the student makes to the agency. Third, there is an international dimension to practice learning, and greater emphasis should be placed on the experience of practice learning in other countries and the messages that might apply within the UK (see, for example, Shardlow and Doel, 2002).

Conclusion

There is a wide variety of forms of off-campus learning. Even as some social policy departments retreat from the field, other (broad social science) departments explore how to make pedagogic sense of the fact that nearly two-thirds of full-time students have regular employment in term time (Universities UK, 2002: 35). Policies and practices for social work placements evolve as much in response to the uneven distribution of opportunities as to professional regulation.

Much of the discourse about off-campus learning has been 'administrative', about the frameworks for support and assessment; some has been pedagogic, about the appropriate learning models for the different educational and training purposes. Little discussion, and even less empirical research, has considered bigger structural questions about the often conflicting roles of HE institutions in relation to the world of work in general and social work in particular.

We conclude with two wishes. First, we note that, despite all the recent developmental work relating to social policy and social science fieldwork (COBALT, 1999; SIP, 2000), 'further work is required to encourage universities to incorporate placement practices in degree courses' (SIP, 2000). We wish, therefore, that the lessons from social work's incorporation of practice into the curriculum could be disseminated more widely.

However, we must sound a note of caution, lest the narrower, clinical dimensions of social work ('learning outcomes', 'contracts', 'supervision', 'feedback', 'appraisal', 'achievement', 'assessment', 'accreditation') dominate. We recognize the fundamental importance of Codes of Good Practice and Guidance frameworks, but wish, second, that students would discover 'a level of insight and understanding into human social life that exceeds whatever might be achieved through attention solely to gathering and reporting data' (Wolcott, 1995: 251). The potential of off-campus learning deserves no less.

10

Interprofessional education

Melanie Ashford and Judith Thomas

Introduction

Interprofessional work and education are in the forefront of the policy agenda
in the UK, particularly in relation to health and social care. Consequently, the
topic is of particular concern to social work educators. Social policy educators may be interested in reviewing the implementation of this policy and
considering the implications for the study of social policy, which may form
part of a curriculum for interprofessional learning.

The focus on interprofessional education (IPE) has arisen from concerns to
improve interprofessional working. Changes in workplace practices now
require members of different professions to work together, for example, in
Primary Care Trusts, Workforce Development Confederations, Mental Health
Partnership Trusts and Children's Trusts (2003b). Legislation, such as the
National Health and Community Care Act (1990), and policy documents,
including *The New NHS: Modern . Dependable* (Department of Health, 1997)
and *A Health Service of All the Talents: Developing the NHS Workforce* (Department
of Health, 2000b), require the development of 'joined-up' delivery of services.
These initiatives, together with a focus on the concerns and needs of the end
user, be they service user, patient or client, have developed with a desire
to ensure that public services are delivered efficiently and effectively. Much of
the policy drive in both practice and education is directed primarily towards
co-operation between different health professionals and the interface between
health and social care. However, social workers also interact with other professionals, such as police officers, probation officers, housing workers, teachers
and lawyers; the need for good collaboration between different services and
workers within them can be seen painfully clearly in the Laming Report (Home
Office, 2003) on Victoria Climbié.

IPE is a complex and evolving pedagogical issue. Evaluations have yet to evidence a direct positive impact on interprofessional working and the care of service users or patients (Freeth *et al.*, 2002). Knowledge and understanding of interprofessional working and learning is a developing but contested field (see, for example, Trevillion and Bedford, 2003). Furthermore, Regan de Bere considers that 'Interprofessional learning and the transference of knowledge to practice are processes, not commodities that can be acquired with sufficient funding and goodwill' (2003: 106). In this chapter we consider some of these complexities. We begin by identifying the confusion over terminology, consider the key policy issues, the issues for higher education institutions (HEIs), for educators, for practice learning, and for students. We illustrate the issues using case studies of IPE in two undergraduate programmes, and conclude by summarizing some key pointers for developing effective interprofessional learning.

Terminology

In order to consider the issues, it is helpful to start by identifying the confusion over terminology and to provide a definition of IPE. Barr points out the confusion over terminology: 'academics marry prefixes (inter-, multi-, cross-, trans-) with adjectives (professional and disciplinary) and nouns (education, training, learning and studies) in seemingly endless permutations. Policy makers and practitioners prefer . . . terms such as "joint training", "shared learning" or "common studies"' (Barr, 2002).

While different models of interprofessional education are considered in this chapter, the definition offered by the Centre for the Advancement of Interprofessional Education (CAIPE) gives a useful starting point: *Occasions when two or more professions learn from and about each other to improve collaboration and the quality of care* (Barr and Horder, 2003). Learning from and about each other to improve collaboration is likely to involve student participation in the form of dialogue and debate. However, there is concern among academics that shared listening, rather than shared learning, is all that is occurring in some 'interprofessional' education. Figure 10.1 illustrates the polarization that can occur.

The ends of the arrow indicate two extremes: at one end students from different professions and on different programmes are in one place listening to a lecture. The other end indicates an integrated programme of study where

Shared listening   Integrated programme of study

Figure 10.1 The spectrum of models for interprofessional education

students are not only in the same place but are engaging with each other and exploring the learning from their particular professional perspective. This is then interwoven with interprofessional practice opportunities. The model of interprofessional learning we advocate relates to the CAIPE definition, rather than shared listening, and the examples used in this chapter use interactive forms of learning.

Policy perspective

A succession of public enquiries has indicated that care breaks down where there is lack of communication and teamwork among the professions, such as Kennedy (2001) and the Laming Report (Home Office, 2003). The relevant governing bodies of the four countries of the UK all stress the need for inter-professional working across health and social care and between social work and a range of other agencies. Examples of recent initiatives that emphasize interprofessional working include:

- Sure Start, a government-funded project to tackle child poverty and social exclusion connecting health, social care, education and community perspectives;
- the Single Assessment Framework for Older People (Department of Health, 2001a), which provides a unified framework for assessment, the decision as to who will undertake this being based on the circumstances of the service user, rather than the task automatically being undertaken by one profession;
- Children's Trusts, which bring together social work, education and health professionals.

Research by Whittington into Diploma in Social Work (DipSW) programmes identifies factors that affect the development of collaborative learning, including 'the degree to which expectations of collaborative practice are clear in regulations and assessment requirements' (Whittington, 2003a: 5). Problems posed by different expectations of professional regulators were noted as well as the perception that the framework for DipSW (CCETSW, 1995) did not support learning for collaborative practice (Whittington, 2003b). However, for the social work degree, the qualifying award for social workers introduced from 2003, the curriculum is based on the benchmarking state-ment developed by the Quality Assurance Agency (QAA, 2000), the National Occupational Standards (NOS) (TOPSS, 2002) and regulations from the Social Care Councils in each of the four UK countries. In all these, specific expectations about interprofessional working are more explicit.

The NOS for social work state that practitioners should be able to 'work within multi-disciplinary and multi-organisational teams, networks and systems' (Key role 5). Interprofessional working is encompassed within the GSCC Codes of Practice that require 'Working openly and co-operatively with colleagues and other professionals, recognising their role and expertise and treating them with respect' (GSCC, 2002a). The QAA benchmarking state-ment for social work refers to 'effective collaborative practice, knowledge of different disciplinary groups, working across professional boundaries, interrela-tionships with other social services, interprofessional and inter-agency collaboration and partnership'. The benchmarking statements for other pro-fessional programmes, such as medicine and nursing, also include expectations of interprofessional learning.

Another component of current policy impacting on IPE is the emphasis now being placed on the views of users or patients. User groups have expressed their support for interprofessional education and practice, believing that they will suffer if professionals are not able to work and be seen to work effectively together. For example, a consultation based on interviews with 28 service users from 11 different organizations commented on the positive aspects of 'professionals communicating well with each other and the service users and keeping everyone informed' (Bryne and Ferguson, 2002). The report identifies improvements that service users felt were needed in joint working:

- learning how to share power properly between professionals and be less protective of their own professions;
- professionals needing to communicate effectively and speak in the same voice;
- professionals needing to have a good knowledge of other professional roles.

(Bryne and Ferguson, 2002: 14)

There is a danger that enhanced interprofessional collaboration may leave patients and service users with even less power, so user participation should be central to interprofessional practice and interprofessional learning. It is doubtful whether this is currently the case.

Thus policy developments in organizational structures, in professional regu-lation and in user participation all point to the need for students from different professional groups to learn to collaborate during their education.

Institutional perspective

Traditional university faculties, schools and departments are not well designed to offer interprofessional learning. Whittington's study highlights 'university structure and climate' (Whittington, 2003a: 5) as a key factor in helping or hindering IPE. Pirrie et al. (1998) comment that institutional structures need to facilitate course development where programmes cross faculties and departments. Institutional support and leadership is important to embed change in educational practices (Baume *et al.*, 2002), so senior managers, deans and associate deans must ensure that resources are available: for example, staff time to plan and experienced people to lead staff development.

Resources, in the shape of both time and budgets, are identified as a key factor for success in developing IPE (Whittington, 2003a). The Common Learning Programme, launched by the Department of Health in England in 2003, gave significant funding for four designated 'leading edge' sites: King's College, London, with Greenwich and South Bank Universities; the Universities of Southampton and Portsmouth; the Universities of Newcastle, Northumbria and Teesside; the Universities of Sheffield and Sheffield Hallam (Department of Health, 2003a). This funding has considerably eased the complex issues of linking learning across professional courses in these institutions. However, most universities must rely on more modest funding to launch IPE.

Another potential problem for social work educators is that interprofessional education initiatives may be driven by the much larger departments of medicine or nursing. Social work, as a junior partner numerically, may then have to put its case firmly to ensure that the social work perspective is embedded in the planning from the start.

Freeth *et al.* (2002) found that many of the published examples of interprofessional learning are based on short, post-qualifying, work-based learning modules rather than the longer qualifying courses at degree or diploma level. While not insubstantial, the difficulties of establishing IPE at post-qualifying level may be considerably fewer than those for any large-scale development at undergraduate level. The potential to involve students from different professional programmes will vary from institution to institution and for different areas of study. Ideally, curriculum planning for each profession and discipline might involve different combinations. For example, an interprofessional module on child protection might involve police, teachers, probation, nursing, health visitors, social work, voluntary agencies, doctors and lawyers, while a module on elder care might focus more specifically on health and social care professionals. However, it is seldom practicable to bring all these groups together in the right combinations at the right time.

Courses may be structured so that modules may be shared by students from different courses (e.g. a module on social policy can be accessed by students from nursing, social work, social policy, politics, economics and criminal justice). Managers may see this type of shared learning providing economies of scale but, if the focus is on shared listening, then opportunities for interprofessional learning, as defined above, will have been lost. However, cost effectiveness is important and providing a lecture to a large group of students from different disciplines may release resources that can be effectively targeted to provide facilitators for follow-up interprofessional seminar groups.

Educator perspective

Whittington's research signals the importance of 'commitment and expertise of faculty and visiting teachers' and also identifying the 'conceptions of collaborative practice and professional or interprofessional identity the course seeks to develop' (2003a: 5). These factors are linked, as commitment is needed for staff to give the time and energy to explore collaboration and values. Staff development opportunities, timetabled peer support and development groups will enable staff to develop their skills and confidence.

The planning process should involve representatives of all the professional groups involved. Values may be reflected in language so terminology and professional jargon need to be debated, and the underlying assumptions can open up essential debates. Where possible, a common language should be negotiated and reflected in module handbooks and teaching resources to ensure that terms derived from one profession do not predominate. Terms such as 'patient', 'service user' and 'clinical' have immediate connotations of a particular perspective.

Underneath terminology lie more complex questions about values. On the one hand, it is suggested that the educator's task is to enable practitioners to work towards a common set of values. This was suggested by practitioners and managers interviewed by DeSouza et al. (2002). They referred to the difficulties experienced when social work students were over assertive in the way they communicated their values. With appropriate guidance from the facilitator, questioning by students from other professions can challenge social work students to critically explore concepts such as 'anti-oppressive practice', 'working in an empowering way' or 'the social model'. However, this needs to be balanced with ensuring that students are confident to assert social models that promote empowerment and not defer to medical models (see Barnes and Hugman, 2002 for a summary of the debates around social work values). On the other hand, work to develop a national framework of values for mental health includes a focus on respect for the diversity of values brought by different professionals (National Institute for Mental Health in England (NIMHE), 2003). Fulford (2004) argues for values-based practice: 'the theory and skills-base for clinical decision-making where legitimately different, and hence potentially conflicting, values are in play'. This relies on process for balanced decision-making where values conflict. Some basic skills to equip students for such an approach might be taught in IPE sessions.

Some key issues for educators were identified in the work undertaken by the Three Centre Research on Interprofessional Practice in Learning and Education (TRIPLE) project, a collaboration between the subject centres for medicine, dentistry and veterinary medicine, health sciences and practice and SWAP (social policy and social work). Interactive approaches were considered essential to give students the opportunity to discuss and debate their approaches, to identify and articulate both shared understanding and differences, and whether the latter are complementary or at times in conflict. However, Helme is clear that skills of facilitation alone are not sufficient for educators. She argues that:

> teaching for interprofessional learning is more than facilitation – because it will entail challenging the judgement and prejudices of students and potentially colleagues. Educators must reflect on their own professional histories and traditions, how these may impact on their teaching and develop strategies to counter this.
>
> (Helme, 1994)

In other words, a developed awareness-in-action of the interplay of personal and professional identities and perspectives is needed.

Interprofessional learning in practice

To ensure that IPE in the classroom is translated into interprofessional practice, a key site for learning will also be the practice placement. Whittington highlights the need to 'Seek practice learning opportunities in a range of agencies . . . in order to maximise available multi-disciplinary and cross-agency learning' (2003a: 11). A good example of this is provided by Torkington and her colleagues in their discussion of the Shared Practice Learning project at the University of Nottingam (2003). However, research into interprofessional placements by DeSouza et al. (2002) identified a range of models and approaches to interprofessional working. These varied from integrated teams with a single management structure who had developed a shared value base to those that shared office space but continued to operate within their own service structures and keep separate records. In these teams, although different professionals may share information, decisions were not necessarily made collaboratively. With such variable approaches to interprofessional working, educators need to prepare students to critically evaluate developments in service delivery and consider how they can effectively contribute to collaborative working. This will be more useful than presenting students with unrealistic expectations of what they will find in practice.

Close working relationships between the university and service agencies are essential. Whittington (2003a: 5) identifies the importance of relationships between HEIs with agencies and professionals. Stuart (2002) argues that it is difficult to get practice-based managers and some practitioners to understand the significance of interprofessional learning, and this can be problematic for all concerned. Balen (2002) planned for this by holding workshops to inform and involve those agencies that had not been involved with the planning.

Whittington also refers to 'the availability, skills and creativity of practice teachers' (2003a: 5) as key factors in developing collaborative learning. In

DeSouza's study (2001) practice teachers identified the need for training to teach and assess interprofessional working. They also recognized the value of developing competence in involving other disciplines in teaching and assessing social work students and their own role in contributing to practice learning in other disciplines (DeSouza *et al.,* 2001).

There are two well-established examples of interprofessional practice teaching programmes at Oxford Brookes and South Bank universities, with practice educators for both social work and nursing. Although developments in this area may have been hampered by the different requirements of professional bodies and established local arrangements for the delivery of programmes, in a survey of practice teaching programmes for social work, Davis and Robertson (2002) identified 16 (out of the 38 that responded) working towards greater integration of different professionals in terms of programme structure and curriculum development.

Student perspective

Student evaluations of interprofessional learning appear positive (e.g. New Generation Project, 2002). Students know they will have to collaborate with other professions in practice as they try to deliver their service, so they are motivated to learn. This is illustrated by the interprofessional education task at Leicester University undertaken by students of medicine, nursing and social work who together interview service users/patients in their homes:

> By undertaking a collective task of investigating patients' circumstances, developing an assessment of their needs and aspirations, identifying barriers and shortcomings in existing services, and compiling a feedback report based on their observations, students are enabled both to experience and to begin to resolve some of the key challenges involved in partnership working.
>
> (Smith and Coates, 2002)

In addition to a perception of relevance, many evaluations of interprofessional education involve practicalities such as the composition of student learning groups, concern about finding time to meet together, and assessment criteria. These may override the perceived learning benefits.

Student attitudes on entry to professional programmes raise questions of the development of professional identity, the timing at which IPE should begin, and whether this should involve exposure to other professionals from the outset. The preliminary findings from one survey identify that students entering social work and occupational therapy hold more negative opinions about interprofessional relationships between health and social care workers than do other disciplines such as nursing and physiotherapy (Miers *et al.,* 2003).

It will be interesting to see if these attitudes change after exposure to inter-professional learning.

Trevillion and Bedford's (2003) work comments on the development of professional identity. In a module for students from health promotion and social work, Trevillion notes that students identified how the programme had 'helped them in relation to assessment, communication and mobilisation'. However, despite 'its explicit intentions, the programme did not seem to problematise professional identity or create new interprofessional identities' (Trevillion and Bedford, 2003: 223). In contrast, on a joint programme for BSc nursing and social work studies, students were reported as having 'focussed less on their learning about roles and relationships and more on their developing internal sense of being a dual practitioner'. Barr suggests that 'the earlier the inter-professional learning in participants' experience, the less they are in a position to share, and the more the teacher needs to provide. The later the learning, the more the participants would be able to set their own agenda and call upon their own resources'. He proposes that objectives for IPE at the pre-qualifying stage might be 'preventive' and 'preparatory'. IPE at post-qualifying level might be more ambitious: effecting change and improving services (Barr, 2002). The link between the development of professional identity and the timing and delivery of interprofessional learning is an area that merits further attention.

Case study 1: University of the West of England, Bristol (UWE): enquiry-based learning for interprofessional education

The Faculty of Health and Social Care has responded to the drive to improve interprofessional collaboration by incorporating interprofessional education into the curriculum of ten pre-qualifying professional programmes (see Table 10.1).

The interprofessional strand permeates the whole programme of these disciplines. It comprises interprofessional modules, interprofessional learning outcomes in other modules and interprofessional working as an element of supervised practice. All interprofessional modules use enquiry-based learning (EBL) (see pp. 72–4) to facilitate interaction between students from different professional programmes and enable the development of transferable skills central to the collaborative process (Boud and Feletti, 1991).

The organization of interprofessional modules is shown in Table 10.2. The timing was determined partly by practical, pragmatic issues such as finding a space in the timetable when students were at the university rather than in practice (Barrett et al., 2003).

The level 3 e-learning interprofessional module allows course teams to use the module in different ways in their programmes, including running it alongside the placement. This gives students the opportunity to integrate inter-professional module learning with their current practice experiences and is the option chosen by the social work degree at UWE.

Table 10.1 Breakdown of student numbers by discipline at UWE
(combined intakes for September 2001 and January 2002)

Discipline	Numbers of students
Adult nursing	457
Physiotherapy	133
Mental health nursing	90
Children's nursing	72
Midwifery	45
Diagnostic imaging	47
Social work	33
Occupational therapy	32
Learning disabilities nursing	17
Radiotherapy	16
Total	942

One challenge facing researchers is that it is not easy to separate issues that relate to IPE from those that can be attributed to the pedagogy of the approach, for example, in this case, EBL. However the points below illustrate how challenges such as devising appropriate learning outcomes using EBL and facilitating such groups manifested themselves in the context of interprofessional learning groups.

In EBL, case scenarios are often used to raise issues, prompt discussion and trigger further enquiry. However, at UWE we found the use of specific case scenarios (e.g. homelessness, hospital admission and asylum seekers) proved problematic. Some groups focused on legal, policy, practical and medical issues where students were engaged more in shared listening to mini presentations than exploring interprofessional working and the potential benefits, tensions and conditions that would support it. This problem was compounded as

Table 10.2 Organization of interprofessional modules at UWE, from 2003

Level	Duration	Mode of delivery
Level 1	Six weeks	Groups of about 15 students meet weekly for two hours, facilitated by staff member. Students undertake associated research between meetings.
Level 2	Six weeks	Two conference days, one at the beginning of the module and one towards the middle. Students undertake self-directed learning and research.
Level 3	Six weeks	Initial face-to-face meeting between students and facilitator followed by a period of online learning. Groups of approximately 15 students and a facilitator discuss issues online.

sometimes the information students fed back was inaccurate or out of date. This can be particularly problematic at level 1 when modules run at the start of the programme before students have had grounding in the ways in which knowledge is created and the critical appraisal of evidence. This prompts questions as to whether these skills should be a prerequisite, so students would have preparation prior to the module. It also links to problems with module learning outcomes that may implicitly or explicitly push students towards the acquisition of factual knowledge rather than exploring collaborative working, which is inevitably more problematic, uncertain and fluid.

To address these problems changes are being made. The learning outcomes are being revised to focus more explicitly on interprofessional working; instead of a case scenario, students start by debating trigger statements such as that shown in Figure 10.2.

While facilitating EBL is challenging (see, for example, Taylor, 1997), the interprofessional dimension adds another level of complexity. At UWE facilitators are drawn from all professional groups; during the development of the curriculum they were supported by a staff development programme and the opportunity to attend a weekly facilitators' support group. All staff are given a facilitators' handbook (UWE, 2001), outlining the need for interprofessional education, the principles of EBL, and approaches to facilitation.

One area that merits further exploration is whether educators from different disciplines and professional backgrounds bring different styles of facilitation. Researchers observed differences in facilitators' responses to dilemmas such as how much direction they should give or whether to ease the group through silences. Further research into the connection between facilitator style and the tradition of the discipline would provide useful information for those involved with staff development and teams planning to use EBL in interprofessional contexts.

Ovreveit *et al.* (1997: 1) claim that:

The reality of modern health and social services is that the care [members of the public] get depends as much on how professionals work with each other as on their individual competence within their own field of expertise.

Recent policy initiatives, therefore, place increasing emphasis on interprofessional collaborative working within the context of health and social care (DoH, 1998; DoH, 1999; DoH 2000a; DoH 2000b). This, according to Barr (1995), can be enhanced through interprofessional education.

Figure 10.2 Trigger for EBL study group, University of West of England (2001) *Interprofessional Module Level 1 Handbook*, Faculty of Health and Social Care

Case Study 2: New Generation Project at the Universities of Southampton and Portsmouth: institution-led programme planning for interprofessional education

The New Generation Project is one of the 'leading edge' sites of the Department of Health-funded Common Learning Programme. It is a partnership between the universities of Southampton and Portsmouth and the Hampshire and Isle of Wight Workforce Development Confederation. The Partnership reaches across fourteen professional programmes, four faculties, two universities and the health and social care organizations that support student learning in practice. It has been designed for all students following health and social care programmes to spend time together, learning from and about each other with the aim of working more effectively in teams when out in practice. The aim is to establish an integrated curriculum for all students studying audiology, medicine, midwifery, nursing, occupational therapy, pharmacy, physiotherapy, podiatry, radiography and social work.

The curriculum contains both 'learning in common' and 'interprofessional learning'. Learning in common includes topics that are common to all the programmes, but which are taught and assessed within the profession-specific programmes. For interprofessional learning students come together in multi-professional learning groups to learn from and about each other, and are assessed on their achievement of interprofessional learning outcomes. There is also an ethos of the centrality of learning in practice. The students learn together in each year of their programme. Four units are built into each course:

- Unit 1 (Year 1) Collaborative learning;
- Unit 2 (Year 2) Interprofessional team working;
- Unit 3 (Year 3) Enabling change in practice;
- Unit 4 (Year 3) Interprofessional problem solving.

Units 2, 3 and 4 are integrated into the overall practice curriculum for each programme. For social work students they also address the National Occupational Standards' key roles, units and elements. Thus, the BSc in Social Work at Southampton has arranged its award as follows:

- Year 1: academic study and preparation for practice;
- Year 2: learning in academic and practice settings (100 days' practice, incorporating 10 days of interprofessional learning halfway through);
- Year 3: learning in practice settings (100 days' practice, incorporating 20 days of interprofessional learning in two 10-day periods), academic study and demonstrating 'fitness for practice'.

In addition to the four units, social work students keep an individual learning portfolio throughout the course. It is presented as a record of overall learning and achievement, with goals for further continual professional development, and 'signed off' by a qualified practice assessor.

Staff development is high on the agenda for this project, focusing on developing the skills of both university and practice staff to support the facilitation of these units. This includes eFacilitation skills for online communication of the units. Staff need skills such as setting ground rules, building student confidence and motivation, dealing with problems and completing reports via the eAssignment system.

Conclusion

We have emphasized in this chapter the central place interprofessional education has in the policy agenda in UK, arising from concerns to improve interprofessional working. We have also stressed the views of service users who consider that professionals should be trained together to encourage collaboration and to provide a more effective service. Given the lack of evidence as to whether IPE is effective in enhancing interprofessional working, and whether this is turn truly benefits the service user or patient, knowledge in this area is still at an early point. Other questions about how IPE relates to professional identity are little explored.

The complexities of developing and implementing strategies for IPE from the institutional, educator, practice and student perspectives have been outlined. We conclude with the pointers for effective IPE proposed by Barr:

1 Put service users at the centre: involve patients and clients in designing, teaching, participating and assessing.
2 Promote collaboration: apply learning to collaborative practice, collaboration within and between professions, within and between organizations and with communities, service users and their carers.
3 Reconcile competing objectives: harmonize, so far as practicable, the aims and methods of interprofessional education with those for multi-professional and uni-professional education.
4 Reinforce collaborative competence: reach beyond modification of attitudes and securing common knowledge bases to ensure competence for collaborative practice.
5 Relate collaboration in learning and practice within a coherent rationale: give reasons why interprofessional learning improves interprofessional practice grounded in theory.
6 Incorporate interprofessional values: be inclusive, equitable, egalitarian, open, humble, mutual, generous and reciprocal.

7 Complement common with comparative learning: include comparative studies to facilitate learning from and about each other, to enhance understanding about respective roles and responsibilities and inform co-working.
8 Employ a repertoire of interactive learning methods: avoid over-reliance on any one method.
9 Count towards qualifications: assess interprofessional education for awards to add value.
10 Evaluate programmes: subject interprofessional education to systematic approval, validation and research.
11 Disseminate findings: inform other developments in interprofessional education.

(Barr, 2002)

Further resources

CAIPE UK Centre for the Advancement of Interprofessional Education. CAIPE is a charitable organization that promotes interprofessional education for health, social care and the related professions as a way of improving collaboration between practitioners working with patients, clients and carers: www.caipe.org.uk

CHIME The Centre for Health Informatics and Multiprofessional Education. A multidisciplinary centre, drawn together through a common focus on research, education, organizational change and technological innovation, linking information quality and governance for health: www.chime.ucl.ac.uk

IPE FDTL4 National projects funded under the Fund for the Development of Teaching and Learning (FDTL) phase 4 contain four projects on interprofessional education. One of them is PIPE (www.pipe.ac.uk) which offers interprofessional education for all pre-registration students in the health professions across three HEIs within South East London Workforce Development Confederation: www.ncteam.ac.uk/projects/fdtl/fdtl4/projects.htm

11

Continuing professional development and education

Pat Higham and Bob Rotheram

Introduction

You probably have 'been there'. We assume that before becoming teachers of social work and social policy, most readers will have worked in local or central government, or the voluntary sector, and have sought some continuing professional development (CPD) or a formal post-qualifying (PQ) award. Perhaps you were a social worker, housing officer or member of a youth offending team. Maybe you were a community worker, policy officer or a social care worker. If so, the chances are that you would have been interested in opportunities to develop yourself professionally. What happened? Were your wishes fulfilled, or were you thwarted?

Let us guess that you studied the social sciences, including some social policy, and some of you acquired a social work qualification. If you are a social policy graduate, you may be developing your career in the growing field of social care. Over time, most of you realized that because policy and practice were evolving at a tremendous pace you were not abreast of all the various 'initiatives'. You may have wanted to change your specialism or acquire a different one. You realized you had not read as many professional journals as you 'should' have. You were vaguely aware that information technology (IT) offered potential professional benefits. Unless you were very lucky, you agreed with colleagues that your employer was not doing much to further your career. You were falling behind, not achieving your potential, and you wanted to do something about it. If you recognize this scenario, perhaps you feel that as a teacher you are now well placed to appreciate the concerns and meet some of the professional development needs of your former colleagues or their successors. But is this true?

Arguably, your own needs were not entirely typical. Assuming that you started teaching in higher education in the last few years, it is likely that your educational background was relatively strong. Given the selection criteria for academic posts, you may well have been engaged in research activity. Although your own experiences will be an advantage in helping you to know what your 'customers' want, your standpoint may not be the sole guide. This parallels a fundamental point made to generations of social work students: individuals differ. What is 'right' for you may not be 'right' for someone else.

The first step in making informed choices is to clarify the differences between 'CPD' and 'PQ'. CPD is a designation that may be more familiar to social policy academics and practitioners than to social workers. CPD implies a broad choice for updating individual skills and knowledge through programmes of academic learning. PQ, a familiar concept to social workers, is post-qualifying study designated by employers and professional statutory bodies for particular professional occupations. PQ tends to be constructed around specific professional and academic awards, and provides a framework which social workers can use to select further study. CPD is a more generic concept that may or may not lead to a specific award. Please note that in this chapter we often subsume 'continuing professional development' and 'post-qualifying awards' under the heading of CPD. This represents a change in the way social workers have conceptualized CPD, because they usually regard PQ as the overarching concept. However, because all social workers and social care workers will be required to undertake CPD (i.e. learning that does not necessarily lead to an award) as part of their re-registration on the Social Care Register, we suggest that the term CPD should include both professionally designated PQ awards and the more broadly based CPD activity.

This chapter reviews some potential participants in CPD for social work and social policy. Then the discussion turns to why these staff might want to learn and how that impacts on the possibilities for CPD. Some space is also devoted to the context for CPD: the background in agencies and higher education, with an examination of some of the implications. Following this, we explore what people might study and consider how they might be enabled to learn. Some practice examples and questions for reflection are provided before the chapter concludes.

Who are the learners?

There are several staff groups who might want to engage in social policy and social work CPD. They include:

- newly qualified workers;
- experienced workers;
- 'returners' to practice;
- recently appointed, or aspiring, first-tier managers;
- senior managers.

Clearly, the motivations of these diverse groups will differ to some extent, even though they might all wish to further their careers. Newly qualified workers may be keen to keep up to date or to extend their knowledge of policy and practice that particularly interests them or that now seems relevant. Experienced practitioners could be seeking a 'refresher' or extension of their knowledge and skills. Potential 'returners' to practice, of whom there probably are many, although no definitive numbers are available (TOPSS England, 2000: 26), may wish to make themselves more employable. New first-tier managers will be aware that their role has changed, and may feel that they are not fully equipped. Senior managers may be eager for more formal management experience. There could be other drivers too, either positive or negative, for example, the prospect of salary increases, the love of learning, fear of being left behind or being pushed by one's employer.

So, prospective students will approach CPD with varying motivations. It is important that you, as a teacher, attempt to discover as early as possible why they want to learn. You should not assume that a particular group of people (such as experienced practitioners) have consistent reasons for further study. A reasonable working hypothesis is that many will wish to progress, yet individuals are likely to differ within a cohort and change their goals over the years. We need to know more about actual choices for CPD. We note that an ESRC funded project is currently researching the nature of learning during the first three years of postgraduate employment, through a longitudinal study of the acquisition of technical knowledge and generic skills by accountants, engineers and nurses at the start of their careers (Eraut *et al.*, 2001–4).

As a provider of CPD to social work and social care, you will have an important advantage over your colleagues who teach undergraduates in non-vocational disciplines. It is our experience that social work and social care students are, in general, very committed to their chosen career path. Usually, they work hard, and many go well beyond the minimum required by the assessment schedule. All this, it appears to us, is characteristic of social work and social care workers seeking continuing professional development.

The context for CPD

In the next section, we examine the CPD framework and the agency background which students bring with them from their workplaces. We consider briefly some implications for the future delivery of CPD, and we discuss changes in higher education and how they might affect what you can offer.

CPD framework

In recent years, CPD opportunities have expanded for employees in social work, social care, social policy and related fields. The framework of post-qualifying (PQ) education developed by the Central Council for Education and Social Work (CCETSW) largely shaped opportunities in social work, while provision in social policy and related areas has been more diverse. The CCETSW post-qualifying framework, introduced in 1991, was designed for the purpose of attaining specific awards such as the Post-Qualifying Award in Social Work (PQSW) rather than for the broader concept of CPD. The PQSW, broadly equivalent in level and size to the final year of a bachelor's degree, is attainable through routes that comprise eclectic mixtures of different courses and portfolio evidence. CCETSW also introduced the Advanced Award in Social Work (AASW), broadly equivalent to Masters level (postgraduate) study.

Even if we ignore qualifications achieved before 1991, social workers' study achievements vary considerably. They may have attained no post-qualifying awards; others may have attained more than one. Non-social work staff in social care agencies, now coming forward for CPD, may be assumed to have none of these qualifications, although they may have attained academic qualifications at different levels in areas that include social policy, sociology, psychology and management studies.

What of the arrangements for supporting the post-qualifying social work awards? After 1991, devolved Post-Qualifying Social Work Consortia, consisting of informal partnerships between higher education institutions and social care agencies, were established in different regions of England and in other UK countries. Each Consortium was responsible for managing processes of registration, mentoring, assessment, accreditation and information. Some Consortia became training bodies, appointing and training mentors and assessors and running their own portfolio programmes.

Some features of these arrangements bear discussion. First, often the Consortia did not realize their potential for promoting and planning post-qualifying study at strategic level because much time was needed to maintain Consortia structures. The CCETSW framework (now regulated by the Care Councils in the four UK countries) was complex and difficult to operate. Take-up and completion rates for awards have been low (GSCC, 2002c), explained partly by complex registration systems and an insufficient supply of mentoring, assessing and supervisory skills. The Consortia's devolved structures emerged before CCETSW fully developed their own quality assurance system – a weakness that made national standardized accreditation and assessment decisions difficult to achieve.

One of the problems of the PQ system (as described above) is that it failed to engage sufficient employers at a strategic level, even though qualifications had to be attained as practice-based awards centred on practice. Managers in social care agencies argue that they cannot afford to release staff because their first priority is to address demanding workloads amidst increasing numbers of staff vacancies. Not only has support from line managers been variable but most social workers have not yet gained any improvement to pay and career opportunities from having completed PQ awards – although this is changing.

Consequently, we argue that the current PQ framework represents poor value for money. Yet we recognize that the framework has its strengths. Regional Consortium partnerships between universities and employers have provided locally responsive study opportunities. Future PQ/CPD arrangements will depend on continuing some form of partnership arrangements between training providers and employers who undertake strategic workforce planning and development. Consortia evolved particular strategies to address the different learning needs of inexperienced newly qualified social workers and experienced social workers who had been qualified for some time but who lacked previous post-qualifying study opportunities. For example, the PQ Wales Consortium developed two routes for attaining PQ1: less experienced staff members are offered a route with structured teaching, learning and mentoring, while more experienced staff are offered assisted portfolio development with opportunities for accrediting prior learning and experience. Social work PQ study benefits from its credit-based design, which Davies and Brynner (2000) argue offers flexibility, openness, and encourages diverse participation by employers, lecturers and trainers.

The successes of the social work PQ framework have been specialist courses like the Practice Teaching Award (PTA), the Approved Social Worker/ Mental Health Award (ASW/MHA) and the Post-Qualifying Award in Child Care (PQCCA). The separately certificated Post-Qualifying Requirement (PQ1) that enables social workers to consolidate and deepen their qualifying level competencies in practice has also proved popular. These specialist awards are more easily related to the actual roles that social workers perform following qualification. We argue that practitioners and employers will find CPD opportunities like these more attractive because the awards are designed to help them meet occupational standards (TOPSS England, 2000) that provide the basis for qualifications, job specifications and appraisal.

From 2000, modernization of the personal social services (Department of Health Social Services Inspectorate, 1998; Department of Health, 2000c; Higham et al., 2001), intended to drive up standards, led to reform of social work education. In 2001, the General Social Care Council (GSCC) took over CCETSW's regulatory functions in England. The GSCC is responsible for setting up and maintaining a Social Care Register on which social workers are registered in England (Brand and Smith, 2001; GSCC, 2002a). Scotland, Northern Ireland and Wales have separate Care Councils and their own country-specific requirements. Social workers are now expected to practise according to Codes of Practice and Care Standards (Department of Health, 2001a; GSCC, 2002a). The social work post-qualifying framework must now take into account the GSCC requirements for registration and re-registration as well as the introduction of a three-year qualifying social work honours degree in place of a two-year diploma.

The registration requirement for social workers heightens the relevance of post-qualifying study. (Those with qualifications in social policy rather than social work will also eventually be required to have their names on the Register if they are employed in a registrable social care role.) Social workers will have to demonstrate first that they have obtained the requisite qualification to be entered on the Register. Then they will have to demonstrate that they have consolidated their qualifying level competences as new workers. They will need to demonstrate post-qualifying occupational standards and qualifications as they move into post-qualifying roles. The GSCC is introducing Post-Registration Training and Learning (PRTL), required of registered social workers as a condition of re-registration. After three years, and subsequently every three years, they will need to demonstrate that they have completed either 90 hours or 15 days of study, training, courses, seminars, reading, teaching or other activity that might be expected to advance their professional development or contribute to the development of the profession. Every registered social worker in England will receive a pro forma that they can use for recording PRTL activities. Social workers on the Register will need to keep a record of PRTL that they have completed. The GSCC may consider failure to meet the PRTL requirements as misconduct (Schedule 3, GSCC, 2003c). These changes raise profound implications for the scale and nature of CPD activity.

The reform of social work education that introduced a three-year social work honours degree as the qualifying award has also led to a GSCC review of the PQ framework. The PQ review (GSCC, 2003b) proposes the following principles to guide future arrangements. Post-qualifying education and training should be: relevant; efficient and effective; meaningful; affordable and value for money; linked to registration requirements, a CPD model and arrangements for other professional groups; flexible; understandable; and accessible. The generic nature of the social work degree suggests that social work PQ may become more specialist.

In January 2004, the GSCC received proposals for a new framework of Post-Qualifying Education and Training (Trevillion, 2004). The proposals recommend a new framework consisting of three types of integrated modular academic and professional qualifications awarded by universities. The awards would comprise a Graduate Diploma in Specialist Social Work at academic Level 3; a Postgraduate Diploma in Advanced Social Work at academic Masters level; and a Masters in Advanced Social Work at Masters level. Each type of award would be associated with specific stages in social workers' careers. For example, social workers would need to complete the specialist stage award before being permitted to attain the new Advanced Awards, a requirement which may prove unpopular over time as more social workers graduate with an honours degree at the qualifying stage.

Universities would be accredited to offer the Graduate Diploma only, or both the Graduate Diploma and the Advanced Awards. In consultation with stakeholders, the GSCC will identify key issues and preferred options for developing an agreed set of generic national standards to underpin the PQ framework, defining specialisms linked to agreed occupational standards, and implementing the principle of regional planning for meeting local and regional needs and building on successful partnerships.

Significantly, although the consolidation of qualifying-level competences in a programme called PQ1 has been very successful, it is not mentioned in the proposed framework. Its position has been questioned with the introduction of the new degree, although it would make good sense for PQ1 or a similar programme to remain as part of induction arrangements for the first appointment following qualification. The Practice Teaching Award is not mentioned specifically, despite calls for its early revision to meet the support needs of the new qualifying degree. Most significant of all is the requirement for regional planning, which might become the central role of the PQ Consortia, perhaps in collaboration with TOPSS England as it becomes a Sector Skills Council with the responsibility for workforce planning across all of social care, including social work. The results of the consultation were announced in summer 2004.

What should CPD students learn?

Three priorities are likely to dominate CPD for social workers and social policy practitioners. They must become confident in their abilities to use research findings for evidence-based practice; to work together with colleagues on an interprofessional inter-disciplinary basis across professional boundaries; and to work in partnership with service users who are the recipients of social care programmes. Some of these features exist in currently available PQ for social workers, for example, the Oxford University MSc in Evidence-Based Social Work (www.apsoc.ox.ac.uk/Courses_EBSW.html), and the University of Birmingham's Community Mental Health Programmes (www.cmh.bham.ac.uk).

Opportunities for study will involve moving away from being concerned only with specific post-qualifying or postgraduate awards towards locating post-qualifying study within a framework of continuing professional development. CPD should be a logical extension of learning beyond the initial qualification. It should consolidate, deepen and broaden knowledge and skills beyond the beginning stage of competence or capability to practice. CPD should first develop a well-assured competence in practice, followed by proficiency, then expertise – as suggested by Benner (1984) in her adaptation of the Dreyfus model of skills acquisition.

CPD priorities for social policy practitioners may overlap with those of social workers because social policy graduates increasingly are employed in new projects that address social exclusion. For example, staff in Connexions, Sure Start, Primary Care Trusts, Youth Offending Teams and neighbourhood renewal programmes have usually held a wide variety of previous posts, and they may now have common interests and objectives. Multi-professional CPD will be vital for the enhanced operation of these important initiatives. Perhaps the best way of developing understanding of multi-professional teamwork is to encourage the development of a wider range of new shared awards that would enable social workers and social policy practitioners to learn together.

Managers seeking CPD will probably have different priorities from practitioners. They are likely to be keen to acquire or further their management skills, informed by up-to-date social policy. Different tiers of management will almost certainly have different needs. We may speculate that senior managers will be concerned mainly with *strategic* matters, including finance and organizational change, in the light of government initiatives. In contrast, new first-tier managers may welcome help with their major change of role. We should note that the NHS is probably more experienced in providing management training for its staff than are social services agencies. This could be relevant where managers on CPD programmes are expected to collaborate with their opposite numbers in the NHS and to provide integrated services. Staff from social work and social care agencies may feel like 'poor relations'.

The SCLDI (Social Care Leadership Development Initiative) programme has run in England since 1999, now funded jointly by the Department of Health through the Social Services Inspectorate, with a contribution from the NHS Health and Social Care Leadership Programmes. The predominant model of learning is action learning sets, and a significant proportion of this work has gone to the HEI sector. The LGA (Local Government Association)/DoH launched the Initiative because local authority employers had failed to recognize the need to invest in senior management development. Approximately 600 senior managers, mostly directors and assistant directors, have participated in the programme. From 2002, the programme broadened to include multi-agency participation. In 2003 the programme was linked to the Social Care Modernization Branch and the NHS leadership centre. In 2004 SCIE (Social Care Institute for Excellence) will offer the programme as CPD for 'top managers' in social care. The Initiative may link with imperatives to become 'Learning Organizations' (discussed in the conclusion). Further information can be found at www.e-scldi.org.uk/infoprog.htm. At the beginning level of CPD management development, a finding from Kearney (2003) suggests that the Practice Teaching Award has been used as a stepping stone to first-line management posts, partly given the lack of other opportunities.

Hence not everyone will have the same agenda when embarking on CPD. As implied earlier, the senior manager and the experienced practitioner will almost certainly have different aims. So, too, will their employers. There may have to be some negotiation between the parties on this. Given the sheer diversity of potential students and the importance of tailoring content to individual needs, it is neither possible nor desirable to try to prescribe closely what CPD should tackle. However, there are a number of likely themes for consideration:

1 CPD for professionals in social work and cognate occupations probably should contain an *appropriate* up-to-date version of the social policy learned in initial qualifying studies. It is very important that such staff have a good understanding of how current policies affect the lives of service users and the operation of agencies. A historical perspective and a reminder that social policy is contested territory will also be valuable. Therefore most CPD programmes will probably revisit topics such as: ideologies of welfare, health, employment and housing. Newer topics such as social exclusion and the environment are likely to figure too, along with comparative international social policy.

2 CPD should include some aspects of transferable key skills (DfES, 2002) such as communication skills, information technology, problem solving and teamwork, which provide employers with some evidence of staff's capacity to transfer from one area of work to another. For IT, some stimulus is likely to be found in Harlow and Webb (2003), a collection of papers on how the welfare services are being affected by rapid technological advances. Furthermore, the requirement of the new degree for all qualified social workers to attain the European Computer Driving Licence or its equivalent will have implications for CPD and IT. Other ideas for CPD are found in the Benchmark Statements for Social Policy and Administration, and for Social Work (QAA, 2000). Although they focus on bachelors degrees with honours, their indicative curricula suggest areas for updating and deepening knowledge in relation to practice.

3 The growing importance of evidence-based practice increases the requirement for social workers to enhance their research capability. The Social Care Institute for Excellence (SCIE), founded to promote the use of research for evidence-based practice, will influence CPD choices for social policy and for social work. The implications may be a rise in demand for more part-time practitioner higher research degrees, CASE (Collaborative Awards in Science and Engineering) studentships (Economic and Social Research Council (ESRC), 2003) which involve an agency partnership for the research topic, and part-time applied 'professional doctorates' based on project work and a shorter dissertation (Thoburn, 1999). Part-time research methods courses at Masters level must become increasingly available as CPD awards for social work and social policy.

4 Social workers and social policy staff who have taken a career break might be encouraged to return to practice if they were offered an easily accessible Return to Practice programme as a refresher. Working in partnership with service users and carers is a predominant theme in social work and social policy, and CPD activity should adopt this focus for its content and its process. Management training could draw on the extensive public sector management literature or on more specialist management sources for first-tier managers (Social Care Institute for Excellence (SCIE), 2001).

You will have noticed the emphasis that the content of a CPD programme should be 'appropriate'. (This is one of the proposed GSCC principles for social work PQ.) What is appropriate? This raises the question of programme delivery. To this we now turn.

How might CPD students be enabled to learn?

It is not easy to teach in higher education, and profound changes have happened since the 1980s that make the day-to-day existence of many teachers

---

Perhaps you might start by reflecting on your own experience of higher education. Does what follows ring any bells?

- The lecturer lectures, making errors along the way. You get confused but have no opportunity (or are too afraid) to ask questions.
- The lecturer gabbles 'to cover the syllabus' but the treatment of the subject is far too brief for most of the audience. You cannot keep up with note-taking and you get lost.
- You have very little real choice of learning opportunities. It is pretty much the standard diet for all. Some of it is of no interest to you, some is trivial, some is too difficult.
- You give an assignment your best shot. The feedback is terse, predominantly negative, and leaves you in the dark about how you might do better next time. You are discouraged.
- You are sick of writing essays: they have become boring and mechanical. You think it neither helpful nor fair to dwell so much on this type of activity. You would like the chance to be assessed in different ways.

in higher education distinctly pressured. For example, staff–student ratios have deteriorated sharply, meaning that careful attention to the needs of individual students is now less feasible. The task of assessment has become a considerable burden at certain times of the year. Added to this, there is a growing pressure to publish in refereed journals and add to the university's research portfolio. Amidst all this, it may be difficult to contemplate, let alone create, CPD programmes, particularly if they are in addition to existing activities.

Gibbs (2001) suggests that experiences like those described in the box on p. 147 have not been rare in higher education. Bearing in mind that your performance as a student was probably better than average, you can perhaps appreciate how unsatisfactory a time some of your contemporaries had. Now is your chance to do things differently. How can you help your CPD students to learn? Detailed advice can be found in easily accessible sources such as Race (1999). Here we provide a few pointers from our combined experience and understanding of the literature on learning and teaching, as well as from the GSCC principles discussed earlier.

CPD programme design

The CPD programme should:

1 be relevant, understandable, efficient and effective, meaningful and be linked to registration requirements, a CPD model, and arrangements for other professional groups. It should:

- have a critical edge;
- be relevant to participants' practice;
- feel up-to-date: current events should be embraced and used;

2 be flexible, accessible, affordable and provide value for money. It should:

- provide a range of learning opportunities;
- allow students some freedom to create their own learning opportunities. In general, it is appropriate to encourage more independence and autonomy at higher educational levels;

3 include a variety of assessment vehicles in 'constructive alignment' (Biggs 1996, as discussed in Chapter 2) with the curriculum;

4 match the programme to the students. Those whose last experience of education was at HE Level 1 or 2 will have very different needs and expectations from those who already have attained postgraduate qualifications.

CPD teaching methods

- Lectures are a poor vehicle for the transmission of information. They are best reserved for inspiring, enthusing, intriguing and provoking.
- Remember that the learning opportunities are more important than your own classroom performance. Get comfortable with the idea of being 'a guide on the side', rather than 'a sage on the stage' (King, 1993).
- Assume the students will be part-time and will appreciate at least some of the programme being organized for distance learning.
- Discussion is crucial in social work and social policy. There are usually no 'right answers' to problems, and it is important to air a range of analyses and remedies.
- Case studies are powerful integrative learning tools, if handled well.
- So are portfolios, with reflective commentary. They may also improve students' promotion chances (and your own!).
- A research project offers the best chance of learners grasping and appreciating research methods, and applying theory to practice.

Examples of teaching methods useful for CPD

How do you teach people you rarely meet?

In a one-term CPD social policy 'refresher' module for graduate social workers up to 100 miles from the study centre, you might 'deliver' the study material by:

- requiring students to buy some books and pressing them to read a broadsheet newspaper regularly, with an eye for social policy-related stories;
- providing (only) a couple of classroom sessions, (at the start) to reorient them to the subject and enthuse them, and (at the end) to reflect on the main themes;
- supplying a modest list of online sources of information (journals, copyright-cleared articles, research reports, etc.) and requiring students to find more (including at their workplace).

You might enable students to engage with the material by:

- publishing a suggested study schedule;
- facilitating an online discussion forum, using a five-stage 'e-moderation' approach (Salmon, 2000);
- communicating individually with students, by email or phone, if necessary.

The power of case studies

These may comprise two lines or 50 pages, be real or synthetic, be a scenario about people or places. Once devised, the main challenge is to steer discussions to achieve the intended learning outcomes.

How much detail? It depends on many factors, including the time available and level of the programme. PQ students might be expected to address a case study of the complexity they meet in practice or sift 10 or so pages of anonymized extracts from an agency file littered with irrelevance.

- Make questions as open as possible.
- Probe for *evidence* for arguments.
- Press for decision-making to be as rational as possible.
- Enable students to *generalize* from the particular case.
- Don't answer questions yourself, or reveal 'what happened', until the students have done their bit.

Action learning sets

These are very suitable for experienced practitioners who can benefit from sharing relevant experiences, reflecting and learning from each other. The action learning set needs to:

- conduct its activities with ground rules that are collectively agreed;
- try to ensure a stable ongoing membership;
- develop trust.

The facilitator needs to spend more time establishing the process rather than preparing learning content. Action learning sets can work together towards certain shared learning goals or they can provide a support mechanism for individual learning. It also is possible to conduct action learning sets online. Burgess (1999) evaluated the perceptions of social services managers who had taken part in action learning sets over four years. The sets were organized around group work processes that introduced participants and their concerns to each other, involved participants in bidding for making contributions to discussions, jointly negotiated issues for discussion, presented issues, identified feelings, clarified facts, sought options, designed an action plan and reviewed progress. The managers reported that participation in the learning sets enabled them to become more reflective and self-empowering but that they had some difficulty relating the learning activity to outcomes that improved services to users. The learning sets did help to open up alternative solutions for situations where professional relationships had become confrontational.

---

e-learning and CPD

- Information technology may help, but don't simply put existing materials on the web and hope that it will do. 'The best computer applications are those that empower students to do what would otherwise be difficult' (Gibbs and Robinson, 1998).
- Start small. If you are new to 'e-tutoring', you may be surprised by the time needed to design, implement and test an e-learning activity.
- Become an e-learner. It is very different from being a classroom student, so try it out sooner rather than later. Maybe you don't have the time or inclination to sign up for a formal programme, but do at least join an online discussion for a while. Even one on a recreational topic will give some insights and may spark ideas.
- If you're stuck for ideas, see Salmon (2002).
- Find out what others are offering. Online programmes in the social work/social policy arena are beginning to happen, e.g. the University of Stirling's Postgraduate Certificate in Drug and Alcohol Studies, and its European Studies in Substance Misuse course (University of Stirling, 2003).

Conclusion: strategic issues

A CPD strategy is an essential tool of good human resources management within the ethos of a 'learning organisation' (Senge, 1990), discussed in more detail in Chapter 14. Currently, too few public service agencies have adopted the philosophy of a 'learning organization' which takes responsibility to develop and value lifelong learning for its staff. There are examples within the health and social care sector. The NHS Scotland is developing a learning organization strategy which includes branded learning centres, a national database of learning opportunities and personal learning credits for staff (NHS Scotland, 2002). The Department of Health will be developing learning resource centres for social work and social care staff in conjunction with the

Practice Learning Task Force and TOPSS England. Current public sector staffing problems in part can be attributable to employers not developing a human resources strategy that enhances staff's potential capability. Employer organizations need to become learning organizations. Both social work and social policy practitioners need CPD opportunities if they are to deliver high-quality practice.

Becoming a learning organization will depend on having an adequate supply of supervisory and mentoring skills, as well as sufficient capacity to assess work-based learning. Qualified social workers will need ongoing 'practice supervision' (similar to 'clinical supervision' for nurses) from an experienced, skilled, professional social worker if they are to develop their professional roles over time. The introduction of skilled social care workers within skill-mix teams creates the need for better practice supervision to support their roles. The current social work Practice Teaching Award should be reworked into a more broadly based Mentors/Assessors/Practice Supervision Award to support work-based learning for social work, social policy and social care practice. A revised award may be the linchpin for ensuring an effective CPD framework.

A streamlined organizational arrangement would enable better regional strategic planning and promotion of CPD by employers. Quality assurance for professional CPD activities (comprising work-based learning and employers' in-service programmes) could be devolved to local universities working in partnership with employers. Together they would ensure that professional learning was fit for purpose, linked to development of professional practice, and based on occupational standards to ensure quality of service delivery. A streamlined framework must contain four components:

1   an award for newly qualified workers that will cover induction standards and the consolidation of competences in the workplace;
2   specialist PQ awards;
3   designated multi-professional awards;
4   agreed processes for updating and maintaining requisite skills and knowledge.

Requirements should sit comfortably within an overall framework of CPD and take place within a learning organization where employers actively support their employees' development.

In conclusion, employers must adopt a clear accountability framework for developing their qualified social workers and social care staff, including those with a social policy qualification; the strategic challenges are to create learning organizations and sufficient work-based mentoring, supervision and assessment to support CPD.

12

Globalization: implications for learning and teaching

Zoë Irving and Malcolm Payne

Introduction

Despite its rather grandiose title the aim of this chapter is not to rehearse the scholarly debates on the processes or project of 'globalization'. These wider debates are skilfully articulated in a number of more general works (for example, Hirst and Thompson, 1999; Held *et al.*, 1999; Held and McGrew, 2002) and works with specific reference to social policy (Deacon *et al.*, 1997; Mishra, 1999; Yeates, 2001; George and Wilding, 2002). The following also does not provide a comprehensive assessment of the implications of globalization for learning and teaching at the more general level. Detailed discussion of the nature and implementation of 'distributed learning' can be found, for example, in Edwards and Usher (2000) and Lea and Nicoll (2002) and analysis of some of the issues arising from a global market in education in Room (2000). Rather, the purpose of this chapter is to identify, within the context of social policy and social work provision in HE, some of the more specific and practical implications of 'the expanding scale, growing magnitude, speeding up and deepening impact of transcontinental flows and patterns of social interaction' (Held and McGrew, 2002: 1).

The perspective on globalization that we take in this chapter, however, acknowledges that concerns about general changes in perception of the world and our relations with other countries and peoples are rising in social policy and social work studies. There are a number of factors in the concerns expressed, including the basic issue that changes in the world economic system are having an impact on relations between countries, affecting their approaches to developing policy and welfare services. Changes in perception arise from a communications revolution in the late twentieth century, leading to information about distant countries and peoples being transmitted more rapidly through television, the Internet and other electronic media. People can also travel increasing distances more often and more quickly. The economic system has changed so that countries are more interdependent, and economic problems in one place can affect other countries more powerfully and more quickly than in previous decades.

So in learning and teaching, social policy and social work students may be particularly concerned to learn about issues in the following areas:

- policy on information and communication technology, with social and ethnic groups having differential access;
- the consequences of faster and easier global travel and changing perceptions of distant countries with migration leading to policy and welfare issues about asylum-seeking and immigration;
- an increasing focus on social development as a concomitant of economic development, and its consequences for practice in the social professions.

At the extreme, the hyperglobalist (to use Held *et al.*'s (1999) term) position might suggest that almost any development in an area can at some point be attributed in some way to processes that are occurring 'out there', beyond national control in the borderless economy. The danger, of course, in attempting to consider everything as a component or consequence of globalization is that we get lost in the analysis and are unable to usefully apply existing scholarship to the concerns of this book. Thus a more restricted and cautious view is adopted here that recognizes that, for a range of reasons not yet fully explained nor agreed upon, international developments are having some impact on the shape of higher education in the UK, both in terms of national policy (DfES, 2003) and in relation to disciplinary developments in social policy and social work, which necessarily impact on course delivery. The developments identified for discussion here are:

- the implications of social, political and economic transnationalization for curriculum content within social policy and social work;
- changes in the professional context of both academics and social workers (and other welfare professionals and the countless other occupations which constitute the employment destinations of our graduates);
- changes in the demand and desire for geographical mobility of students and graduates.

These three aspects of change are illustrative of the impact of processes of globalization on areas such as knowledge transfer, the labour market and cultural awareness. The remainder of this chapter is thus divided into three sections. The first examines some of the issues arising from the growing internationalization of the disciplines. The second section provides examples of the impact of the 'global market' in higher education with regard to social policy and social work provision. The final section addresses the student experience in the context of pressures and opportunities to 'think global'.

Relevance and suitability: two challenges

Is globalization important to students? On one hand, everyday public discourse may lead them to accept or perhaps even to exaggerate its importance as a contemporary 'hot issue'. Globalization is not a new set of processes, but concern about them has been rising. Transport and communication have been developing and leading to change over many centuries, and countries were always economically interdependent.

Concern about globalization has, in part, grown because inequalities between countries are emphasized by the growing pace of change: countries with more powerful economies are enabled by the communication revolution to gain more cultural and economic influence. This issue underlies the public debate about policy responses to globalization and professional responses to its consequences for welfare systems. People in less powerful countries fear that their economic interests and important aspects of their culture will be compromised. Another social change associated with globalization is more rapid and wide-scale migration of people in search of greater economic prosperity and to avoid the impact of war, famine and social disturbances. Concerns about globalization are associated with concerns about post-modern trends in many societies, in which culture, solidarity and shared experience seem increasingly fragmented. People worry about how diversity in ethnic origin and social and psychological attitudes will affect the cohesiveness and security of the society in which they live.

Higher education teachers, therefore, may need to reflect both caution in accepting the relevance of globalization explanations, while facilitating consideration of suitable issues in appropriate ways. Programmes of education in social policy and social work need to allow students to engage with the various theses about globalization and related ideas such as post-modernism and post-colonial theory. Students need to engage critically with over-simple ideas that globalization leads to growing cultural uniformity and dominant cultures suppressing diversity. They may also need to look at opportunities generated by globalization, such as wider awareness of minority cultures, and the possibility that cheaper and more flexible communication media, such as the Internet and desktop publishing, permit greater awareness and representation of alternative cultures and perceptions.

Relevance

Unification of the HE sector, widening participation and changes to student financing mean that increasing numbers of students are now drawn from areas local to universities. Many students may not have had opportunities to travel widely either within or beyond the UK. This experience of the world is in direct contrast to that of more privileged students whose experience of other countries and cultures is broad and who may have deferred entry in order to travel and work abroad. In addition, increasing numbers of students from minority ethnic groups are found within the category of 'home' students. Their experience adds yet another dimension to the experience of 'other' cultures. Interest in welfare arrangements in Islamic countries within comparative study and the place of religion and culture in the study of values in social work are two examples of how student experiences might be related to content. The overall challenge for learning and teaching is in communicating the relevance of the study of a range of global issues within this diversity of 'global'

Getting to grips with the tools of comparative analysis

In a student intake where local and minority ethnic students form a substantial proportion, students taking the 'Comparative Social Policy' module at the University of Surrey, Roehampton, engage in a series of in-class unassessed problem-solving activities. A worksheet provides explanatory notes and a summary of key points, prescribed reading, excerpts of statistical tables and accompanying questions, which take students through a staged learning process. Most effective where students work in pairs, this approach allows students to apply knowledge of individual countries and theoretical approaches covered earlier in the taught elements. Students are able to build confidence in their own critical and analytical skills and improve familiarity with and appreciation of statistical material.

These exercises aim to engage students in the study of both the nature of cross-national variation in different areas of social policy and the explanation of divergent patterns of welfare. Thus the relevance of particular welfare arrangements to types of welfare outcomes and the relative importance of explanatory factors and frameworks are demonstrated. The learning and teaching methods emphasize accessibility on the part of students to the processes and information sources used by social policy analysts.

Contact: Judith Glover, University of Surrey, Roehampton, j.glover@roehampton.ac.uk. Further details of this example can be found on the SWAP website at: www.swap.ac.uk/links/casestudies.asp

experience. The example given in the box opposite outlines one method of communicating this relevance using an active approach to student learning.

Suitability

Attention to the effects of globalization on human welfare clearly requires some space within curriculum design, but in the context of the demands of professional accreditation and a social policy curriculum which is already felt by many teachers to be overloaded, the inclusion of yet more content is problematic. Taking an international perspective in the social work curriculum has also been problematic. The short (two-year) length of the professional qualification, the Diploma in Social Work, during the 1990s and the need to focus primarily on practice requirements in a national legal and administrative context limited the possibilities for including international content. However, the QAA benchmark statement applied to the new social work degree-length qualification starting in 2003 proposes the inclusion of material on 'The location of contemporary social work within both historical and comparative perspectives, including European and international contexts' (QAA, 2000). Moreover, the benchmark statement includes substantial contextual material that might benefit from international comparators. More widely, social work curriculum standards in the US have, since 2001, contained the requirement to prepare 'social workers to recognize the global context of social work practice' (Council on Social Work Education (CSWE), 2003). Prior to this, from 1994, they stated that 'effective social work education programs recognize the interdependence of nations and the need for worldwide professional cooperation' (CSWE, 1994). These provisions have led to an explosion in American texts providing comparative information of interest to American students, and placing social work practice in an international context. Examples are the Greenwood Press international handbooks (Watts *et al.*, 1996; Mayadas *et al.*, 1997) featuring chapters describing provision in a range of countries, and more integrated works, such as Midgley (1997); Van Wormer (1997); Ramanathan and Link (1999); Healy (2001).

Research and teaching interest in global/international issues in social policy is increasing, and is observable in the recent publication of undergraduate texts (Yeates, 2001; George and Wilding, 2002), which add to previous contributions (Deacon *et al.*, 1997; Mishra, 1999), and the launch in 2003 of the 'International and Comparative Social Policy Special Interest Group' under the auspices of the Social Policy Association. This group has combined existing interest in comparative social policy with more recent disciplinary developments in the study of supranational organizations and social policy in the global context. However, a contrasting view on the place of globalization in the social policy curriculum was expressed by one respondent to the SWAP social policy project who commented: 'What is bad practice in social policy?

Bad practice is having a lecture hall of 200 people who are then told about globalisation.' Undoubtedly there are aspects of globalization which are not among the specific concerns of social policy and social work but the changing international landscape of welfare provision and a global concern for human wellbeing most certainly are.

It is likely that globalization or global/international issues will develop further as discrete areas of study, but at present study is more likely to be integrated within existing teaching on social policy and social work degrees. In the social policy curriculum, the most obvious current place to locate study of globalization and related topics is in modules covering comparative issues, since these have already expanded following the publication of the bench-marking statement which recommends that 'all social policy courses should contain a significant comparative element although not necessarily in the form of a specialist unit. Comparative approaches should inform the subject matter' (QAA, 2000: 2). The focus on comparative study is broadened further in both the 'knowledge and understanding' and the 'subject specific skills and abilities' sections of the statement where knowledge of the 'international and supra-national dimensions of social policy' and understanding and application of theories and concepts to 'international contexts' are listed.

For many teaching teams, one of the thorny issues arising from the social policy benchmarking statement relates to the location of the 'comparative element' in teaching: whether this area of study is best addressed within modules or through provision of a stand-alone module. Is its subject matter too complex to be dealt with in a single lecture on a theory module? Does fleeting reference to contrasting welfare arrangements in other industrialized countries provide students with sufficient awareness of global issues? Is comparative analysis possible or even appropriate at undergraduate level where supply of library materials is often limited and students' contextual knowledge may be least developed? This latter question is particularly important in rela-tion to learning outcomes: is it fair to expect students to produce much more than derivative work when they may have little more than a few key text books to inform their thinking? An example of developing international and comparative approaches early in an undergraduate social policy course using a problem-based approach is given on p. 74.

There is no reason why global/international issues must be pigeonholed as an element of comparative study, however, and many reasons why this should not be the case. A 'specific unit' covering comparative issues is not a prescrip-tion of the social policy benchmarking statement, and it may be the case that the configuration of expertise and interest within a particular course team suggests provision of international/global studies units as the more appropriate approach to examine the relevant concepts, theories and methods. Many 'global issues' represent vehicles through which core elements of social policy and social work study can be effectively delivered to students. One example of this is the study of immigration and welfare which allows exploration of areas such as ideology and politics, policy development, international relations, racism and cultural difference and so on (see the box below for an example). The terms 'international' and 'global' in module titles also seem to appeal to students, even though the actual content may not be as 'exotic' as they imagine.

Immigration and welfare

Work with asylum seekers and refugees is no longer a peripheral activity in social work and related professions. Work is emerging in and across the full range of welfare contexts, in statutory and voluntary social work agencies and in mainstream and specialist provision. In children and families work, in mental health, in criminal justice settings, in community care contexts, it is likely that matters concerning immigration status will have to be confronted by practitioners. Workers are often unprepared to deal with the practical and ethical issues this work raises and are ill equipped to manage the complex situations those subject to immigration control find themselves in.

A module is targeted at students on professional courses who will enter social work, youth and community work, health, housing and other welfare arenas. It is delivered at level 2 and 3 of a degree programme and builds on level 1 work, which focused on the historical, ideological and legislative framework of immigration control in the UK.

The module aims to develop that understanding of the legislative and ideological framework by focusing on the ways asylum and immigration impact on professional practice. The module explores the relationship between immigration control, asylum policy and the delivery of health, education, social housing, social security, criminal justice and childcare and mental health services. As well as looking at the relevant policies, students are expected to consider their own role as welfare providers in the internal policing of immigration and in the gatekeeping of services to this vulnerable group. Teaching methods include lectures, use of case study material from a variety of practice settings/scenarios and a visit to an immigration tribunal. Students are assessed by way of a case study example, which explores the tension between their professional value base and the practical application of immigration control. Student feedback is extremely positive: without exception students experience the visit to the tribunal as a devastatingly graphic way to understand the impact of immigration and asylum policy on people's lives.

Contact: Debra Hayes, Manchester Metropolitan University, D.Hayes@mmu.ac.uk

The professional context

One area of change in the professional context for academics is the impact of institutional strategies to keep afloat in the supposed rising tide of globalization. These strategies can include a wide range of bi-lateral and multi-lateral international relationships between institutions and the expected involvement of departments, schools and individual academics in supporting teaching, research and networking activities. A variety of social work cross-national activities has developed, particularly those funded by the European Union. Unplanned and unfocused activity developed as a result of grant aid has sometimes been transitory. Attempts to maintain long-term relationships require a mutuality in commitment over a period of time to develop more complex and equal relationships (Askeland and Payne, 2001a). Consequently, more complex relationships, including research and staff mobility alongside student mobility, may gain greater support in universities. Certainly, issues of the validity of cross-national knowledge in social work are usefully raised by cross-national connections (Askeland and Payne, 2001b) and cross-national analysis (Payne, 2001). Social work courses in American universities have developed links internationally as a result of the curriculum requirements, and information about some of these is contained in Healy et al. (2003).

An example of more recent developments of this kind is the setting-up of the Worldwide Universities Network (WUN) in 2000. In contrast to the European Union (EU) ERASMUS programme which aimed to create a European university network through student and staff mobility and the development of joint teaching initiatives, the WUN programme (www.wun.ac.uk) primarily exists to enhance research capability within research-led institutions in the UK, the US and, more recently, China, with planned expansion to universities in a number of European countries. It is an example of institutions capitalizing on the opportunities offered within a shrinking world: combining and thus strengthening research-related activities; developing wider and deeper partnerships with corporate organizations; and, with a budget of $1 million, providing a range of postgraduate student and staff exchange options lasting between six weeks and six months. Since the WUN mission is 'to develop a global research alliance', teaching-related developments are directed towards research training and employability, hence 'the need to equip students with the skills to function in an international context'. Objectives in relation to distributed learning and the transfer of know-how are stated to include the sharing of 'distributed learning materials and to work together in developing new material – enhancing pedagogical effectiveness, increasing student choice, augmenting efficiency and creating better learning outcomes' (WUN, 2003).

The WUN objectives also include the development of a virtual graduate school which currently offers an online Masters in Public Policy and Management, the first course developed under contract to the UK's e-University and accredited by the University of York (*The Independent*, 2002). It is interesting that such a course is the pioneer for the virtual graduate school given recent debates within the social policy academic community regarding the (re)location of social policy on the disciplinary map and the recruitment problems and consequent viability struggles currently being experienced by some social policy courses. With a budget of $2 million, this postgraduate programme is to be a completely virtual learning experience for students. Modules are authored by academics in the UK and US, and course material includes downloads from the BBC archives and access to York University's e-library. Designed for adult learners, the learning process includes individual and online collaborative activities with support from course tutors.

Among the modules offered is 'Globalization and Social Policy' (see box on p. 162), which could be considered a totally globalized learning experience. For the purposes of this chapter, this e-module represents a practical example of the design of a unit of study on the topic of 'globalization' while the development of the wider Masters programme illustrates both the significance of social policy in the global context and the process by which a global market in higher education is emerging. However, as critics (including the UK author of the 'Globalization and Social Policy' module) would point out, reflecting a wider critique of 'globalization' itself, WUN is currently driven by the better-off Anglo-American universities who also form the majority of partners. Thus knowledge transfer in this context could be considered a one-way process from North to South: the authors of the Public Policy and Management course are Anglo-American, the course texts and other materials are drawn from Anglophone sources, but some of the potential consumers of this material are likely to be sponsored by administrative institutions and non-governmental organizations in the South. (In addition to the technical requirements for access to the course, the full Masters fees are £9,000 per UK student, but the UKeU website states that 'prices will vary from country to country depending on the arrangements we have with local partners'.*)

To reinforce the direction of the transfer, the first point made on the 'our courses' section of the UKeU website is that 'participation on a UKeU course does not grant non-UK students any right of abode in the UK', which itself highlights a range of issues which could be discussed on relevant social policy and social work courses. Despite these drawbacks, the WUN model of international collaboration demonstrates that there is at least momentum (and possibilities for funding) in the development of a global approach to teaching and learning. Cogent arguments could be presented which support the extension of a similar but modified model to undergraduate teaching and to less research-rich institutions in the North and a wider range of institutions in the South.

---

* Since this chapter was written, the UKeU has closed.

The Worldwide Universities Network
Masters in Public Policy and Management:
Globalization and Social Policy module

The module is divided into three sections:

1   Debates are reviewed around the concept of 'globalization' and its implications for social welfare and policy.
2   Social policy at the global level is considered, examining the way global institutions address international social issues from poverty alleviation to pensions, health and labour rights.
3   The social policy agenda is considered in the context of globalization in Western Europe, Central and Eastern Europe, Latin America and East Asia. In addition to the learning outcomes and process for the module outlined below, each of the ten units has its own specific key question, outcomes, summary of activities to be undertaken by the student, core and additional readings and BBC resources accessed via the web.

Learning outcomes

● Understand the terms of the debate on globalization and social policy.
● Access and analyse critically the social policy agenda of major international organizations.
● Examine critically the international politics of key social policy issues: poverty alleviation, pensions, health and labour standards.
● Examine critically the influence of globalization on the making of social policy in different regional and national contexts.

Learning process

In addition to reading the online authored material, students will:

● undertake private study of two textbooks covering the module as a whole and three required readings per unit;
● submit several short work tasks for comment by the online tutor;
● access and evaluate web-based materials on the global social policy debate;
● participate in online group discussion and debate from study questions posed for each unit.

Contact: Bob Deacon, University of Sheffield,
b.deacon@sheffield.ac.uk

Student mobility

Student exchange programmes are well established, particularly in the European and US context and within specific international partnerships developed at the institutional level. The nature and uptake of these exchanges is diverse and variable, but the simple exchange of small numbers of students undertaking study of specific modules or units on cognate degrees in partner countries is the most common format. In social work, placements in a foreign country are often arranged and supervised from a university in partnership with a UK university (see box below). More recently, the trend has been towards bilateral exchange rather than exchange within a network of partners, which could include more than a dozen institutions with more than one in any one country.

For social policy and social work students in the UK, specific issues arise in relation to the uptake of exchange opportunities. At the general level, changes in student financing impact on students' capacity to suspend paid work and housing commitments in order to study abroad; and on degrees recruiting significant proportions of mature students, family responsibilities can also present barriers to substantial time spent away from home. In fact, these obstacles to uptake and the decline in financial support for the EU ERASMUS exchange programme have been recognized for some time (Bradley and Harris, 1993), and, over the last decade, incentives to maintain links have

---

Experiencing the 'other' in European exchanges

Exchanges with partner universities for ten-day group visits in European countries were established at Manchester Metropolitan University for youth and community students. The idea at first was to give students experience of planning and organizing a visit. Students benefited particularly from travelling abroad, in many cases for the first time, in staying with foreign students and having them stay at their own homes, and in carrying out a project. As the visits developed, each participating university organized a conference on a theme agreed in advance as part of the visit. Students from each country brought a presentation on related issues in their own country, and visited relevant agencies in the country they travelled to. This gave a clearer academic focus to the visit and allowed students to extend their ideas beyond general impressions of 'foreignness' to specific comparisons in particular policy and practice areas. From these exchanges, staff teaching visits to other countries developed, as well as a staff research conference and arrangements for professional placements in other countries.

virtually vanished. The investment of time and effort required of individual exchange co-ordinators has largely gone unnoticed at the institutional level and even the most committed 'Europeanists' have tired (and in some cases retired). These factors, combined with substantial decreases in the levels of EU funding for student exchange, suggest a decline in opportunity just at the time when expansion is needed.

For UK students the benefits of study in other European countries are numerous, most obviously in terms of building confidence and acquiring language skills. However, as many co-ordinators continue to find, the demand for exchange places in the UK far outweighs the demand of UK students to study abroad. Options that may address these obstacles are the development of programmes which make greater use of distributed learning approaches (see, for example, http://cms.euromodule.com, the pages of the University of Central Lancashire and its European ERASMUS partners in the fields of social work and policy) or those which involve bringing the international experience to the student (see the box below). The trade-off here is clearly the

---

Social Security in Europe: the roadshow model of European student exchange

Developed by members of the European Institute of Social Security (EISS) and funded through the EU ERASMUS and later Tempus and Socrates programmes, the 'Social Security in Europe' course ran from 1988 to 2001. The course was accessed by up to six students from each EU country (and later Poland, Hungary and the Czech Republic) and taught in English. An intensive teaching timetable allowed teaching sessions to be undertaken by members of the EISS – academics from a range of European countries and disciplines including economics, law, sociology and social policy. The location of the course rotated around the institutions to which the EISS members were associated. Students were accommodated by the host institution, all together in halls or dispersed around the university town. Teaching took place over one to two weeks with each contributor visiting the host institution and delivering two sessions on one day. Assessment included group work where an international mix of students produced a study on a particular issue, e.g. pensions reform in Europe, as well as written work and oral exams.

The benefits of an integrated model of cross-national study are found in the mix of student participants, the range of perspectives and expertise within the teaching team and the opportunity for students from the host institution to access the course without the need to travel. Many of the students participating in this programme went on to postgraduate study and employment within the EU and various national government departments.

removal of language acquisition for the UK students but increased up-take may be worth the cost.

Conclusion

This chapter has attempted to outline some of the issues arising from the impact of globalization on the design and delivery of social policy and social work courses in terms of curriculum content, institutional and professional context and opportunities for enhancing the student experience. As an area of study, globalization is clearly relevant for students of the two disciplines in terms of both the backdrop to their lives and as an increasingly important context in which social policy and the practice of welfare professions is shaped and enacted. In many ways students may be fully aware of the global context in which they undertake daily activities, the goods they consume, the films they watch and the places they visit. Some of them may even be directly involved in activities which aid understanding of global issues such as voluntary or paid work abroad, and protest movements.

The task for teachers, then, is to draw upon existing experience and understanding and identify ways in which academic concerns can be made both attractive and accessible to students. Notwithstanding the QAA regulatory framework, the place of global/international study in the social policy and social work curriculum can present difficulties in relation to the space for and place of these aspects of study. For course teams, an acceptable resolution of these difficulties may emerge from an imaginative interpretation of benchmark recommendations which privileges neither comparative nor international study but considers them as possibilities for the design and organization of units of study which can be made appropriate to all levels of university teaching. At the institutional level, it is clear that national pressures are being exerted upon universities to further internationalize their activities and, while these pressures are mostly directed towards research-based income generation and related consortium building among the better-off institutions, all universities and their constituent faculties, schools and individual academics are feeling the ripple effects.

Although the push to optimize international links in the academic world may provide opportunities to fund and develop a wide range of innovative and worthy programmes of study and student exchange in social policy and social work, increasing demands on the time and range of activities undertaken by academics seem to mitigate against the involvement of even the most highly motivated individuals. Thus the role of senior managers in academic schools and departments in recognizing the professional investment required by such developmental activities and supporting them in the various relevant institutional committees is crucial if an international learning experience is to be achieved.

Useful websites

General

www.eswin.net/
The European Social Welfare Information Network provides information about social work in a range of European countries and links to international issues.

www.gaspp.org
Pages of the Globalization and Social Policy Programme which links research centres in Finland, England, Canada and India and has a research, advisory, education and public information remit (also linked to *Global Social Policy* journal).

www.hometown.aol.com/egeratylsw/globalsw.html
The site for a 'global social work community', an American site with a social development emphasis.

www.iassw.soton.ac.uk/Generic/default.asp?lang=en
The website of the International Association of Schools of Social Work represents the main international collaborative body of social work educators.

www.ifsw.org/
The website of the International Federation of Social Workers contains up-to-date information about international issues for social workers and the international code of ethics and definition of social work.

www.iucisd.org/
The website of the Inter University Consortium on International Social Development covers social development issues in social work.

www.socialcritic.org/review.htm
A range of papers and excerpts by many well-known and not so well-known authors on social change, globalization and related topics.

www.socialworker.com
A site for American social work students, the New Social Workers Online.

www.socialworksearch.com
An American social work search site that covers an international range of websites.

www.uclan.ac.uk/facs/health/socialwork/socialpolicy/links/comparative.htm
Comparative Social Policy at the University of Central Lancashire, resources to support students and pages supporting social policy and social work modules on

their Socrates exchange programme, including papers free to download and links to other relevant sites.

www.york.ac.uk/depts/spsw/spa/

Social Policy Association (with link to International and Comparative Group pages, www.sheffield.ac.uk/socst/ICSP).

Key institutions

European Union: http://europa.eu.int
International Labour Organization: www.ilo.org
International Monetary Fund: www.imf.org
Organisation for Economic Co-operation and Development: www.oecd.org
World Bank: www.worldbank.org
World Trade Organization: www.wto.org

Organizations with an interest in globalization

Asia Europe Dialogue on Alternative Political Strategies: www.ased.org
Bretton Woods Project: www.brettonwoodsproject.org
Corp Watch: www.corpwatch.org
Globalise Resistance: www.resist.org.uk
Global Policy Forum: www.globalpolicy.org
Trade Observatory: www.wtowatch.org/
World Development Movement: www.wdm.org.uk

Asylum and immigration related sites

www.asylumsupport.info

Independent website run by Frank Corrigan containing very useful policy information, and updates and links to many relevant organizations and documents.

www.ercomer.org

The European Research Centre on Migration and Ethnic Relations, including a virtual library.

www.homeoffice.gov.uk/rds/immigration1.html

Website of the Home Office (UK), Research Development and Statistics Directorate, where a range of occasional papers and research reports can be found.

Also:

Commission for Racial Equality (UK): www.cre.gov.uk
International Organization for Migration: www.iom.int
The Refugee Council: www.refugeecouncil.org.uk/
United Nations Office of the High Commissioner for Human Rights: www.
   unhchr.ch
United Nations Office of the High Commissioner for Refugees: www.
   unhcr.ch

Acknowledgements

The authors would like to thank Sue Morris, Alex Robertson and Adrian Sinfield for providing further information on examples included in the chapter.

13

International perspectives

Karen Lyons

Introduction

Chapter 12 has focused on the resources for teaching about globalization and some of the approaches to 'internationalizing' the UK curricula in social policy and social work. It is clear that there has been a significant growth in the number of texts available which address international social policy issues, often from a comparative perspective, and that the development of the Internet has added a new dimension to the availability of resources and the opportunities for imaginative forms of teaching, learning and assessment. While the emphasis and examples in the previous chapter have tended to concentrate on social policy, it can be argued that these resources and opportunities are equally available in the area of social work education. However, assumptions that social work is essentially a 'local' activity, bound by national legislation and traditions, as well as professional requirements regarding course content and assessment, may have operated in addition to other constraints to limit development of international perspectives, at least at the qualifying stage of social work education.

The aim of this chapter is to argue the case for the 'internationalization' of social work education while also emphasizing the relevance of social policy resources and teaching to an approach that recognizes the impact of supranational events and agreements on local issues and professional practices. Not least of these is the effect of global trends in relation to national governments' thinking and policies on the changing balance between the state and the 'independent' or 'third' sectors in welfare provision (Teeple, 2000; Klug, 2001). Given the centrality of the state in the UK welfare system (with implications for the training and employment of social workers and other welfare professionals) the chapter commences with a comparative perspective on the role of the state in welfare, before focusing more specifically on definitions and rationale in relation to the concept of 'internationalization'. The chapter concludes with a discussion of some aspects of implementation, including a note on the role of international professional associations.

A comparative perspective on the role of the state in welfare

It is assumed that education in social policy and for social work produces people, whom we might broadly term 'welfare professionals', who (for at least part of their careers) are likely to work in central or local government departments. Alternatively, they may work in non-governmental or private organizations which are either contracted by the state to 'supply services' or which complement the (social) services that the state provides. It is therefore relevant to consider the role that the state plays in welfare provision in different societies (with resulting implications for the role of the voluntary, private and informal sectors).

It would be timely first to say a little more about the use of the term 'welfare' in an international context. This may be understood differently by people in different places and based within different traditions. Thus, an American text about welfare policy (aimed at social workers) has defined welfare as 'the state of collective well-being of a community or society' (Van Wormer, 1997: 4), and includes sections on 'social welfare functions and structures'; 'care through the lifecycle'; and 'world (welfare) policy issues'. (The last section includes chapters on marginalized populations, human rights and sustainable development.) Meanwhile, Bull (2000) has pointed out the very limited common understanding of 'welfare' in the US as meaning the financial assistance to lone parents which has been the focus of recent change in federal legislation and much debate among state policy makers and social workers alike. While UK academics, practitioners and public took on something of this meaning (as reflected in the growth of 'welfare rights work' since the late 1960s), it is relatively more likely that UK policy literature and teaching will relate to a range of services commonly held to be part of 'the welfare state' (Powell and Hewitt, 2002).

In this connection we can note that much recent literature has focused on changes to the state's role in welfare policy and provision resulting from the rise to dominance of neo-liberalism in the late 1980s and early 1990s, as illustrated in the case of New Zealand by Kelsey's account (1997), and also discussed from a Canadian standpoint (but taking an international perspective) by Teeple (2000). The association between the state and fiscal arrangements is strong in much of the literature. For example, an appendix on 'The structure of welfare in Member States' (Hantrais, 1995) summarized the social security systems of European Union (EU) countries; and fiscal arrangements

Classical models of the welfare state and the role of social work therein

The Middle European model

- social integration and opportunities for human development produced by a solidaristic civil society (corporations, communities) supported by the State;
- social market economy;
- social work:
  - helping people to organise different kinds of self-help in their living world (*Lebenswelt*) in order to provide a setting for social integration amid human growth based on the idea of civilisation (*Bildung*);
  - an expression of a solidaristic caring society.

The Anglo-American model

- managing and solving problems of the poorest of the poor and very needy people in accordance with the principle of individual self-determination;
- open capitalism;
- social work:
  - helping people to solve their everyday problems by therapies, guidance and counselling;
  - entity of various problem solving methods and techniques of guidance and counselling connected to the principles of human rights.

The Nordic model

- social security for all people provided by the State through comprehensive systems of national insurance and welfare services;
- state capitalism/market socialism;
- social work:
  - helping people to use the complex systems of benefits and services according to their needs;
  - an instrument of social policy in terms of promoting welfare equality and social security.

(Hamalainen, forthcoming)

(tax, pension and income support systems) were also the basis for Esping Anderson's classic comparative study and resulting typology of 'welfare states' (1990). This was largely, though not exclusively, rooted in European models and examples and has subsequently been critiqued and modified (e.g. Abrahamson, 1993; Hill, 1996). However, it has served as a basis for much subsequent comparative analysis, and also provided a framework for emerging work on a 'comparative science of social work' (see, for example, Hamalainen, forthcoming, and the box on p. 171).

It has also been suggested that other countries not generally credited with having 'a welfare state', such as the US and Japan, may in fact have a weak form of one, since some provisions are made to prevent destitution, although welfare benefits of various kinds (including healthcare) are considerably more targeted and conditional than in conventionally defined welfare states (Van Wormer, 1997). Additionally, as changes over the past decade or so have shown, welfare states (including provision of social services) are not static entities. Just as they have been changing in the West, the change in welfare systems has been even more dramatic in the countries of the Former Soviet Union (FSU) and more recently China. (See, for example, Chytil and Popelkova re the Czech Republic (2000); and Yuen-Tsang and Wang (2002) and Leung and Wang (2002) re China.) Both countries could be said to have previously had strong forms of welfare states (though not within the framework of a democratic political system as understood in the West) relative to emerging residual and market-oriented systems.

We can also question how far the concept of state provision of welfare is mainly a twentieth-century phenomenon of the developed world, given the limited extent to which countries with low per capita income and often high rates of indebtedness can meet the requirements of even basic healthcare and education for all – let alone the demands of social care for vulnerable populations. (Having said this, it is striking how many countries in the world have at least some educational opportunities for students of social policy and social work.) However, development of public welfare services of various kinds can be attributed at least in part to political will and public values, and is not solely a function of a country's wealth, as demonstrated in the cases of the US and some Indian states (Lyons, 1999b).

There has been a recent increase in texts that discuss the role of the state in relation to welfare systems and social work and which take European and international comparative perspectives (for instance, Adams et al., 2000; Cochrane et al., 2001). Much of this literature illustrates the shift towards social services provision by voluntary (not for profit), private (commercial) and informal (family and 'community') sectors, sometimes termed 'the mixed economy of welfare'. Such a welfare mix has long been established in the social care field in some European countries, such as Spain and Greece (Feu, 2000; Soumpasi 2002), but it is gaining ground even in the traditionally strong welfare states of Scandinavia (see, for instance, Blomberg et al. (2002) for a

Swedish example and Hamalainen and Niemela (2000) re Finland). Some of this literature relates these policy and organizational shifts to demographic changes, and to the implications for women in particular, as well as to wider issues of changing labour markets and population mobility.

We can note here the role of 'subsidiarity' in development of welfare systems. This has been a familiar concept in many European countries throughout the twentieth century, but mainly came into the English vocabulary in the context of developments in the European Community (now the EU). The term (with origins in late nineteenth-century Catholic teaching) means that responsibility should rest at the lowest level capable of meeting needs (whether through the family, or associations or public bodies, including churches), rather than functions being taken over by the state (Cannan et al., 1992). The principle of subsidiarity has had a considerable influence on shaping the organization of social services in countries such as France, Germany and the Netherlands (Lorenz, 1994). The move to a mixed economy of care in the UK might therefore be seen as bringing this country more into line with its continental neighbours (although this was not the motivation for the changes). For instance, parallels have been drawn between 'community care' in the UK and subsidiarity in Germany (Kornbeck, 1997); and concerns about the increased dependence on the informal sector (with implications particularly for women's roles and responsibilities) have also been echoed in other countries.

The implications for welfare of different societal value systems between (broadly) Western 'individualistic' and Eastern 'family and community' orientation have also been noted elsewhere and have had a bearing on views about the role of the state in welfare and more specifically on social services provision, social work education and social work approaches (see, for instance, Tsang and Yan, 2001, and Yuen-Tsang and Wang, 2002).

Definitions and rationale

It is appropriate at this point to consider the meaning of 'international perspectives' in social policy and social work education and to assert that much of the literature and teaching in this area to date has been of a comparative nature rather than specifically international. A comparative approach can be justified on a number of grounds, not least the idea that comparative research and study contribute to the development of international perspectives, and, pragmatically, that welfare professionals are increasingly engaged in various forms of cross-national activity. Such activities either afford the opportunity to learn about another country's welfare arrangements or require knowledge of that country's systems and culture(s). One such example in relation to social work is the case of inter-country adoption (Selman, 1998) although, as the author suggests, all good practice requires knowledge of European and international conventions and ethical codes. This last point also raises the question of how far 'international' perspectives are largely evident in some British curricula and texts as European perspectives or as perspectives from other advanced industrial countries where English is the dominant language. Both of these possibilities can also be explained and justified as follows.

In the first case, as part of the EU, British policies (and thus, in some areas, social work practice) are increasingly subject to European directives and policy initiatives. As indicated in the previous chapter, European Community funding played a significant role in stimulating the formation of European networks that facilitated student and staff exchanges and curriculum development, including in the fields of social policy and social work. These funding incentives can be seen as promoting wider EU policy goals of harmonization of educational systems, encouragement of labour mobility and establishment of a European social as well as economic identity.

However, it could be argued that European developments have prompted *regional* (continental) perspectives in curricula and constituted a form of 'Europeanization' rather than internationalization (Lyons, 2002). It may also open educators to charges of taking a 'Euro-centric' view that lacks appreciation of the wider context within which welfare policies are developing, and of failing to take sufficient account of the population diversity and interconnections outside the region that are increasingly evident in many European countries. Having said this, research, teaching and learning about social work education itself provide an interesting case example of both a comparative approach to study and of 'Europeanization'.

The boxed text on p. 175 suggests that social work education in the UK is moving closer to European norms; and, overall, comparative research in this area gives some evidence of a wider trend towards harmonization of training for social workers within the EU (at least according to the three criteria stipulated in the 1989 Directive). This suggests movement towards achievement of the goal of the directive – namely, to establish parity of professional qualifications as the basis for labour mobility in a range of professional fields.

Turning now to the second possibility (that internationalization is approached primarily from the perspective of other advanced industrial countries that share the English language), this might be justified on the grounds that we are then comparing 'like with like'. However, the assumption that a shared language reflects common origins and ways of thinking might distort or neglect real differences in how countries have developed and the factors shaping current policies. On more pragmatic grounds, a shared language does at least facilitate access to literature and academic and professional interchange – although such exchange should not be undertaken uncritically. For instance, for much of the second half of the twentieth century the academic field of social work was dominated by the availability of American social work literature and it may still be more influential than material from European countries. Some American writers (e.g. Midgley, 1983) have cautioned against the dangers of professional imperialism, but it seems likely that US ideas and

Case example: British social work education in a European context

- A new three-year degree replaces the two-year Diploma in Social Work in England in 2003, and in Wales, Northern Ireland and Scotland in 2004.

- Additionally, new bodies, the Care Councils (of England, Northern Ireland, Scotland and Wales) now have responsibility for the registration of social workers.

Both developments reflect a national response to concerns about social work standards.

But the moves also represent belated conformity with requirements of an EC (1989) General Directive about professional education and qualifications (Barr, 1990):

1   education for a minimum of three years at undergraduate level;
2   courses in a university/higher education institution;
3   qualification should be followed by subsequent registration.

Many EU countries already met these requirements but others (e.g. Austria, France) have had to make changes related to, for example:

- the status of the institutions within which social work is taught;
- the variety of routes and qualifications leading to posts in the broad area of social services and eligibility for particular titles and/or registration.

Comparative study of social work education – even within the EU – therefore presents a complex picture requiring some understanding of:

- the higher education systems of different countries;
- the naming, organization and roles of 'social workers'.

Variations from British arrangements and assumptions include different:

- job titles and boundaries between occupational groups;
- educational traditions and recent changes in qualifying training (such as distinctions between social work and social pedagogy in e.g. Germany, Spain, Denmark, Finland);
- specific aspects of social work education including selection and placements.

resources are now influential in how welfare policies and educational programmes are developing, both in the Former Soviet Union countries (personal
communications) and elsewhere in the world, including China (Yuen-Tsang
and Wang, 2002).

It can also be argued that the influence of the US on British policy is still significant and, notwithstanding Britain's place in the European Union, there was
evidence in the late 1990s of interest by British politicians in American developments. One such example concerned federal and state approaches to work-
fare and to child poverty. However, in this case, the resulting British policies also
demonstrated the influence of a range of 'local factors', including public attitudes
and 'Euro-influences', which might serve to modify exact replication of policies
(Lyons, 2000). Conversely, there may also be an awareness of the British influence on the origins of welfare systems in countries as diverse as Australia, Canada
and South Africa that can make current welfare arrangements seem superficially
familiar and more comprehensible. Taking the case of social work, there may be
an assumption about similarity in the education of social workers influencing
(among other factors) the current drive to recruit social workers from these
three countries (personal communications). While this policy is understandable
in terms of the shortages facing UK departments (and the personal choice/
opportunities it affords to individuals for exposure to different systems and new
experiences), it also raises ethical issues. These include the effect of depriving the
'sending country' of resources needed to staff their own social services, following investment in the training of such personnel. The teasing out of such
assumptions and ethical dilemmas, and the identification of reasons for differences in policies and practices (or different perspectives on the same
policy/practice), provide a useful basis for development of analytical and critical
skills informed by international perspectives.

The boxed text on p. 175 leads on to a consideration of the place for
teaching and learning about social policy and social work in less developed
countries. It can be argued that any course or module in the social field which
aims to incorporate international perspectives must give some recognition to
the web of relationships which exist between countries and continents and
which often span the North–South and East–West divides. As well as possible
ideological differences, these divisions reflect the global imbalance in the distribution of wealth and power that affects both the development of 'in-country'
welfare services and the motivation for migration to more favoured destinations. In relation to the latter, the presence of both temporary migrants (in
the form of overseas students) and of indigenous students from ethnic minority
communities in some UK universities raises challenges and opportunities in
terms of developing relevant teaching and learning opportunities (see Chapter
12) and will be returned to in the section on implementation.

However, there is another element in the teaching and learning process
that perhaps shifts our thinking from primarily a comparative approach to
considering international dimensions of a social problem and international (as

opposed to national or regional/European) responses. This is the examination of the roles and policies of international governmental and non-governmental bodies, including organizations such as the International Monetary Fund (IMF) and the United Nations (UN). There is a variety of mechanisms that affect, or seek to regulate, the relationships between states, the distribution of (welfare) resources and the internationally agreed principles on which social affairs should be conducted (including those pertaining to issues of human rights and citizenship) (Lyons, 1999b). It can also be observed that over the last decade we have seen the development of a whole range of social problems that transcend the borders of individual states. These require responses from politicians and welfare professionals (as well as often personnel in the criminal justice area), at cross-national and international levels as much as at the national or local level. Examples of such international problems include child labour, human trafficking, drug smuggling, the sexual exploitation of children, families and communities fractured by war or AIDS, and environmental pollution.

These are in addition to (or are aspects of) the more conventionally acknowledged issues that are often the focus of social policies and interventions, such as poverty and illiteracy, variable health and housing standards, changing family forms and roles, the 'greying of the planet' and the special needs of particular populations – all of which also have international dimensions (Lyons, 1999b). None of these 'global' problems are amenable to solution or alleviation by individual countries, nor indeed by individual occupational groups, but even preliminary consideration of them at the higher education stage throws into sharp relief the need for all social policy and social work students to develop some awareness of the interconnected nature of the postmodern world and the challenge to understand better the aetiology of problems so that the slogan, 'think globally: act locally' has some meaning.

Implementation issues and resources for internationalizing the curriculum

Before proceeding to suggestions for resources, it may be useful to briefly consider the term 'international social work' – as opposed to the notion of international *perspectives* in and on social policy and social work. International social work is as yet a nebulous and 'under-developed' term. This was indicated in a study carried out by Nagy and Falk (2000). The researchers' findings (see the box on p. 178) give an indication of the varied understandings of this term and all 12 categories might be considered as aspects of international social work or as resources for this activity or as the means through which international perspectives might be included in social policy and social work education.

> ## What do we understand by the term 'international social work'?
>
> In 1995–6 Falk and Nagy (2000) carried out research into the teaching of 'international social work'. Postal questionnaires were sent to schools of social work in 20 countries, resulting in 96 responses.
>
> One aim of the survey was to explore the meaning of the term 'international social work'. The researchers grouped their findings into 12 categories as follows:
>
> 1 international events and social forces – problems faced by world's population;
> 2 implications of increasing interdependence of nations;
> 3 role of governments internationally and of international non-governmental organizations (INGOs);
> 4 influence of multi-nationals and global financial organizations;
> 5 comparative social policies, structures, values and cultural assumptions;
> 6 practice approaches, programmes and methods used in other countries;
> 7 range of international practice opportunities;
> 8 struggles for a more just world and support for human rights;
> 9 working with immigrants and refugees;
> 10 educational exchanges – educators, students, practitioners;
> 11 international consultation projects;
> 12 international seminars and conferences.

The findings also suggest an association in the minds of respondents between international activities and cross-cultural communication – the latter being related to a European concept, 'inter-cultural learning' (Aluffi-Pentini and Lorenz, 1996). A similar association has been made in the recent requirements of the American Council on Social Work Education (CSWE), which include the requirement that all social work qualifying courses should enable students to recognize the global context of social work practice *and* to work in the context of diverse cultures (CSWE, 2002). In the UK, feedback from a five-year retrospective study of social workers who had completed a top-up degree leading to the award of a BA International Social Work Studies at the University of East London (UEL) gave rise to two useful findings:

- that, while it had been anticipated that students taking this course might be aiming for 'specialist work' in the international field, the majority were still working in East London;

- that the main value of the course was seen as the development of skills and confidence in cross-cultural communication.

In relation to the latter, cross-cultural learning had mainly been derived from the students' experience of a three-month project period abroad researching some aspect of social work policy or practice. Unlike other student 'placements' abroad such as those discussed in Chapter 9 (usually based on formalized institutional contracts and arranged through staff) this programme required students to set up their own projects, enabling them to choose locations suited to their personal and family connections, language abilities, etc. The student-initiated model of project work has been retained in a more recently established MA course. (For a fuller discussion of models and the issues associated with placements or project work abroad, see Lyons and Ramanathan, 1999.) There is also some indication from recruitment patterns to the MA and work destinations of initial cohorts that this course may be serving as a 'specialist international social work course' equipping students to work 'abroad' and/or in international organizations.[*]

While the development of specific award-bearing courses about 'international social work' (Healy, 2001) (or international social policy) might thus be seen as specialist courses, more suited to students at the post-qualifying stage, evidence from the undergraduate award and other recent experience suggests that it is important for undergraduates qualifying in social policy or social work also to have exposure to some of the elements which might be contained in more specialist courses. This might be in the form of selected option modules/units (or aspects of core modules), but it would seem preferable if it could be through an integrated approach that is informed by global and comparative thinking permeating all aspects of the teaching. The previous chapter has suggested that this can pose dilemmas in relation to the literature available to staff and students, but in developing international courses it has been necessary to think creatively about what constitutes resources for such an approach.

It is suggested that some of the learning which needs to inform staff and student thinking about international perspectives is available from the news and media reports on current affairs – although the opportunity for exposure to newspapers, journals and/or the media in different countries provides an important reminder of the different perspectives from which the same or a similar problem can be viewed. A second source of new ideas and information is often the students themselves who, besides sometimes having had experience of a particular country or issue, often show considerable resourcefulness in tracking down information, for example, from embassies and from agencies 'abroad' (not to mention the web). A third resource is the plethora

---

[*]   The BA International Social Work Studies at UEL was phased out (in 2003) in favour of the more recently established MA International Social Work with either Community Development Studies or Refugee Studies.

of organizations and associations which either have 'branches' or counterparts in other countries or are international in character.

Some of the many branches of the United Nations have a particular relevance to the work in the social welfare field, as has already been mentioned. However, there are many other organizations that operate across a range of countries, have a wide remit in the broad field of humanitarian aid and welfare work, and generally produce publicity and other materials that can be selectively used, including to provide case examples. These include the Red Cross/Red Crescent, Amnesty International, Oxfam, Caritas and International Social Services. Additionally, there are three international associations which have particular relevance to education in the social policy and social work fields, namely, the International Council of Social Welfare (ICSW), the International Association of Schools of Social Work (IASSW) and the International Federation of Social Workers (IFSW) More detailed information about the origins and functions of these organizations has been given elsewhere (Lyons, 1999b), but it may be useful to give some brief examples of their roles and work.

All three of these bodies have primarily institutional memberships, although in the case of both IASSW and IFSW there is also limited provision for individual membership. The ICSW has a membership of voluntary organizations concerned with social policy and provision, drawn from over 70 countries, and sees its role as promoting social development and enabling communication between voluntary and governmental sectors and between the local level and international level. It thus has links with other bodies in the international and regional fields, such as the European Platform of Social NGOs. The IASSW has a membership of schools and individuals, also drawn from over 70 countries. It aims to 'promote excellence in social work education, research and scholarship globally, to enhance human well being' (IASSW, 2004), to facilitate international exchange and to represent social work education at an international level. Examples of its work include a recent survey of social work education worldwide (Garber, 2000) and leading a joint (with IFSW) Task Force on 'Global Standards' for social work education (see the box on p. 181). Some of its work is carried out through regional associations, which may also carry out specific projects. For instance, the European Association of Schools of Social Work (EASSW) is initiating (in 2003) an enquiry into the 'transferability' of social work qualifications.

By far the largest of the three organizations is the International Federation of Social Workers. This now has a membership of national associations from 77 countries and, including individual members ('Friends'), it apparently speaks for more than 490,000 social workers worldwide. Apart from representation on a number of bodies with cognate concerns, the IFSW also operates task groups and committees on a range of areas, for instance, in relation to human rights, and on ethical issues. It periodically produces policy statements and other material to guide and inform members. Examples include the recent adoption

---

Global Qualifying Standards: suggested core curriculum

The IASSW/IFSW issued a Discussion Document on Global Standards, presented to the General Assemblies of both organizations at the Joint Congress (Adelaide, 2004). The document includes suggestions for a universal core curriculum, as summarized below:

- knowledge and skills in assessment and intervention (at micro, mezzo and macro levels);
- social work's origins, purposes and development;
- how socio-economic factors impact on human functioning and development;
- application of knowledge, skills, values and ethics to confront inequality and injustices;
- person in environment transaction and life span development: bio-psycho-social and cultural factors influencing behaviour;
- knowledge of welfare policies and services;
- knowledge and skills in social work research and application in practice;
- knowledge of related occupations to facilitate interprofessional collaboration;
- supervised fieldwork education.

The document also makes reference to the expectation that qualifying courses will prepare students for generalist practice in a range of settings and with diverse populations; and to be critically self-reflective and morally active practitioners. (Regrettably the document does not yet include an explicit recommendation for inclusion of comparative or international perspectives.)

The full document is available on the websites of both organizations (IASSW, 2004; IFSW, 2004).

---

of a new Policy Statement on Displaced Persons, and current work on a Policy Statement on Globalization (aimed at countering the negative effects of globalization) and on a new Statement on Principles (related to human rights and social justice) and Ethics (professional conduct), both presented to the General Meeting in Australia in 2004.

These associations play an important role in sponsoring opportunities for international exchange and networking, not least through regional and international conferences, as well as through posting material on their websites. They also jointly sponsor publication of the journal *International Social Work* and support other means of disseminating research findings and good practice. For example, IASSW supported academics in the development of *The Caribbean Journal of Social Work* (established in 2002). Overall, these associations provide another source of information and ideas for use in developing international perspectives, particularly in relation to social work but also of some use in social policy teaching and learning.

Conclusion

Finally, it may be useful to quote here a short extract from the IFSW Interim Policy Statement on Globalization. Having given a short definition, the statement goes on to recognize that:

> Globalisation is a continuing process which, while advancing global technological development and communications, also has a negative impact on the balance of economic, political and cultural power between individuals and communities. Social Workers see and work with the consequences of these processes.
>
> (IFSW, 2002: 3)

Such a statement articulates the view that globalization has sometimes unacknowledged effects at local and national levels and for this reason (among others) it is important for all welfare professionals to have some understanding both of this process and of the ways in which international institutions may be contributing to, or seeking to address, the consequences of the process. Students of social policy and social work can also be challenged to develop more sophisticated and critical understanding of national problems, policies and systems through the integration of comparative and international perspectives into their courses. Additionally, there is scope for the development of specialist knowledge and skills in the particular fields of international social policy and social work for a minority of students, whether they subsequently choose to work at home or abroad or in international organizations. There has been some suggestion of insularity on the part of British people, of language problems and of attitudes among staff and students that may not support 'internationalization' – not to mention timetable constraints and concern about preparation for the UK workforce. However, the need for cross-cultural skills as part of a wider repertoire of anti-oppressive principles and strategies has already been recognized in British social work education; and it is interesting to note in the professional press that two local authorities are currently developing opportunities for study periods or voluntary work abroad (Kent and Essex, respectively) as part of a personnel policy aimed at staff development and retention (Tarpy, 2003).

In conclusion, while we still need further research and theorizing in this area (particularly in social work), there has been a significant expansion in the range of articles, texts and other resources available, and opportunities for all staff and students to participate in some form of international activity (for example, through conference attendance) are increasing. Current events, other research and literature, and experience in this field all suggest that the time is right to promote comparative and international perspectives in social policy and social work education with the aim of producing welfare professionals who are more globally aware and able to work collaboratively with a view to improving welfare services for all users.

Resources: useful websites

General

Division for the Advancement of Women: www.un.org/womenwatch/daw/index.html
One World: www.oneworld.net/
PRAXIS – Resources for Social and Economic Development: http://caster.ssw.upenn.edu/%7Erestes/praxis.html
Social Work Search: www.socialworksearch.com/
Women Watch: www.un.org/womenwatch
World Wide Web Resources for Social Workers: www.nyu.edu/socialwork/wwwrsw/

Institutions

United Nations Children's Fund: www.unicef.org
United Nations Development Fund for Women: www.unifem.org
United Nations Development Programme: www.undp.org
United Nations Educational, Scientific and Cultural Organization: www.unesco.org
United Nations International Research and Training Institute for the Advancement of Women (INSTRAW): www.un-instraw.org
United Nations Research Institute for Social Development: www.unrisd.org

Associations

International Association of Schools of Social Work (IASSW): www.iassw.soton.ac.uk
International Council on Social Welfare (ICSW): www.icsw.org/
International Federation of Social Workers (IFSW): www.ifsw.org

14

Developing the university as a learning organization

Imogen Taylor

Introduction

> An organisation bent on encouraging learning needs to focus not just on the circumstances which make learning necessary, but its own systems and structures to support learning, and the culture within which learning is embedded.
>
> (Cayley, 2000: 39)

In this book, we have focused on the development of effective learning and teaching in social work and social policy. To become and to continue to be effective requires from the individual educator continuing attention, commitment and a related expenditure of time and energy, as well as the capacity to critically reflect on practice and to integrate feedback from a range of stakeholders. However, this is not sufficient to develop and sustain effectiveness and a university must examine its own structures and systems that support learning and the culture in which it is embedded (Cayley, 2000).

In this chapter, I will argue that in addition to focusing on the individual educator and what she or he can do to self-manage change, we must consider the higher education institution (HEI) as a learning organization. Here the learning of both staff and students is viewed as a core activity embedded in a stimulating and supportive culture. The HEI as a learning organization acknowledges that for the educator to provide an effective learning opportunity for the student, that educator him/herself must be provided with effective learning opportunities and resources. The learning opportunities may be formally planned or occur informally and they may be explicit or tacit. The learning opportunities may be provided directly by the HEI, or the HEI may support access to the opportunities provided by other stakeholder groups, which in social policy and social work are likely to include professional accrediting bodies, discipline-based associations, subject centres or government departments. The knowledge being explored may be about either generic or discipline-based material that will contribute to the process of learning and teaching, or it may be knowledge about policy or practice developments that will contribute to the content of teaching and learning. Without an effective organization to support learning, it is unrealistic and unreasonable to expect the individual educator to develop and/or sustain his or her own learning.

I begin by identifying New Labour policies that promote the learning organization and examine the concept of the learning organization as it occurs in the literature. I then draw on the concept of the scholarship of learning and teaching to provide the link between the organization and the individual practitioner and examine a four-dimensional model for the scholarship of learning and teaching developed by Trigwell *et al.* (2000). I suggest five strategies to support the development of the scholarship of learning and teaching and note that the style of academic management will be important to these. Finally, prompted by Fielding (2001), I raise what is for many of us an increasingly pressing question: whether we live to work or work to live.

Modernization and the learning organization

The term 'learning organization' regularly appears in New Labour policies. The modernization agenda draws on the discourse of lifelong learning prioritized in the White Paper *The Learning Age: A Renaissance for a New Britain*:

> The skills of the workforce are vital to our national competitiveness. Rapid technological and organisational change means that, however good initial education and training is, it must be continuously reinforced by further learning throughout working life.
>
> (Department for Education and Employment, 1998: 3, 4)

New Labour policies designed to modernize public sector services typically assume that lifelong learning is delivered by the learning organization. As Maggie Pearson, Deputy Director of Human Resources for the Department of Health (DH), said in an interview for the *Times Higher Education Supplement*: 'Delivering a workforce for the future is a key part of the delivery contract signed between the DH and Number 10. The commitment to creating a learning organization comes right from the top' (Sanders, 2002). Alan Milburn, then Minister of Health, expands on this in his foreword to the White Paper *Working Together–Learning Together – A Framework for Lifelong Learning for the National Health Service*:

> Learning and development are key to delivering the Government vision of patient centred care in the National Health Service. Lifelong learning is about growth and opportunity, about making sure that our staff, the teams and the organisations they relate to, and work in, can acquire new knowledge and skills, both to realise their potential and to help shape and change things for the better.
>
> (Department of Health (DH), 2001b)

This White Paper identifies the characteristics of the successful learning organization:

- a well-resourced learning strategy;
- a regularly reviewed system of appraisal and personal development planning;
- non-discriminatory and flexible access to education and training;
- provision of a learning infrastructure that is accessible in terms of time and location;
- demonstration of strong links between education, training and development and career progression and reward;
- a variety of development methods to enable staff to build on skills and expertise;
- regular evaluation and monitoring of learning activity.

(Department of Health, 2001b)

Unfortunately, there are two problems with this framework. First, the confident assertion that these are the characteristics of a successful learning organization lacks any evidence base. Second, as we will see in the next section, the learning organization literature is inadequately theorized. For example, the Department of Health's emphasis is on formal learning which, although important, neglects the equally if not more important dimension of informal, unplanned learning (Eraut, 2000).

The learning organization

Interest in the learning organization initially peaked in the early 1990s. The basic premise is that in a global economy, maintaining a competitive edge depends on the process of continuous improvement, and the most effective insurance against being left behind by the rapid pace of change is to embed within the organization processes which facilitate learning (Senge, 1990). A learning organization was defined by Senge as 'a group of people continually enhancing their capacity to create what they want to create' (1991: 42), a collective undertaking which involves people making choices. Senge's thesis is that organizations reflect how we think and interact and if organizations are to be vibrant and productive then we need to change our patterns of thinking and interacting 'so that learning can become a way of life rather than an episodic event' (Senge, 1991: 38).

These ideas are compelling for social work and social policy educators who, as we have seen in Chapter 1, are faced with a context of rapid change in both the policy and practice context and the higher education context. However, beyond these broad brush ideas the learning organization is inadequately conceptualized (Eraut, 2001) in three key ways.

First, possibly because the learning organization was developed in relation to the private sector, the literature tends to assume a common understanding of an organization. Yet, given the huge structural changes occurring in public sector organizations today, including HEIs, it is important to consider what we mean by an 'organization'. An organization has been defined as, 'The planned co-ordination of the activities of a number of people for the achievement of some common, explicit purpose or goal, through division of labour and function and through a hierarchy of authority and responsibility' (Schein, 1989: 15). This might indicate a more coherent and controlled structure than is typically found in HEIs. Is there a common purpose in a context where the rewards of

---

The learning organization literature – key themes:

- Success depends on the organization's ability to see things in new ways, gain new understandings and produce new patterns of behaviour, on a continuing basis and in a way that engages the organization as a whole (Dovey, 1997).
- Learning is a way of life rather than an episodic event (Senge, 1991).
- Learning is a collective undertaking which involves people making choices, 'a group of people continually enhancing their capacity to create what they want to create' (Senge, 1991: 42).
- Learning organizations are concerned with empowerment of the workforce (Longworth and Davies, 1996).
- Learning organizations are those 'which encourage the wheel of learning, which relish curiosity, questions and ideas, which allow space for experiment and reflection, which forgive mistakes and promote self-confidence' (Handy, 1989: 199).

the Research Assessment Exercise drive a preoccupation with research and where the White Paper, The Future of Higher Education (Department for Education and Skills, 2003) has been criticized as furthering the split between research and teaching? Is there a clear hierarchy of authority and responsibility in a complex and diffuse structure where, particularly in the pre-1992 universities, the academic is used to having a large measure of autonomy? Is planned co-ordination across the entire organization possible or even desirable?

There is some evidence that learning and teaching activities are becoming co-ordinated through tools such as learning and teaching strategies or widening participation strategies. In 1999 HEFCE allocated £50 million as a funding entitlement for HEIs to develop learning and teaching strategies, and in 2002 another £50 million was allocated for the next three years. All 134 English HEIs submitted their strategies in June 2002 and received their entitlements. The strategies reveal considerable development since 1998 when they were first reviewed (Gibbs and Habeshaw, 2002).

The second problem related to the lack of conceptualization of the learning organization is that the literature tends to focus on individuals learning in the organization and processes through which learning takes place rather than on how the organization learns or how different levels of the organization learn from each other (Taylor, 2004). Gould (2000), for example, in research undertaken in a national child care agency, found that developing an organizational memory was important. It could identify where in an organization similar issues were being addressed or where expertise might lie that could be mobilized by others in the organization. Managing knowledge in this way means that it is systematically collected and held, and thus less vulnerable to individuals who leave and take knowledge with them.

The third problem with the learning organization literature is that it prioritizes learning that is planned and formal. Undoubtedly this will have an important role in 'providing concepts and theories . . . to make sense of . . . experience and understand issues and alternative perspectives more clearly' (Eraut et al., 1998: 8). However, this denies findings from research into the development of professional expertise that most workplace learning is non-formal and unplanned (Eraut et al., 1998, 2000) where learning occurs continually, but employees do not think about their jobs as learning because what they learn is their practice. Eraut and his colleagues in their research into the learning of nurses, engineers and accountants in their first three years of employment are finding that learning opportunities are heavily dependent on the frequency and nature of interpersonal encounters in the workplace and the nature and structuring of work. They identify four key factors that shape formal and informal learning: the work activity structure; the distribution of activities over time and space; the structure and patterns of social relations in the workplace; and the outcomes of work, their evaluation and the attribution of credit or blame (Eraut, 2002).

The scholarship of learning and teaching

Another way of thinking about learning and teaching beyond the role of the individual academic is offered by the developing literature about the scholarship of learning and teaching (Healey, 2000). Trigwell and his colleagues (1999) offer a four-dimensional model for the scholarship of learning and teaching, helpful for our discussion in this chapter:

- the conceptions of learning and teaching held by the lecturer;
- the extent to which the lecturer engages with the scholarly contribution of others, including the literature of learning and teaching and particularly learning in that discipline;
- the extent of reflection on the lecturer's own learning and teaching within the discipline;
- the quality of communication and dissemination of aspects of practice and theoretical ideas about teaching and learning.

(Trigwell *et al.*, 1999: 163)

I will argue that these four dimensions are crucial not only to the development of effective social work and social policy academics but also to the practice of social work and social policy graduates in the field. In the following section, I discuss each dimension in depth and highlight where we have the opportunity to mirror the practice we espouse in the way we teach. I then go on to discuss strategies to support the development of the scholarship of learning and teaching.

Conceptions of learning and teaching held by the lecturer

If lecturers are to engage with learning and teaching concepts, they need to be given the tools to do so, including knowledge of the basic concepts. Young (2003) in her research into teaching practices in undergraduate social policy programmes found that lecturers were happier talking about teaching content than methods. She found that although terms such as 'curriculum development', 'learning objectives and outcomes' and 'transferable skills' were used, there was very little use of technical conceptions of learning to describe approaches to teaching. She comments on the 'ordinariness' of the way lecturers talk about their work, and how they might describe teaching as going well or going badly. She contrasts this with the use of the specialist disciplinary language of social policy exemplified in the recent publication of the dictionary of social policy (Alcock *et al.*, 2002a).

Young's findings (2003) in social policy mirror those of Entwistle and Walker (2002) who point out that when academics discuss teaching they use pragmatic languages which draw on 'craft knowledge'. This is largely tacit knowledge based on their experiences as students, and even exceptional teachers rarely use precise conceptual language. Young (2003) reminds us that the language does exist and cites the index of Biggs' (1999) guide to teaching as evidence of this. Academics are similar to other professionals in this respect. Eraut (1994) had earlier formulated the view that professionals draw on tacit as opposed to explicit knowledge in developing professional expertise.

The risk of the absence of a set of concepts and a shared specialist language for discussing teaching is that it can engender the belief that teaching is common sense and we all know how to do it. This view of teaching as common sense is particularly powerful when it resonates with a view of the profession as common sense. Jacqui Smith, Minister of State at the time of introduction of the new social work degree in England, says that 'the new award will require social workers to demonstrate their practical application of skills and knowledge and their ability to deliver a service . . . the emphasis must be on practice and the practical relevance of theory' (Department of Health, 2002b: i). She held strongly to a 33 per cent increase in the required number of days students must spend in placement in spite of an outcry from educators and employers concerned among other things about the capacity to meet this requirement.

Engaging with the contribution of others in the discipline

The literature suggests collaboration is least developed in relation to teaching in contrast to an emphasis on collaboration in the development of research teams (Young, 2003). Teaching in universities continues to be a largely hidden and private activity. Interestingly, Neumann (2001) in his review of disciplinary differences found that scholars in the 'hard' disciplines were more likely to collaborate in teaching than those in the 'soft', and of course the latter includes social policy and social work. This is somewhat anomalous given the emphasis both disciplines would place on team and community practice and the importance of group and collective action. It seems possible that the professional focus of social work education, the imperative to meet professional requirements and the regular quality audits by the Care Councils might contribute to more of an ethos of collaboration in social work than social policy.

Young (2003) enquired into opportunities for academics to share ideas about teaching with colleagues. She found there was a range, including a large minority of academics who feel isolated and unable to discuss teaching with colleagues although they may be in a culture that encourages discussion of research. She found a greater number who participate in more formal events where teaching practices are discussed; these might include departmental 'away days', team or course meetings, university-wide staff development events, learning and teaching committee meetings, teaching review meetings and conferences. The importance of informal exchange also emerged in the interviews.

Reflection on learning and teaching

There has been a proliferation of literature, influenced by the work of Schön (1983), on the nature of reflection both in relation to teaching and learning as well as practice, particularly in professions such as social work, nursing and education. The term 'reflection' is contested (Ixer, 1999). However, the following definition may be useful, since it highlights several elements of reflection: 'The process by which a thought, feeling or action is brought into consideration. The creation of meaning and conceptualisation from the experience. The possibility of looking at things in a new way' (Brockbank and McGill, 1998: 57). The process under discussion may until then have been tacit rather than explicit. Bringing it to consciousness enables the opportunity to name and understand the experience and to look at it in a new way which may result in changing actions.

Healey's (2000) discussion of geography suggests there is likely to be a continuum which appears likely to be generalizable to social work and social policy. At one end are the lecturers with no awareness of ideas about learning and teaching, who do not reflect on their own practice and who do not discuss teaching with colleagues. At the other end are those who strive to improve learning and teaching by consulting the literature, reflecting on their own teaching and their students' learning and sharing their ideas and practice with their peers.

Once again echoing the discussion of the first dimension of the scholarship of learning and teaching, it is argued that 'Reflecting on your teaching, and seeing what is wrong and how it may be improved, requires you to have an explicit theory of teaching' (Biggs, 1999: 6). Biggs (1999) also suggests it is important to be aware of research on teaching. Ballantyne et al. (1999) emphasize that reflection is not a straightforward tick-box process. They suggest that 'the complexity and situatedness of teaching . . . involves making sense of contradictions and dilemmas; wrestling with ideas and methods; interacting with students and colleagues; and juggling the demands of teaching in an increasingly crowded portfolio of professional responsibilities' (Ballantyne et al., 1999: 238).

Communication and dissemination of practice

The fourth dimension of the Trigwell et al. model of the scholarship of learning and teaching refers to the 'quality of the communication and dissemination of aspects of practice and theoretical ideas about teaching and learning in general, and teaching and learning within their own discipline' (1999: 163). They perceive a continuum with at one end the lecturer prepared to formally communicate his or her ideas and practice to peers and at the other end the lecturer who keeps practice to him or herself.

Taylor suggests there is an important but not much discussed reason for academics to develop knowledge of learning and teaching: 'Academics could contest issues related to practices and conditions of their teaching more cogently and credibly if they were to utilise this information quite systematically to develop their expertise as teachers-of-a-discipline' (1999: 53). Interestingly this may resonate with social policy and social work academics who are likely to view advocacy as a skill for their students to develop for practice with oppressed groups such as people with learning disabilities or mental health problems.

Strategies to support the development of the scholarship of learning and teaching in social policy and social work

Teamworking

Social policy and social work graduates are likely to be working in practice in teams and, as discussed in Chapter 10, these are likely to be interprofessional teams. Undergraduate and Masters programmes often include teaching about teamwork and certainly teamwork will usually be identified as a transferable skill. Yet, as academics we are unlikely to work collaboratively (Young, 2003). Elton (1998) argues that the most important dimension of excellence in university teaching is the excellence of the work of the course team, but he also argues that 'The absence of team work in most universities makes it virtually impossible at present for any department in any university to lay claim to teaching excellence' (p. 4).

Young (2003) suggests that where collaboration can be found in relation to teaching this tends to be around the planning of new programmes, but once validated there is a return to more individualized work. In social work across the UK, all programmes leading to the new award were validated in either 2003 or 2004. This provided an unparalleled opportunity to share good practice and problems in teaching and learning, although the time constraints under which the degree was introduced may have mitigated against this (Burgess, forthcoming). It is to be hoped that the research into the new degree commissioned by the Department of Health will examine the realities of teaching teams, their impact and their sustainability.

Peer observation

Young's (2003) social policy interviewees were not specifically asked about peer observation but did on occasion refer to it, expressing some ambivalence about peer observation being required and concerns about processes being mechanistic and burdensome. Would these findings be any different with a group of social work educators? Certainly in social work priority is traditionally given to the value of observation as an approach to learning about practice (Le Riche and Tanner, 1998) and this has been given added impetus by the new degree and the Department of Health's (2002b) requirement that students 'shadow' experienced social workers as part of assessed preparation for direct practice in placement. The author's own experience with peer observation is that a formal scheme can provide a useful opportunity to reflect with a colleague on teaching; informal opportunities to work alongside colleagues and observe them at work have provided invaluable teaching models. Two aspects, however, are particularly important. First is the opportunity to choose who to observe depending on the learning that is being sought. The academic who excels in the lecture theatre may differ from the academic who excels at facilitation. In discussion of the first dimension of the model for scholarship and learning, we looked at the issue of a shared set of basic concepts about learning and teaching to enable discussion. From my experience I would argue that observation may allow for a form of apprenticeship where modelling can occur without the necessity of discussion. Second, it is important that the scheme operates outside formal appraisal processes if Handy's statement – about the importance of the learning organization allowing space for experimentation, forgiving mistakes and promoting self-confidence – are to be taken seriously (1989).

Staff development

Programmes are usually structured for beginning academics; in most HEIs participation is required and will result in accreditation by the Institute for Learning and Teaching (ILTHE). However, there is a significant backlog of established academics appointed when such programmes did not exist or were not required. Ideally, they will elect to undertake staff development on learning and teaching or to engage in a conference on a topic such as assessment or working with large groups. Gibbs and Coffey critique the limits of 'centralized generic training programmes' which are not 'embedded in disciplinary and departmental communities of practice' (2001: 20).

Brokerage and dissemination: the role of the subject centre

In 2000, the UK Higher Education Funding Councils established the discipline-based Learning and Teaching Support Network Subject Centres. In the Social Policy and Social Work Subject Centre (SWAP) our aim is to 'improve learning and teaching' within our subjects. One of our objectives in doing this is to engage discipline members in learning both about subject content as well as methods. The SWAP team does this by disseminating information and brokering change. We carry these activities out in two key ways. First, we established and support the SWAP website (www.swap.ac.uk), which carries a range of discipline-based information and is regularly updated. Second, we recognize the value of working with discipline-based groups to broker change. At its most intensive, we will work with a group within one HEI who are keen to focus on a process of change, for example in the development of e-learning. We also recognize the value of bringing together academics regionally and nationally to explore shared issues, and, for example, over the period of intense activity in planning the new social work degree, we offered working conferences to social work educators. From 2004 the SWAP becomes part of the Higher Education Academy.

The core aims of the Higher Education Academy are to:

- provide strategic advice and co-ordination for the higher education sector, government, funding bodies and others on polices and practices that will impact on and enhance the student experience;
- support and advance curriculum and pedagogic development across the whole spectrum of higher education activity;
- facilitate the development and increase the professional standing of all staff in higher education.

(Wagner, 2003)

Increasing the evidence base

In the fields of social policy and social work the emphasis on evidence-based practice is increasing. However, in our academic departments, 'The bad news is that not only do departments not have the knowledge to [be responsible for the professional development of academic staff that is necessary for transformative learning], there is little knowledge to call upon' (Harvey and Knight, 1996: 166). We have very little research about learning and teaching in higher education and we have even less discipline-based research. There are some hopeful signs of change. In 2003, the ESRC Teaching and Learning Research Programme Phase III (www.tlrp.org/) focused on post-compulsory education although it was disappointing in that ultimately only 12 projects were funded and none of these specifically focused on education for social policy or social work. The Department of Health has commissioned an evaluation of the new social work degree and promises the future commissioning of small-scale focused studies related to the degree. The Social Care Institute for Excellence has commissioned knowledge reviews into learning and teaching in social work education including reviews on communications skills, law, partnership working, interprofessional working and human growth and behaviour (www.scie.org.uk). The Scottish Institute for Excellence in Social Work Education is commissioning projects to contribute to change in social work education in Scotland (www.sieswe.org/).

Rewarding excellent teaching

Young (2003) found in her study that questions on reward for effort in teaching provoked more strong feeling than any other interview topic. There

A social work or social policy department that is a learning organization might include the following activities:

- team meetings;
- reflection days;
- curriculum review;
- peer observation;
- staff appraisal;
- induction and mentoring for new staff;
- rotation of experienced staff through key roles;
- an active staff development programme;
- a reward structure that acknowledges improvement and excellence in learning and teaching;
- firm and fair management of staff;
- research and teaching and learning seminars;
- links to HEI: e-learning expertise; Learning and Teaching and Academic Support Units;
- links to national associations: the Social Policy Association; the Joint University Council Social Work Education or Social Policy Committees;
- links to Care Councils responsible for professional accreditation; and to employers and their organizations;
- links to the Social Work and Social Policy Learning and Teaching Support Network and other relevant subject centres.

was a strongly held view that teaching is devalued in comparison with research and this is reflected in promotion processes, even where teaching is one of the criteria for promotion. Initiatives to increase the status of teaching were viewed with some scepticism. Gibbs and Habeshaw (2002) note that in 1994 only 2 per cent of promotion decisions were made primarily on grounds of teaching excellence and 38 per cent of HEIs reported not making any such promotions. Since then the picture has changed and the proportion of institutions including recognition and reward mechanisms in their learning and teaching strategy increased from 12 per cent in 1998 to 65 per cent in 2000.

The importance of academic management

Before moving to the final section of this chapter, it is important to very briefly refer to the importance of academic management. Ramsden discusses the importance of transformational leadership; he suggests that departments that had:

firm and fair management of staff, and recognition and development of staff as high priorities were more likely to contain teachers who reported student focused approaches to teaching. They were also less likely to report teacher-focused approaches. Moreover students in these units rated the teaching more highly.

(1998: 66)

Further research is necessary in this area.

Conclusion

In this chapter, I have tried to emphasize the impact on the effectiveness of the individual social policy or social work educator of the learning organization comprising four interacting arenas:

1 the national policy and professional requirements that drive learning and teaching in the subject, particularly through the evaluation of outcomes;
2 the institutional and departmental structures, policies and procedures of the HEI, that distribute work activities over time and space;
3 the impact of the social relations of the workplace;
4 the perspective on change by the individual educator (as outlined by Taylor (1999) in Chapter 1).

To end, Michael Fielding (2001) critiques Senge (1990) for omitting to discuss a key question:

Do we live to work or work to live? Do HEIs exist, adapt, and change for economic purposes first and individual development second? Or should the emphasis be on staff and students first, their needs and personal development, with the organisation playing a subordinate role?

Bibliography

Abrahamson, P. (1993) 'Welfare pluralism: towards a new consensus for a European social policy', *Cross National Research Papers,* 2 (6), pp. 5–22.

Adams, A., Erath, P. and Shardlow, S. (2000) *Fundamentals of Social Work in Selected Countries,* Russell House Publishing, Lyme Regis.

Ahmad B. (1990) *Black Perspectives in Social Work,* Venture, Birmingham.

Albanese, M. and Mitchell, S. (1993) 'Problem-based learning: a review of the literature on its outcomes and implementation issues', *Academic Medicine,* 68 (1), pp. 52–81.

Alcock, P., Erskine, A. and May, M. (eds) (2002a) *The Blackwell Dictionary of Social Policy,* Blackwell, Oxford.

Alcock, P., Erskine, A. and May, M. (eds) (2002b) *The Student's Companion to Social Policy,* Blackwell, Oxford.

Alcock, P., Erskine, A. and May, M. (eds) (2003) *The Student's Companion to Social Policy,* 2nd edn, Blackwell, Oxford.

Aluffi-Pentini, A. and Lorenz, W. (1996) *Anti-racist Work with Young People: European Experiences and Approaches,* Russell House Publishing, Lyme Regis.

Arnstein, S. (1969) 'A ladder of citizen participation', *Journal of the American Institute of Planners,* 35 (4), pp. 216–24.

Ashford, M. and Young, P. (2003) 'The role of ICT in social policy' in P. Alcock, A. Erskine and M. May (eds) *The Student's Companion to Social Policy,* 2nd edn, Blackwell, Oxford.

Ashworth, P., Bannister, P. and Thorne, P. (1997) 'Guilty in whose eyes? University students' perceptions of cheating and plagiarism in academic work and assessment', *Studies in Higher Education,* 22 (2), pp. 187–203.

Askeland, G. A. and Payne, M. (2001a) 'Broadening the mind: cross-national activities in social work', *European Journal of Social Work,* 4 (3), pp. 263–74.

Askeland, G. A. and Payne, M. (2001b) 'What is valid knowledge for social workers?', *Social Work in Europe,* 8, (3), pp. 13–23.

Association of University Teachers (2003) *Survey on Staff Stress,* www.aut.org.uk/index.cfm?articleid=257 [accessed 16 February 2004].

Badger, L. W. and MacNeil, G. (2002) 'Standardised clients in the classroom: a novel instructional technique for social work educators', *Research on Social Work Practice,* 12 (3), pp. 364–74.

Baldwin, M. (2000) 'Does self-assessment in a group help students to learn?', *Social Work Education,* 19 (5), pp. 451–62.

Balen, R. (2002) *MA/PG Dip/PG Cert Child Welfare and Protection,* Case study for SWAP website, www.swap.ac.uk/Links/casestudy.asp?casefind=csrbalen [accessed 3 February 2003].

Ballantyne, R., Dain, D. and Packer, J. (1999) 'Researching university teaching in Australia: themes and issues in academics' reflections', *Studies in Higher Education,* 24 (2), pp. 237–57.

Bangemann, M. Cabral da Fonseca, E., Davis, P. *et al.* (1994) Bangemann Report, *Europe and the Global Information Society,* www.cyber-rights.org/documents/bangemann.htm, p. 26 [accessed 6 April 2003].

Barnes, D. and Hugman, R. (2002) 'Portrait of social work', *Journal of Interprofessional Care,* 16 (3), pp. 277–88.

Barnes, J. (2002) *Focus on the Future: Key Messages from Focus Groups about the Future of Social Work Training,* Department of Health, www.doh.gov.uk/Home/fs/en [accessed 16 February 2004].

Barnett, R. (1997) *Higher Education: A Critical Business,* The Society for Research into Higher Education and Open University Press, Buckingham.

Barr, H. (1990) *In Europe 1: Social Work Education and 1992,* Central Council for Education and Training in Social Work, London.

Barr, H. (1995) *Evaluating Interprofessional Education,* Bulletin 10, Centre for the Advancement of Interprofessional Education, London.

Barr, H. (2002) *Interprofessional Education, Today, Yesterday And Tomorrow: A Review.* Health Sciences and Practice Subject Centre, www.health.ltsn.ac.uk/publications/occasional paper/occasionalpaper01.pdf [accessed 13 July 2004].

Barr, J. and Horder, J. (2003) 'Quality Improvement. Ensuring Quality in Interprofessional Education', *CAIPE Bulletin,* winter, Centre for the Advancement of Interprofessional Education.

Barrett, G., Greenwood, R. and Ross, K. (2003) 'Integrating interprofessional education into ten health and social care programmes', *Journal of Interprofessional Care,* 17 (3), pp. 293–301.

Bartholomew, A., Davis, J. and Weinstein, J. (1996) *Interprofessional Education and Training: Developing New Models,* Central Council for Education and Training in Social Work, London.

Bates, A. W. (2000) *Managing Technological Change – Strategies for Colleges and University Leaders,* Jossey-Bass Inc., San Francisco, California.

Baume, C., Martin, P. and Yorke, M. (eds) (2002) *Managing Educational Development Projects,* Kogan Page, London.

Becher, T. (1989) *Academic Tribes and Territories: Intellectual Enquiry and the Culture of Disciplines,* Society for Research in Higher Education/Open University Press, Buckingham.

Becher, T. and Trowler, P. R. (2001) *Academic Tribes and Territories,* 2nd edn, Society for Research in Higher Education and Open University Press, Buckingham.

Beckmann, A. and Cooper, C. (2002) *Globalisation and Education: Rethinking Pedagogy in Britain,* paper presented at the Social Policy Association Annual Conference, University of Teesside, Middlesbrough, 16–18 July.

Beetham, H. (2002) *Understanding e-learning: Skills for e-learning,* University of Bristol, www.ics.ltsn.ac.uk/pub/eLearning/UnderstandingE-learning.doc [accessed 3 April 2003].

Benner, P. (1984) *From Novice to Expert,* Addison-Wesley, London.

Bennett, J. B. (1998) *Collegial Professionalism: The Academy, Individualism and the Common Good*, Oryx Press, Phoenix, Arizona.

Beresford, P. (1994) *Changing the Culture, Involving Service Users in Social Work Education*, Paper 32.2, Central Council of Education and Training in Social Work, London.

Beresford, P. (2003) *It's Our Lives: A Short Theory of Knowledge, Distance and Experience*, Citizen Press in association with Shaping Our Lives, London.

Beresford, P. and Croft, S. (1986) *Whose Welfare: Private Care or Public Services?*, Lewis Cohen Urban Studies Centre, Brighton Polytechnic, Brighton.

Beresford, P. and Croft, S. (1987) 'Are we really listening? 'The Client Speaks', by J. Meyer and N. Timms (1970) in T. Philpot (ed.) *On Second Thoughts: Reassessments of the Literature of Social Work*, Community Care/Reed Publishing, London, pp. 50–5.

Biggs, J. (1996) 'Enhancing teaching through constructive alignment', *Higher Education*, 32 (3), pp. 347–64.

Biggs, J. (1999) *Teaching for Quality Learning at University*, Society for Research into Higher Education (SRHE) and Open University Press, Buckingham.

Biggs, J. (2003) *Teaching for Quality Learning at University*, 2nd edn, Society for Research into Higher Education (SRHE) and Open University Press, Buckingham.

Blomberg, S., Edebalk, P. G. and Petersson, J. (2002) 'The withdrawal of the welfare state: elderly care in Sweden in the 1990s', *European Journal of Social Work*, 3 (2), pp. 151–63.

Boezerooy, P. (2003) *Keeping up with our Neighbours: ICT Developments in Australian Higher Education*, LTSN Generic Centre, www.ltsn.ac.uk/genericcentre/index.asp?docid=17732 [accessed 1 April 2003].

Bogo, M. and Vayda, E. (1998) *The Practice of Field Instruction in Social Work: Theory and Process*, 2nd edn, University of Toronto Press, London.

Bornat, J. (1997) 'Representations of Community' in J. Bornat, J. Johnson, C. Pereira, D. Pilgrim and F. Williams (eds) *Community Care: A Reader*, Macmillan, Basingstoke, pp. 22–33.

Boud, D. and Feletti, G. (eds) (1991) *The Challenge of Problem-based Learning*, Kogan Page, London.

Boud, D. and Feletti, G. (eds) (1997) *The Challenge of Problem Based Learning*, 2nd edn, Kogan Page, London.

Boud, D. and Miller, N. (eds) (1996) *Working with Experience: Animating Learning*, Routledge, London.

Boud. D., Cohen, C. and Walker D. (eds) (1993) *Using Experience for Learning*, The Society for Research into Higher Education and The Open University Press, Buckingham.

Bradley, G. and Harris, R. (1993) 'Social work in Europe: an ERASMUS initiative', *Social Work Education*, 12, (3), pp. 51–66.

Brand, D. and Smith, G. (2001) *Social Care Registration Project: Consultation Paper on Proposals for a Draft Registration Scheme for the Social Care Workforce*, NISW (National Institure of Social Work), London.

Braye, S. and Preston Shoot, M. (1995) *Empowering Practice in Social Care*, Open University Press, Buckingham.

Braye, S., Lebacq, M., Mann, F. and Midwinter, E. (2003) 'Learning social work law: an enquiry-based approach to developing knowledge and skills', *Social Work Education*, 22 (5), pp. 479–92.

Bridges, D. (1994) 'Transferable skills: a philosophical perspective' in D. Bridges (ed.) *Transferable Skills in Higher Education*, University of East Anglia, Norwich.

Brina, C. (2002) *Employing Computer Conferencing at Undergraduate Level*, case study for SWAP, www.swap.ac.uk/links/casestudy.asp?casefind=Cscbrina [accessed 25 March 2003].

British Educational Communications and Technology Agency (Becta) (2003) *About Freedom of Information*, www.becta.org.uk/foi/foi/index.cfm#about_becta [accessed 2 April 2003].

Brockbank, A. and McGill, I. (1998) *Facilitating Reflective Learning in Higher Education*, Society for Research into Higher Education and Open University Press, Buckingham.

Brown, G. (2001) *Assessment: A Guide for Lecturers*, LTSN Generic Centre, York.

Brown, G., Bull, J. and Pendlebury, M. (1997) *Assessing Student Learning in Higher Education*, Routledge, London.

Brown, S. and Glasner, A. (eds) (1999) *Assessment Matters in Higher Education: Choosing and Using Diverse Approaches*, The Society for Research into Higher Education and Open University Press, Buckingham.

Bryne, H. and Ferguson, H. (2002) 'Informing the new social work degree at UWE: a service user consultation project: executive summary', *British Educational Research Journal*, 29 (1), pp. 105–24.

Bull, D. (2000) 'Foreword' in R. Link and A. Bibus, with K. Lyons (eds) *When Children Pay: US Welfare Reform and its Implications for UK Policy*, CPAG, London.

Bulmer, M., Lewis, J. and Piachaud, D. (eds) (1989) *The Goals of Social Policy*, Unwin Hyman, London.

Burgess, H. (1992) *Problem-led Learning for Social Work: The Enquiry and Action Approach*, Whiting & Birch, London.

Burgess, H. (2004) 'Re-designing the curriculum for social work education: complexity, conformity, chaos, creativity, collaboration?', *Social Work Education*, 23 (2), pp. 163–83.

Burgess H. and Jackson S. (1990) 'Enquiry and action learning', *Social Work Education*, 9 (3), pp. 3–19.

Burgess, H., Baldwin, M., Dalrymple, J. and Thomas, J. (1999) 'Developing self-assessment in social work education', *Social Work Education*, 18 (2), pp. 133–46.

Burgess, R. C. (1999) 'Reflective practice: action learning sets for managers in social work', *Social Work Education*, 18 (3), pp. 257–70.

Burrell, G. and Morgan, D. (1979) *Sociological Paradigms and Organisation Analysis*, Heinemann, London.

Butler A., Elliott T. and Stopard N. (2003) 'Living up to the standards we set: a critical account of the development of anti-racist standards', *Social Work Education*, 22 (3), pp. 271–82.

Butler, S. S. and Coleman, P. A. (1997) 'Raising our voices: a macro practice assignment', *Journal of Teaching in Social Work*, 15 (1–2), pp. 63–80.

Cahill, M. (1994) *The New Social Policy*, Blackwell, Oxford.

Callender, C. and Kemp, M. (2000) *Changing Student Finances: Income, Expenditure and the Take-up of Student Loans among Full- and Part-time Higher Education Students in 1998/9*, Department for Education and Employment, London, RR213.

Candy, P. C. (1997) 'Some issues impacting on university teaching and learning: implications for academic developers' in S. Armstrong, G. Thompson and S. Brown (eds) *Facing up to Radical Changes in Universities and Colleges*, Kogan Page, London.

Cannan, C., Berry, L. and Lyons K. (1992) *Social Work and Europe*, Macmillan, Basingstoke.

Castells, M. (2000) *The Rise of the Network Society*, 2nd edn, Blackwell, London.

Cayley, L. (2000) *Fostering the Effectiveness of Work-related Training*, unpublished PhD dissertation, University of Sussex, Brighton.

Central Council for Education and Training in Social Work (CCETSW) (1988) *Accreditation of Agencies and Practice Teachers in Social Work Education,* CCETSW, London.

Central Council for Education and Training in Social Work (CCETSW) (1989) *Rules and Requirements for the Diploma in Social Work (Paper 30),* CCETSW, London.

Central Council for Education and Training in Social Work (CCETSW) (1991a) *The Teaching of Child Care in the Diploma in Social Work,* CCETSW, London.

Central Council for Education and Training in Social Work (CCETSW) (1991b) *Rules and Requirements for the Diploma in Social Work (Paper 30)* 2nd edn, CCETSW, London.

Central Council for Education and Training in Social Work (CCETSW) (1995) *Assuring Quality in the Diploma in Social Work –1,* CCETSW, London.

Central Council for Education and Training in Social Work (CCETSW) (1996) *Assuring Quality in the Diploma in Social Work –1,* 2nd edn, CCETSW, London.

Central Council for Education and Training in Social Work (CCETSW) (1998) *Report on a Conference on User Involvement,* CCETSW, London.

Central Council for Education and Training in Social Work (CCETSW) (2001) *Annual Report for 1999–2000,* CCETSW, London.

Chand A., Clare J. and Dolton R. (2002) 'Teaching anti-oppressive practice on a diploma in social work course', *Social Work Education,* 21 (1), pp. 7–22.

Channer, Y. (2000) 'Understanding and managing conflict in the learning process: Christians coming out' in V. E. Cree and C. Macaulay (eds) *Transfer of Leaning in Professional and Vocational Education,* Routledge, London.

Chytil, O. and Popelkova, R. (2000) 'Social policy and social work in the Czech Republic' in A. Adams, P. Erath and S. Shardlow (eds) *Fundamentals of Social Work in Selected Countries,* Russell House Publishing, Lyme Regis.

Clapton, G. (2000) 'In praise of the process recording' in V. E. Cree and C. Macaulay *Transfer of Learning in Professional and Vocational Education,* Routledge, London.

Clark, A. *et al.* (2002) *Making Connections: Work-based Learning, Employability and the Professional, Academic and Personal Development of Students,* University of Birmingham, C-SAP, Birmingham.

Clarke, J. (1998) 'Consumerism' in G. Hughes (ed.) *Imagining Welfare Futures,* Routledge, London.

Clarke, T. (2000) *Debate on the Future of Social Policy,* www.social.policy@jiscmail.ac.uk [accessed 25 June 2002].

Clifford, D. (2003) *E-learning at Liverpool John Moores University: a case study in learning and teaching about assessment,* www.swap.ac.uk/links/casestudy.asp?casefind=csdclifford, [accessed 16 February 2004].

COBALT (1999) *Report of survey of practice in Community Based Learning,* Community-Based Learning Teamwork, University of Liverpool, Liverpool www.bham.ac.uk/cobalt.

Cochrane, A., Clarke, J. and Gewirtz, S. (eds) (2001) *Comparing Welfare States,* Sage, London.

Coleman, G. (1991) *Investigating Organisations: A Feminist Approach,* School for Advanced Urban Studies, Bristol.

Coleman M., Collings, M. and McDonald P. (1999) 'Teaching anti-oppressive practice on the Diploma in Social Work', *Social Work Education,* 18 (3), pp. 297–308.

Collins, H. M. (1989) 'Learning through enculturation' in A. Gellatly, D. Rogers and J. A. Sloboda (eds) *Cognition and Social Worlds,* Clarendon Press, Oxford.

Collis, A. (1978) Fieldwork Survey, JUC (Joint University Council) Social Administration Committee, London.

Cosis Brown, H. (1998) *Social Work and Sexuality: Working with Lesbians and Gay Men*, Macmillan, Basingstoke.

Coulshed, V. (1989) 'Developing the process curriculum', *Issues in Social Work Education*, 9 (1 and 2), pp. 21–30.

Council on Social Work Education (CSWE) (1994) 'Curriculum policy statement for Master's degree programs in social work education' in CSWE (ed.) *Handbook of Accreditation Standards and Procedures*, Alexandria, Virginia.

Council on Social Work Education (CSWE) (2002) *Educational Policy and Accreditation Standards,* CSWE, Alexandria, Virginia.

Council on Social Work Education (CSWE) (2003) *Educational Policy and Accreditation Standards*, www.cswe.org/

Crawshaw M. (2002) 'Disabled people's access to social work education', *Social Work Education*, 21 (5), pp. 503–14.

Cree, V. E. (2000) 'The challenge of assessment' in V. E. Cree and C. Macaulay (eds) *The Transfer of Learning in Professional and Vocational Education,* Routledge, London.

Cree, V. E. and Davidson, R. D. (2000) 'Enquiry and action learning: a model for transferring learning' in V. E. Cree and C. Macaulay (eds) *Transfer of Learning in Professional and Vocational Education*, Routledge, London.

Cree, V. E. and Macaulay, C. (eds) (2000) *Transfer of Learning in Professional and Vocational Education*, Routledge, London.

Cree, V. E., Macaulay, C. and Loney, H. (1998) *Transfer of Learning. A Study*, Central Council for Education and Training in Social Work and Scottish Office, Edinburgh.

Crisp, B. R. (1999) 'Not in the classroom: Teaching social work research to off campus students', *Advances in Social Work and Welfare Education*, 2 (2), pp. 34–41.

Crisp, B. R., Anderson, M. R., Orme, J. and Green Lister, P. (2003) *Knowledge Review 1: Learning and Teaching in Social Work Education. Assessment*, Social Care Institute for Excellence, London.

Critical Social Policy (2001) *In and Beyond New Labour* (Special Issue), *Critical Social Policy*, 21 (4), Issue 69, November.

Croft, S., Adshead, L. and Beresford, P. (2005) *What Service Users Want From Specialist Palliative Care Social Work*, York Publishing, York.

Cropper, A. (2000) 'Mentoring as an inclusive device for the excluded: black students' experience of a mentoring scheme', *Social Work Education*, 19 (6), pp. 597–607.

Cust, J. (1995) 'Recent cognitive perspectives on learning-implications for nurse education', *Nurse Education Today*, 15, pp. 280–90.

Cuthbert, R. (2002) 'The impact of national developments on institutional practice' in S. Armstrong, G. Thompson and S. Brown (ed.) *The Effective Academic*, Kogan Page, London.

Danbury, H. (1994) *Teaching Practical Social Work*, 3rd edn, Arena, Aldershot.

Darvill, G. (2004) 'Employability and Recruitment', *Social Policy Association News*, June, pp. 12–15.

Davies, H. and Kinloch, H. (2000) 'Critical incident analysis: facilitating reflection and transfer of learning' in V. E. Cree and C. Macaulay (eds) *Transfer of Learning in Professional and Vocational Education*, Routledge, London.

Davies, P. and Bynner, J. (2000) *The Impact of Credit-based Systems of Learning on Learning Cultures*, ESRC, City University and University of London, London.

Davis, J. and Robertson, J. (2002) *Working and Learning Together in Practice Teaching and Learning*, Interprofessional Practice Teaching Working Group, www.swap.ac.uk/docs/ac/jointpracticeteaching.rtf [accessed 31 October 2003].

Deacon, B. with Hulse, M. and Stubbs, P. (1997) *Global Social Policy*, Sage, London.

Dearing (1997) *Higher Education in the Learning Society*, Report of the National Committee of Inquiry into Higher Education, Department for Education and Employment.

Deliberations Forum (2003) *'Long, Thin' Versus 'Short Thick' Modules*, www.jiscmail.ac. uk/lists/deliberations-forum.html.

Department for Education and Employment (DfEE) (1998) *The Learning Age: A Renaissance for a New Britain*, HMSO, London.

Department for Education and Skills (DfES) (2002) *Education and Skills: Delivering Results. A Strategy to 2006*, DfES Publication Unit, Sudbury.

Department for Education and Skills (DfES) (2003) *The Future of Higher Education*, DfES, London.

Department of Health (DoH) (1997) *The New NHS: Modern . Dependable*, HMSO, London.

Department of Health (DoH) (1998) *Modernising Social Services: Promoting Independence, Improving Protection*, Department of Health, London.

Department of Health (DoH) (1999) *National Service Framework for Mental Health: Modern Standards and Service Models*, DoH, London.

Department of Health (DoH) (2000a) *The NHS Plan: A Plan for Investment. A Plan for Reform*, HMSO, London.

Department of Health (DoH) (2000b) *A Health Service of All the Talents: Developing the NHS Workforce*, HMSO, London.

Department of Health (DoH) (2000c) *A Quality Strategy for Social Care: Consultation*, HMSO, London.

Department of Health (DoH) (2001a) *National Service Framework for Older People*, HMSO, London.

Department of Health (DoH) (2001b) *Working Together–Learning Together – A Framework for Lifelong Learning for the NHS*, HMSO, London.

Department of Health (DoH)★ (2002a) *Reform of Social Work Education*, DoH, London, www.doh.gov.uk/Home/fs/en [accessed 14 March 2002].

Department of Health (DoH)★ (2002b) *The Requirements for Social Work Training*, DoH, London, www.doh.gov.uk/Home/fs/en [accessed 23 March 2003].

Department of Health (DoH)★ (2003a) *Common Learning*, www.doh.gov.uk/Home/fs/en.

Department of Health (DoH)★ (2003b) *Children's Trusts*, www.doh.gov.uk/Home/fs/en.

Department of Health/Social Services Inspectorate (DoH/SSI) (1998) *The Quality Protects Programme: Transforming Children's Services, LAC. (98) 2*, HMSO, London.

Desai, M. (2000) 'Curriculum planning for history of philosophies of social work', *The Indian Journal of Social Work*, 61 (2), pp. 221–39.

DeSouza, P., Taylor, P. and Thomas, J. (2002) *Interprofessional Student Placements – Opportunities and Implications for Teaching and Practice*, Report for Faculty of Health and Social Care, University of the West of England, Bristol.

Dewulf, S. and Baillie, C. (1999) *CASE Creativity in Art, Science and Engineering: How to Foster Creativity*, Department for Education and Employment (also reproduced in 2002 as part of the Imaginative Curriculum Project, LTSN working paper, www.ltsn.ac.uk).

Dick, E., Headrick, D. and Scott, M. (2002) *Practice Learning for Professional Skills: A Review of Literature*, Scottish Executive, Edinburgh.

★ Since completion of the manuscript, the Department of Health has changed the structure of its website and it is no longer possible to 'deep link'. The editors recommend that readers use the search facility on the DoH home page to find the document referenced.

Dickson, A. (1995) Letter to the Vice-Chancellor of Manchester University, 18 May 1978, in D. Scott and N. Shenton, *Enterprise in Higher Education: Some critical perspectives from social policy*, Department of Social Policy and Social Work, University of Manchester, p. 29.

Diggins, M. (2004) *Teaching and Learning Communication Skills in Social Work Education: A Resource Guide*, Social Care Institute for Excellence, London.

Dillenburger, K., Godina, L. and Burton, M. (1997) 'Training in behavioral social work: a pilot study', *Research on Social Work Practice*, 7 (1), pp. 70–8.

Doel, M. and Shardlow, S. M. (2005) *Modern Social Work Practice*, 3rd edn, Ashgate, Aldershot.

Dominelli, L. (1997) *Anti-racist Social Work*, Macmillan, London.

Dominelli, L. (2002) *Anti-Oppressive Social Work Practice*, Palgrave, Basingstoke.

Dovey, K. (1997) 'The learning organisation and the organisation of learning', *Management Learning*, 28 (3) pp. 331–49.

Driver, S. (undated) *Multiple Choice Assessment on a Government and Institutions Module*, www.swap.ac.uk/links/casestudy.asp?casefind=cssdriver [accessed 16 February 2004].

Ducatel, K., Webster, J. and Hermann, W. (2000) 'Information, infrastructures or societies' in K. Ducatel, J. Webster and W. Hermann (eds) *The Information Society in Europe: Work and Life in an Age of Globalization*, Rowan & Littlefield, Oxford.

Economic and Social Research Council (ESRC) (2003) *CASE Studentships* 2003, ESRC, www.esrc.ac.uk/ESRCContent/postgradfunding/case_studentships.asp [accessed 17 August 2003].

Edwards, H., Smith, B. and Webb, G. (eds) (2001) *Lecturing: Case Studies, Experience and Practice*, Kogan Page, London.

Edwards, K. and Kinsey, E. (1999) 'The place of NVQ4 in the training continuum', *Social Work Education*, 18 (3), pp. 271–85.

Edwards, R. (2002) 'Distribution and interconnectedness, the globalisation of education' in M. Lea and K. Nicoll (eds) *Distributed Learning, Social and Cultural Approaches to Practice*, Routledge/Falmer/Open University Press, London.

Edwards, R. and Usher, R. (2000) *Globalisation and Pedagogy*, Routledge/Falmer, London.

Ehrenberg, L. M. (1983) 'How to ensure better transfer of learning?', *Training and Development Journal*, 37, pp. 81–3.

Electronic Government Services for the 21st Century (2000) www.number-10.gov.uk/su/delivery/indexFrame.htm [accessed 20 March 2004].

Elton, L. (1998) 'Dimensions of excellence in university teaching', *The International Journal for Academic Development*, 3 (1), pp. 3–11.

Entwistle, N. (1988) *Styles of Learning and Teaching: An Integrated Outline of Educational Psychology for Students, Teachers and Lecturers*, David Fulton, London.

Entwistle, N. and Ramsden, P. (1983) *Understanding Student Learning*, Crook Helm, Beckenham, Kent.

Entwistle, N. and Walker, P. (2002) 'Strategic alertness and expanded awareness within sophisticated conceptions of teaching' in N. Nativa and P. Goodyear (eds) *Teacher Thinking, Beliefs and Knowledge in Higher Education*, Kluwer, Dortrecht, Netherlands.

Eraut, M. (1994) *Developing Professional Knowledge and Competence*, Falmer, London.

Eraut, M. (2000) 'Non-formal learning, implicit learning and tacit knowledge in professional work' in F. Coffield (ed.) *The Necessity of Informal Learning*, Policy Press, Bristol.

Eraut, M. (2001) 'Learning challenges for knowledge-based organisations' in J. Stevens (ed.) *Workplace Learning in Europe*, Chartered Institute of Personnel and Development, London.

Eraut, M., Alderton, J., Cole, G. and Senker, P. (1998) 'Learning from other people at work' in F. Coffield (ed.) *Skill Formation*, Policy Press, Bristol.

Eraut, M. (2002) *Conceptual Analysis and Research Questions: Do the Concepts of 'Learning Community' and 'Community of Practice' Provide Added Value?'*, paper presented at the Annual Conference of the American Educational Research Association, New Orleans, April.

Eraut, M., Steadman, S., Furner, J., *et al.* (2001–4) 'Learning during the first three years of postgraduate employment', ESRC (TLRP), Universities of Brighton and Sussex.

Erskine, A. (1998) 'The approaches and methods of social policy' in P. Alcock, A. Erskine and M. May (eds) *The Student's Companion to Social Policy*, Blackwell, Oxford.

Erskine, A. (2003) 'The approaches and methods of social policy' in P. Alcock, A. Erskine and M. May (eds) *The Student's Companion to Social Policy*, 2nd edn, Blackwell, Oxford.

Esping Anderson, G. (1990) *The Three Worlds of Welfare Capitalism,* Polity Press, Oxford.

Everitt, A. and Gibson, A. (1994) *Researching in the Voluntary Sector; Making It Work*, ARVAC, Wivenhoe.

Fawcett, M. (1996) *Learning through Child Observation*, Jessica Kingsley, London.

Feu, M. (2000) 'The development of social work in Spain' in A. Adams, P. Erath and S. Shardlow (eds) *Fundamentals of Social Work in Selected Countries*, Russell House Publishing, Lyme Regis.

Fielding, M. (2001) 'Learning organisation or learning community? A critique of Senge', *Reason in Practice*, I (2), pp. 17–29.

Franklyn-Stokes, A. and Newstead, S. E. (1995) 'Undergraduate cheating: who does what and why?', *Studies in Higher Education*, 20 (2), pp. 159–72.

Freeth, D., Hammick, M., Koppel, I., Reeves, S. and Barr, H. (2002) *A Critical Review of Evaluations of Interprofessional Education*, JET, www.health.ltsn.ac.uk/.

Freire P. (1972) *The Pedagogy of the Oppressed,* Penguin, Harmondsworth.

Freire, P. (1983) 'Education and conscientizacao' in M. Tight (ed.) *Education for Adults: Adult Learning and Education*, Open University/Croom Helm, Beckenham, Kent.

Fulford, K. W. M. (2004) 'Ten principles of values-based medicine' in J. Radden (ed.) *The Philosophy of Psychiatry: A Companion*, Oxford University Press, New York.

Fullan, M. (1993) *Change Forces – Probing the Depths of Educational Reform*, Falmer Press, London.

Garber, R. (2000) 'World census of social work and social development: interim report' in B. Rowe (ed.) *Social Work and Globalization*, Special Issue, *Canadian Social Work*, 2 (1).

Gardiner, D. (1989) *The Anatomy of Supervision*, The Society for Research into Higher Education and Open University Press, Buckingham.

General Social Care Council (GSCC) (2002a) *Codes of Practice for Social Care Workers and Employers*, GSCC, London, www.gscc.org.uk/codes_copies.htm.

General Social Care Council (GSCC) (2002b) *Guidance on the Assessment of Practice in the Work Place*, GSCC, London.

General Social Care Council (GSCC) (2002c) *Social Work Education and Training Annual Quality Assurance Report 2001–2*, GSCC, London.

General Social Care Council (GSCC) (2003a) *Social Work Education and Training Data Pack 2002–3*, www.gscc.org.uk/news_story.asp?newsID=87 [accessed 16 February 2004].

General Social Care Council (GSCC) (2003b) *The Review of Post-Qualifying Education and Training,* GSCC, London.

General Social Care Council (GSCC) (2003c) *GSCC (Registration of Social Workers) Rules 2003*, GSCC, London.

Gentle, P. (2001) 'Course cultures and learning organisations', *Active Learning in Higher Education,* 2 (1), pp. 8–29.

George, V. and Wilding, P. (2002) *Globalization and Human Welfare*, Palgrave, Basingstoke.

Gibbs, G. (1982) *Twenty Terrible Reasons for Lecturing,* Occasional Paper no. 8, Oxford Polytechnic, Oxford.

Gibbs, G. (2001) *Analysis of Strategies for Learning and Teaching,* Research Report, HEFCE, London.

Gibbs, G. and Coffey, M. (2001) 'Students give top marks to the trained', *Times Higher Education Supplement,* 20, 9 November.

Gibbs, G. and Habeshaw, T. (2002) *Recognising and Rewarding Excellent Teaching,* Centre for Higer Education Practice, Open University, Milton Keynes.

Gibbs G. and Robinson D. (1998) 'Computer-aided learning as a tool: lessons from educational theory' in M. Henry (ed.) *Using IT Effectively: a Guide to Technology in the Social Sciences,* UCL Press, London.

Gibelman, M., Gelman, S. R. and Fast, J. (1999) 'The downside of cyberspace: cheating made easy', *Journal of Social Work Education,* 35 (3), pp. 367–78.

Glastonbury, B. and LaMendola, W. (1992) *The Integrity of Intelligence: A Bill of Rights for the Information Age,* St Martin's Press, New York.

Gooding, C. (1996) *Disability Discrimination Act 1995,* Blackstone, London.

Goodyear, P. (2002) 'Psychological foundations for networked learning' in C. Steeples and C. Jones (eds) *Networked Learning: Perspectives and Issues,* Springer Verlag, London.

Gore, A. (1991) 'Computers, networks and public policy: infrastructure for the global village', *Scientific American,* 265, September, pp. 108–11.

Gore, A. (1994) 'Basic principles for building an information society', *Global Issues: Communications the Information Society Journal,* http://usinfo.state.gov/journals/itgic/ 0996/ijge/ijge0996.htm [accessed 6 April 2003].

Gough, D. A., Kiwan, D., Sutcliffe, S., Simpson, D. and Houghton, N. (2003)*A Systematic Map and Synthesis Review of the Effectiveness of Personal Development Planning for Improving Student Learning: Provisional Summary,* LTSN Generic Centre in collaboration with The Evidence for Policy and Practice Information Co-ordinating Centre, Social Sciences Research Unit, Institute of Education, University of London, www.ltsn.ac.uk/ application.asp?app=resources.asp&process=full_record&section=generic&id=231 [accessed 16 February 2004].

Gould, N. (2000) 'Becoming a learning organisation: a social work example', *Social Work Education,* 19 (6), pp. 595–96.

Gould, N. (2003) 'Caring professions and information technology' in E. Harlow and S. Webb (eds) *Information and Communication Technologies in the Welfare Services,* Jessica Kingsley, London.

Gould, N. and Taylor, I. (eds) (1996) *Reflective Learning for Social Work: Research, Theory and Practice,* Arena, Aldershot.

Green Lister, P. (2000) 'Mature students and transfer of learning' in V. E. Cree and C. Macaulay (eds) *Transfer of Learning in Professional and Vocational Education,* Routledge, London.

Gutierrez, L. and Alvarez, A. L. (2000) 'Educating students for multicultural community practice', *Journal for Community Practice,* 7 (1), pp. 39–56.

Hall, D. and Hall, I. (1996) *Practical Social Research: Project Work in the Community,* Macmillan, Basingstoke.

Hall, I. and Hall, D. (2002) 'Incorporating change through reflection: community-based learning' in R. McDonald and J. Wisdom (eds) *Academic and Educational Development: Research, Evaluation and Changing Practice in Higher Education*, London, Kogan Page.

Hamalainen, J. (forthcoming) 'Social care service and social work in transition' in B. Littlechild and K. Lyons (eds) *Locating the Occupational Space for Social Work*, Venture Press/BASW Monograph Series, Birmingham.

Hamalainen, J. and Niemela P. (2000) 'Social policy and social work in Finland' in A. Adams, P. Erath and S. Shardlow (eds) *Fundamentals of Social Work in Selected Countries*, Russell House Publishing, Lyme Regis.

Handy, C. (1989) *The Age of Unreason*, Arrow Business Books, London.

Hantrais, L. (1995) *Social Policy in the European Union*, Macmillan, Basingstoke.

Hargeaves, A. (1994) *Changing Teachers, Changing Times*, Cassell, London.

Harlow E. and Webb S., (eds) (2003) *Information and Communication Technologies in the Welfare Services*, Jessica Kingsley, London.

Harris, J. (1989) 'The Webbs, the COS and Ratan Tata' in M. Bulmer, J. Lewis and D. Piachaud (eds) *The Goals of Social Policy*, Unwin Hyman, London.

Harris, R. J. (1985) 'The transfer of learning in social work education' in R. J. Harris (ed.) *Educating Social Workers*, Association of Teachers in Social Work Education, Leicester.

Hartley, J. (1998) *Learning and Studying. A Research Perspective*, Routledge, London.

Harvey L. and Knight P. (1996) *Transforming Higher Education*, SRHE and Open University Press, Buckingham.

Haughton, E. (2002) 'Gender split', *Education Guardian*, 5 March, www.education. guardian.co.uk/itforschools [accessed 1 October 2003].

Hawkins, P. (1994) 'The changing view of learning' in J. Burgoyne, M. Pedler and T. Boydell (eds) *Towards the Learning Company – Concepts and Practices*, McGraw-Hill, Maidenhead, pp. 9–27.

Healey, M. (2000) 'Developing the scholarship of teaching in higher education: a discipline based approach', *Higher Education Research and Development* 19 (2), pp. 169–89.

Healy, L. M. (2001) *International Social Work: Professional Action in an Interdependent World*, Oxford University Press, New York.

Healy, L. M. (2002) *International Social Work: Professional Action in an Interdependent World*, Oxford University Press, New York.

Healy, L. M., Asamoah, Y. and Hokenstad, M. C. (eds) (2003) *Models of International Collaboration in Social Work Education*, CSWE, Alexandria, Virginia.

HEFCE (2002) 'Successful student diversity', www.hefce.ac.uk/pubs/hefce/2002/02_48. htm.

Held, D. and McGrew, A. (2002) *Globalization/Anti-globalization*, Polity Press, Cambridge.

Held, D., McGrew, A., Goldblatt, D. and Perraton, J. (1999) *Global Transformations, Politics, Economics and Culture*, Polity Press, Cambridge.

Helme, M. (2004) *Thinking about the Wood as well as the Trees, the Dance as well as the Dancers*, presentation on the Three-centre Research on Interprofessional Practice in Learning and Education (TRIPLE) project to the Mental Health in Higher Education Conference on Interprofessional Education for Mental Health, www.mhhe.ltsn.ac.uk/news/ workshop.asp?ref=666.

Henderson, J., Lloyd, P. and Scott, H. (2002) '"In the real world we're all put on the spot at some time or other, so you need to be prepared for it": An exploratory study of an oral method of assessing knowledge of mental health law', *Social Work Education*, 21 (1), pp. 91–103.

Henkel, M. (2000) *Academic Identities and Policy Change in Higher Education*, Jessica Kingsley, London.

Her Majesty's Stationery Office (HMSO) (2003) *Freedom of Information Act 2000*, www.hmso.gov.uk/acts/acts2000/20000036.htm [accessed 2 April 2003].

Heron, E. (2002) *Assessment of 'Theories of welfare' using a VLE Case Study for SWAP*, www.swap.ac.uk/links/casestudy.asp?casefind=csEHeron [accessed 12 February 2003].

Heron, E. and McManus, M. (2003) 'Political literacy and the teaching of social policy: a study into the political awareness and political vocabularies of first year under-graduates', *Social Policy and Society*, 2 (1), pp. 23–32.

Higgison, C. A. and Harris, R. A. (2002) *Online tutoring – the OTiS Experience: A JISC Guide for Tutors*, JISC, Higher Education Funding Council, Bristol.

Higham, P. E. with Sharp, M. and Booth, C. (2001) 'Changes in the quality and regula-tion of social work education: confronting the dilemmas of workforce planning and competing qualifications frameworks', *Social Work Education*, 20 (2), pp. 187–98.

Higher Education Funding Council for England (HEFCE) (2002) *Successful Student Diversity*, www.hefce.ac.uk/publications.

Hill, M. (1996) *Social Policy: a Comparative Analysis*, Harvester Wheatsheaf, Hemel Hempstead.

Hirst, P. and Thompson, G. (1999) *Globalization in Question*, 2nd edn, Polity Press, Cambridge.

Hobson, E. H. (1996) 'Encouraging self-assessment: writing as active learning' in T. E. Sutherland and C. C. Bonwell (eds) *Using Active Learning in College Classes: A Range of Options for Faculty*, Jossey-Bass, San Francisco, California.

Hoggett, P. (2001) 'Agency, rationality and social policy', *Journal of Social Policy*, 30 (1), pp. 37–56.

Hollister, C. D. and McGee, G. (2000) 'Delivering substance abuse and child welfare con-tent through interactive television', *Research on Social Work Practice*, 10 (4), pp. 417–27.

Holman, B. (1993) *A New Deal for Social Welfare*, Lion Publishing, Oxford.

Home Office (2003) *The Victoria Climbié Inquiry: Report of an Inquiry by Lord Laming* (also known as the Laming Report), HMSO, London.

Honey, P. and Mumford, A. (1992) *The Manual of Learning Styles*, Peter Honey, Maidenhead.

Horwath, J. and Shardlow, S. M. (2000) 'Empowering learners through open (distance) programmes: an evaluation of a practice teaching programme', *Social Work Education*, 19 (2), pp. 111–23.

Huber, M. T. (1999) *Disciplinary Styles in the Scholarship of Teaching: Reflections on the Carnegie Academy for the Scholarship of Teaching and Learning*, paper read at 7th International Symposium, Improving Student Learning Through the Disciplines, University of York.

International Association of Schools of Social Work (IASSW) (2002) *Discussion Document on Global Qualifying Standards*, IASSW and IFSW, www.iassw.soton.ac.uk/en/Global QualifyingStandards/Globalstandardsaugust2002.pdf.

International Association of Schools of Social Work (IASSW) (2004) www.iassw-aiets.

International Federation of Social Workers (IFSW) (2002) 'Countering the negative effects of globalisation', *IFSW News* 2/3, Berne, Switzerland.

International Federation of Social workers (IFSW) (2004) www.iassw.soton.ac.uk/Generic/GlobalQualifyingStandards.asp?lang=en.

Irving, Z. and Young, P. (forthcoming) 'When less is more: the dominance of subject con-tent in the teaching of undergraduates social policy', *Social Policy and Society*, 4 (1), p. 18.

Ixer, G. (1999) 'There's no such thing as reflection', *British Journal of Social Work*, 29, pp. 513–27.

Jackson, B. (1997) 'Managing to help teachers change: an agenda for academic managers' in S. Armstrong, G. Thompson and S. Brown (eds) *Facing up to Radical Changes in Universities and Colleges*, Kogan Page, London.

Jackson, N. (2001) *Implications of Benchmarking for Curriculum Design and the Assessment of Student Learning*, LTSN working paper, www.ltsn.ac.uk.

Jackson, N. (2002a) *Designing for Creativity: a Curriculum Guide*, LTSN working paper, www.ltsn.ac.uk/application.asp?app=resources.asp&process=full_record&section=generic&id=58.

Jackson, N. (2002b) *Using Complexity Theory to Make Sense of the Curriculum*, www.ltsn.ac.uk/application.asp?app=resources.asp&process=full_record&section=generic&id=55.

Jackson, N., Wisdom, J. and Shaw, M. (2003) *Using Learning Outcomes to Design a Course and Assess Learning,* Imaginative Curriculum project team, LTSN working paper, www.ltsn.ac.uk/application.asp?app=resources.asp&process=full_rtecord&section=generic&id=58.

Jenkins, A. (2002) *Designing a Curriculum is Like Creatively 'Controlling' a Ouija Board,* LTSN working paper, www.ltsn.ac.uk.

Jordan, B. and Jordan, C. (2000) *Social Work and the Third Way*, Sage, London.

Kearney, P. (2003) *The Roles and Functions of Practice Teachers*, draft paper, SCIE/NOPT, London.

Kelsey, J. (1997) *The New Zealand Experiment: a World Model for Structural Adjustment?*, 2nd edn, Auckland University Press, Auckland.

Kennedy, D. and Duffy, T. (2000) 'Understanding the effort' in C. Higgison (ed.) *Practitioners' Experiences in Online Tutoring: Case Studies from the OTiS e-Workshop*, Heriot-Watt University, Edinburgh, and The Robert Gordon University, Aberdeen, http://otis.scotcit.ac.uk/casestudy/ [accessed 3 April 2003].

Kennedy, I. (2001) *Learning from Bristol: the Report of the Public Inquiry into Children's Heart Surgery at the Bristol Royal Infirmary 1984–1995*, Department of Health, London.

King, A. (1993) 'From sage on the stage to guide on the side', *College Teaching*, 41 (1), pp. 30–5, www.classroomtools.com/king.htm [accessed 9 January 2003].

Kirk, K. (2002a) *Experiential Learning Online?* Case study for SWAP, www.swap.ac.uk/links/casestudy.asp?casefind=cskatekirk [accessed 25 March 2003].

Kirk, K. (2002b) 'A Holistic Approach to Support for Learning', *Learning and Teaching in Action*, 1 (3), autumn, Learning and Teaching Unit, Manchester Metropolitan University, www.ltu.mmu.ac.uk/ltia/issue3 [accessed August 2003].

Klug, W. (2001) 'Social work and the Third Sector: the example of the German welfare state' in A. Adams, P. Erath and S. Shardlow (eds) *Fundamentals of Social Work in Selected Countries*, Russell House Publishing, Lyme Regis.

Kneale, P. E. (1997) 'The rise of the "strategic student": How can we adapt to cope?' in S. Armstrong, G. Thompson and S. Brown (eds) *Facing up to Radical Changes in Universities and Colleges*, Kogan Page, London.

Knight, P. (2002) *The Idea of a Creative Curriculum*, Imaginative Curriculum Network paper, www.ltsn.ac.uk/genericcentre.

Knight, P. T. (2000) 'The value of a programme-wide approach to assessment', *Assessment and Evaluation in Higher Education*, 25 (3), pp. 237–51.

Knight, P. T. and Trowler, P. (2000) 'Departmental-level cultures and the improvement of learning and teaching', *Studies in Higher Education*, 25 (1).

Knowles, M. S. (1983) 'Andragogy: an emerging technology for adult learning' in M. Tight (ed.) *Education for Adults: Adult Learning and Education*, Open University/Croom Helm, Beckenham, Kent.

Kolb, D. A. (1976) *Learning Style Inventory: Technical Manual*, Institute for Development Research, Newton, Massachusetts.

Kolb, D. A. (1984) *Experiential Learning: Experience as the Source of Learning and Development*, Prentice Hall, New Jersey.

Koprowska, J., Hicks, L., McCluskey, U., Fisher, T. and Wishart, J. (1999) *Facts, Feelings and Feedback: a Collaborative Model for Direct Observation*, video and accompanying booklet, University of York, York.

Kornbeck, J. (1997) 'Community care in the United Kingdom, subsidiarity in Germany: only a matter of words?', *Social Work in Europe*, 4 (2), pp. 1–11.

Kornbeck, J. (2002) 'Reflections on the exportability of social pedagogy', *Social Work in Europe*, 9 (2), pp. 37–49.

Le Riche, P. and Tanner, I. (1998) *Observation and its Application to Social Work*, London, Jessica Kingsley.

Lea, M. and Nicoll, K. (eds) (2002) *Distributed Learning, Social and Cultural Approaches to Practice*, Routledge/Falmer/Open University Press, London.

Learning and Teaching Support Network (LTSN) Generic Centre (2002) *Guide to Curriculum Design: Personal Development Planning*, www.ltsn.ac.uk/application.asp?app=resources.asp&process=full_record&section=generic&id=56 [accessed 16 February 2004].

Leung, J. and Wang, Y. C. (2002) 'Community-based service for the frail elderly in China', *International Social Work*, 45 (2), pp. 205–16.

Levin, E. (2004) *Involving Service Users and Carers in Social Work Education*, Social Care Institute for Excellence, London.

Lewis, I. M. P. (2002) 'Speech transcript', Minister with responsibility for Adult Learning and Skills, from 'e-Citizen', *The e-Summit*, www.e-envoy.gov.uk/ [accessed 3 April 2003].

Light, G. and Cox, R. (2001) *Learning and Teaching in Higher Education: The Reflective Professional*, Paul Chapman, London.

Link, R. and Bibus, A. with Lyons, K. (2001) *When Children Pay: US Welfare Reform and its Implications for UK Policy*, CPAG, London.

Lister, P. (2003) 'It's like you can't be a whole person, a mother who studies', *Social Work Education*, 22 (2), pp. 125–38.

Logan, J. (2001) 'Sexuality, child care and social work education', *Social Work Education*, 20 (5), pp. 563–75.

Longworth, N. and Davies, W. (1996) *Lifelong Learning: New Visions, New Implications, New Roles for People, Organisations, Nations and Communities in the 21st Century*, Kogan Page, London.

Lorenz, W. (1994) *Social Work in a Changing Europe*, Routledge, London.

Lyons, K. (1999a) *Social Work in Higher Education: Demise or Development?*, Centre for Evaluative and Developmental Research, Ashgate, Aldershot.

Lyons, K. (1999b) *International Social Work: Themes and Perspectives*, Ashgate, Aldershot.

Lyons, K. (2000) 'UK policy designed to combat child poverty' in R. Link and A. Bibus, with K. Lyons (eds) *When Children Pay: US Welfare Reform and its Implications for UK Policy*, CPAG, London.

Lyons, K. (2002) 'European and international perspectives in British social work education: past developments and future prospects', *Social Work in Europe*, 9 (2), pp. 1–9.

Lyons, K. and Ramanathan, C. (1999) 'Models of field practice in global settings' in C. Ramanathan and R. Link (eds) *All Our Futures: Principles and Resources for Social Work Practice in a Global Era,* Wadsworth, Belmont, California.

Macaulay, C. and Cree, V. E. (1999) 'Transfer of learning: concept and process', *Social Work Education,* 18, (2), pp. 183–94.

McCann, G. (2002) 'Globalisation can be good', *The Independent,* 2 May, www.wun. ac.uk/news/article.php?id=19 [accessed 12 August 2004].

McCarthy, D. and Hurst, A. (2001) *A Brief Guide on Assessing Disabled Students,* LTSN Generic Centre, York.

McDonald, P. and Coleman, M. (1999) 'Deconstructing hierarchies of oppression', *Social Work Education,* 18 (1), pp. 19–32.

Macdonald, R. and Wisdom, J. (eds) (2002) *Academic and Educational Development: Research, Evaluation and Changing Practice in Higher Education,* London, Kogan Page.

Macey, M. and Moxon, E. (1996) 'An examination of anti-racist and anti-oppressive theory and practice in social work education', *British Journal of Social Work,* 26 (3), pp. 297–314.

McNay, I. (1997) *The Impact of the 1992 RAE on Institutional and Individual Behaviour in English Higher Education: the Evidence from a Research Project,* HEFCE M 5/97, Bristol.

Maidment, J. and Cooper, L. (2002) 'Acknowledgement of client diversity and oppression in social work student supervision', *Social Work Education,* 21 (4), pp. 399–407.

Manthorpe, J. and Stanley, N. (1999) 'Dilemmas in professional educations: responding effectively to students with mental health problems', *Journal of Interprofessional Care,* 13 (4), pp. 355–65.

Marotta, S. A., Peters, B. J. and Paliokas, K. L. (2000) 'Teaching group dynamics: an inter-disciplinary approach', *Journal for Specialists in Group Work,* 25 (1), pp. 16–28.

Marsh, P. and Triseliotis, J. (1996) *Ready to Practice? Social Workers and Probation Officers: Their Training and First Year at Work,* Avebury, Aldershot.

Martin, E. (1999) *Changing Academic Work: Developing the Learning University,* Society for Research in Higher Education and Open University, Buckingham.

Masuda, Y. (1982) *Information Society: As Post-Industrial Society,* World Future Society. Information pack (2001) available from www.jisc.ac.uk/mle/reps/infopack.html, Office of the e-Envoy, www.e-envoy.gov.uk/EStrategy/MonthlyReports/fs/en [accessed 22 December 2003].

Mathias, H. and Rutherford, D. (1983) 'Decisive factors affecting innovation: a case study', *Studies in Higher Education,* 8 (1).

Mayadas, N. S., Watts, T. D. and Elliott, D. (eds) (1997) *International Handbook on Social Work Theory and Practice,* Greenwood, Westport, Connecticut.

Mayor, M. and Swaan, J. (2002) 'The English language and "global" teaching' in M. Lea and K. Nicoll (eds) *Distributed Learning, Social and Cultural Approaches to Practice,* Routledge/Falmer/Open University Press, London.

Mercer, G. (2002) 'Emancipatory disability research' in C. Barnes, M. Oliver and L. Barton (eds) *Disability Studies Today,* pp. 228–49, Polity Press, Cambridge.

Meyer, J. E. and Timms, N. (1970) *The Client Speaks: Working Class Impressions of Casework,* Routledge & Kegan Paul, London.

Mezirow, J. (1983) 'A critical theory of adult learning and education' in M. Tight (ed.) *Education for Adults: Adult Learning and Education,* Open University/Croom Helm, Beckenham, Kent.

Midgley, J. (1983) *Professional Imperialism: Social Work and the Third World,* Heinemann, London.

Midgley, J. (1997) *Social Welfare in Global Context*, Sage, Beverly Hills, California.

Miers, M., Pollard, K., Clarke, B., Means, R., Ross, K. and Thomas, J. (2003) *Interprofessional Learning in the Academic Environment and in Practice Settings*, conference paper, University of the West of England, Bristol, 15 July.

Mishra, R. (1989) 'The academic tradition in social policy: the Titmuss years' in M. Bulmer, J. Lewis and D. Piachaud (eds) *The Goals of Social Policy*, Unwin Hyman, London.

Mishra, R. (1999) *Globalization and the Welfare State*, Edward Elgar, Cheltenham.

Montalvo, F. F. (1999) 'The critical incident interview and ethnoracial identity', *Journal of Multicultural Social Work*, 7 (3/4), pp. 19–43.

Moss, B. (2000) 'The use of large group role play techniques in social work education', *Social Work Education*, 19 (5), pp. 471–83.

Moss, B. (2003) 'Planning problem based learning opportunities for students in social work and nursing at Staffordshire: a case study in learning and teaching about assessment in social work education', www.swap.ac.uk/links/casestudy.asp?casefind=csbmoss [accessed 16 February 2004].

Moxley, D. P. and Thrasher, S. P. (1996) 'The intervention design seminar: structure, content and process', *Journal of Teaching in Social Work*, 13 (1/2), pp. 73–92.

Mutch, A. and Brown, G. (2001) *Assessment: A Guide for Heads of Department*, LTSN Generic Centre, York.

Nagy, G. and Falk, D. (2000) 'Dilemmas in international and cross-cultural social work education', *International Social Work*, 43 (1), pp. 49–60.

Napier, L. and Fook, J. (2000) *Breakthroughs in Practice: Theorising Critical Moments in Social Work*, Whiting & Birch, London.

National Council of Work Experience (NCWE) (2003) *A code of good practice: A definition of quality work experience*, National Council of Work Experience, www.work-experience. org [accessed 25 February 2004].

National Organisation for Practice Teaching (NOPT) (2003) *Code of Practice*, www.nopt. org/ac2002.htm [accessed 25 February 2004].

Neumann, R. (2001) 'Disciplinary differences and university teaching', *Studies in Higher Education* 26 (2), pp. 135–46.

New Generation Project, 2002 (new part of the Health Care Innovation Unit, www. hciu.soton.ac.uk; www.hciu.soton.ac.uk/; reference originally at www.mhbs.soton. ac.uk/newgeneration/IPEYear2Evaluation; www.mhbs.soton.ac.uk/newgeneration/ IPEYear2Evaluation [accessed 4 August 2003].

Newman, M. (2003) *A Pilot Systematic Review and Meta-analysis on the Effectiveness of Problem-based Learning*, LTSN-01 commissioned report, www.ltsn-01.ac.uk/docs/pbl_report. pdf.

NHS Scotland (2002) *Learning Together. NHS. Education for Scotland*, Scottish Executive Health Department, Edinburgh.

NIMHE (National Institute for Mental Health in England) (2003) *National Framework of Values for Mental Health*: Draft available at the Mental Health Foundation conference website: www.connects.org.uk/conferences (log-in required).

Office of the E-Envoy (2002), *Report to the Prime Minister from the e-Minister and e-Envoy*, The Cabinet Office, e-Government Unit, www.e-government.cabinetoffice.gov.uk/ Home/Homepage/fs/en [accessed 23 October 2003].

Oliver, M. (1996) *Understanding Disability*, Macmillan, Basingstoke.

Ovretveit, J., Matthias, P. and Thompson, T. (1997) *Interprofessional Working for Health and Social Care*, Macmillan, London.

Oxford University, MSc in Evidence-Based Social Work (EBSW), Department of Social Policy and Social Work, University of Oxford, 2004, www.apsoc.ox.ac.uk/Courses_EBSW.html [accessed 17 August 2003].

Parker, J. and Bradley, G. (2003) *Social Work Practice: Assessment, Planning, Intervention and Review*, Learning Matters, Exeter.

Parton, N. and O'Byrne, P. (2000) *Constructive Social Work: Towards a New Practice*, Palgrave, London.

Payne, M. (2001) 'Knowledge *bases* and knowledge *biases* in social work', *Journal of Social Work*, 1 (2), pp. 133–46.

Petracchi, H. E. (1999) 'Using professionally trained actors in social work role-play simulations', *Journal of Sociology and Social Welfare*, 24 (4), pp. 61–9.

Petracchi, H. E. and Patchner, M. E. (2001) 'A comparison of live instruction and interactive televised teaching: A 2-year assessment of teaching an MSW research method course', *Research on Social Work Practice* 11 (1), pp. 108–17.

Phillipson J. (1992) *Practising Equality: Women, Men and Social Work*, CCETSW, London.

Piaget, J. (1972) *Psychology and Epistemology*, trans. P. Wells, Penguin, Harmondsworth.

Pirrie, A., Elsegood, J. and Wilson, V. (1998) *Evaluating Multidisciplinary Education in Health Care*, SCRE research report 89, SCRE, Edinburgh.

Powell, M. and Hewitt, M. (2002) *Welfare State and Welfare Change*, Open University Press, Buckingham.

Prosser, M. and Trigwell, K. (1999) *Understanding Learning and Teaching: The Experience in Higher Education*, SRHE and Open University Press, Buckingham.

Quality Assurance Agency (QAA) (1995) *Subject Overview Report: – Social Policy and Administration*, Quality Assurance Agency, www.qaa.ac.uk/revreps/subjrev/All/qo_9_95.htm [accessed 16 February 2004].

Quality Assurance Agency (QAA) (1998) *Quality Assurance in UK Higher Education: A Brief Guide*, QAA, Gloucester.

Quality Assurance Agency (QAA) (2000) *Benchmarking Statement for Social Work*, www.qaa.org.uk/crntwork/benchmark/socialwork [accessed 19 September 2003].

Quality Assurance Agency for Higher Education (QAA) (2001a) *Progress Files for Higher Education*, QAA, Gloucester, www.qaa.ac.uk/crntwork/progfileHE/contents.htm [accessed 16 February 2004].

Quality Assurance Agency in Higher Education (QAA) (2001b) *Code of Practice for the Assurance of Academic Quality and Standards in Higher Education: Placement Learning*, QAA, Gloucester, www.qaa.ac.uk/public/cop/copplacementfinal/precepts.htm [accessed 23 March 2003]

Quality Assurance Agency (QAA) (2001c) *Benchmark Statement: Health Care Programmes. Phase 1. Nursing*. QAA, Gloucester.

Race, P. (1999) *2000 Tips for Lecturers*, Kogan Page, London.

Rafferty, J. and Waldman, J. (2003) *Building Capacity to Support the Social Work Degree: a Scoping Study for the Department of Health eLearning Steering Group*, Department of Health, August, full study available online, www.swap.ac.uk/elearning/develop4.asp [accessed 27 August 2003].

Ramanathan, C. S. and Link, R. J. (eds) (1999) *All Our Futures: Principles and Resources for Social Work Practice in a Global Era*, Brooks/Cole Wadsworth, Belmont, California.

Ramsden, R. (1998) *Learning to Lead in Higher Education*, Routledge, London.

Regan de Bere, S. (2003) 'Evaluating the implications of complex interprofessional education for improvements in collaborative practice: a multidimensional model', *British Educational Research Journal*, 29 (1), pp. 105–24.

Risler, E. A. (1999) 'Student practice portfolios: integrating diversity and learning in the field experience', *Arete*, 23 (1), pp. 89–96.

Rodgers, B. N. (1963) *A Follow-up Study of Social Administration Students of Manchester University 1940–1960*, Manchester University Press, Manchester.

Rogers, J. (1989) *Adults Learning*, 3rd edn, Open University Press, Buckingham.

Room, G. (2000) 'Globalisation, social policy and international standard-setting: the case of higher education credentials', *International Journal of Social Welfare*, 9, pp. 103–19.

Rosenberg, M. J. (2001) *e-Learning, Strategies for Delivery Knowledge in the Digital Age*, McGraw-Hill, New York.

Rowntree, D. (1987) *Assessing Students: How Shall We Know Them?*, Kogan Page, London.

Rudenstine, N. (1996) *The Internet is Changing Higher Education*, Harvard Conference on the Internet and Society, 29 May, http://usinfo.state.gov/journals/itgic/0996/ijge/gjcom2.htm [accessed 6 April 2003].

Rustin, M. (1994) 'Flexibility in higher education' in R. Burrows and B. Loader (eds) *Towards a Post-Fordist Welfare State*, Routledge, London.

Sainsbury, E. E. (1966) *Fieldwork in Social Administration Courses*, National Council of Social Services, London.

Salmon, G. (2000) *E-Moderating: The Key to Teaching and Learning Online*, Kogan Page, London.

Salmon, G. (2002) *E-tivities: The Key to Active Online Learning*, Kogan Page, London.

Sanders, C. (2002) 'Harassed, pulled every which way but committed to her workers', *Times Higher Education Supplement*, 7 June.

Sapey, B. and Turner, R. (2004) *Access to Practice: Overcoming the Barriers to Practice Learning for Disabled Social Work Students*, SWAP, Southampton.

Savin-Baden, M. (2003) *Facilitating Problem-based Learning: Illuminating Perspectives*, The Society for Research into Higher Education and The Open University Press, Buckingham.

Schein, E. H. (1989) *Organisational Psychology*, Prentice-Hall, New Jersey.

Schön, D. (1983) *The Reflective Practitioner: How Professionals Think in Action*, Maurice Temple Smith, London.

Schön, D. (1987) *Educating the Reflective Practitioner: Towards a New Design for Teaching and Learning in the Professions*, Jossey Bass, San Francisco.

Scott, D. (2003) 'Fieldwork placements and the social policy curriculum' in P. Alcock, A. Erskine and M. May (eds) *The Students Companion to Social Policy*, 2nd edn, Blackwell, Oxford.

Scott, D. and Shenton, N. (1995) *Enterprise in Higher Education: Some Critical Perspectives from Social Policy*, Department of Social Policy and Social Work, University of Manchester.

Scottish Organisation for Practice Teaching (SCOPT) (2003) Code of practice, www.scopt.uk/code.html.

Secker, J. (1993) *From Theory to Practice in Social Work*, Avebury, Aldershot.

Selman, P. (1998) 'Intercountry adoption in Europe after the Hague Convention' in R. Sykes and P. Alcock (eds) *Developments in European Social Policy: Convergence and Diversity*, Policy Press, Bristol.

Senge, P. (1990) *The Fifth Discipline: The Art and Practice of the Learning Organisation*, Century Business, London.

Senge, P. (1991) 'The learning organisation made plain', *Training and Development*, October, pp. 37–44.

Shardlow, S. and Doel, M. (1996) *Practice Learning and Teaching*, Macmillan, Basingstoke.

Shardlow, S. M. and Doel, M. (eds) (2005) *Learning to Practise Social Work: International Approaches*, Jessica Kingsley, London.

Shardlow, S. M. and Doel, M. (2005) *Practice Teaching and Learning*, 2nd edn, Palgrave, Basingstoke.

Sharpe, M. and Danbury, H. (1999) *The Management of Failing DipSW Students*, Ashgate, Aldershot.

Shaw, M. (2002) *Contexts for Curriculum Design: Working with External Pressures*, www.ltsn. ac.uk/application.asp?app=resources.asp&process=full_record&section=generic&id=57.

Shenton, N. (1987) *Survey of Fieldwork in Social Administration/Social Policy Courses in Higher Education – a Preliminary Report*, University of Manchester, Manchester.

Shorrock, R. (2002) 'The student experience' in S. Armstrong, G. Thompson and S. Brown (eds) *The Effective Academic*, Kogan Page, London.

Sieppert, J. D. and Krysik, J. (1996) 'Computer-based testing in social work education: a preliminary exploration', *Computers in Human Services*, 13 (1), pp. 43–61.

Singh, G. (2000) *Developing Black Perspectives in Practice Teaching,* Coventry University/ CCETSW, London.

Skehill, C. (2003) 'Using a peer action learning approach in the implementation of communication and information technology in social work education', *Social Work Education*, 22, (2), pp. 177–90.

Smith, R. and Coates, M. (2002) *Partnership in Practice: A Joint Training Initiative Between Social Work and Health*, Case study for SWAP, www.swap.ac.uk/Links/casestudy. asp?casefind=cssmithcoates [accessed 3 February 2003].

Snow, R. (2002) *Stronger Than Ever: Report of the First National Conference of Survivor Workers UK*, Asylum, Stockport.

Social Care Institute for Excellence (SCIE) (2001) *Practice Guide for Managing Practice*, www.elsc-bestpracticeguides.org.uk/first_line/firstline.asp [accessed 12 July 2003].

Social Services Inspectorate/Department of Health (SSI/DoH) (2001) *Modern Social Services: a Commitment to Deliver*, The 10th Annual Report of the Chief Inspector of Social Services 2000/2001, www.doh.gov.uk/scg/ciann_10.htm [accessed 16 February 2004].

Sociologists in Placements (SIP) (2000), *Placement Practice in Social Science; a Learning Resources pack*, Sociologists in Placements, www.unn.ac.uk/academic/ss/sip.

Soumpasi, A. (2002) *Social Services and Social Work in Greece,* course work for UEL MA ISW course, unpublished.

Spicker, P. (2000) *An Introduction to Social Policy*, www2.rgu.ac.uk/publicpolicy/intro duction/index.htm [accessed 25 March 2003].

Stuart, G. (2002) *Embedding Practice Based, Interprofessional Education into the Curriculum*, case study for SWAP, www.swap.ac.uk/Links/casestudy.asp?casefind=csgstuart [accessed 3 February 2003].

SureStart, www.surestart.gov.uk/ [accessed 17 February 2004].

SWAP (2003) *Key Elements in Best Practice in Practice Learning*, www.swap.ac.uk/learning/ practiceSW1.asp?version=norm [accessed 25 February 2004].

Tait, M. (2000) 'Using a reflective diary in student supervision' in V. E. Cree and C. Macaulay (eds) *Transfer of Learning in Professional and Vocational Education*, Routledge, London.

Tarpy, L. (2003) 'Postcards from abroad', *Care and Health,* 30, 26/2–11/3, pp. 32–3.

Taylor, I. (1996) 'Facilitating reflective learning', in N. Gould and I. Taylor (eds) *Reflective Learning for Social Work,* Arena, Aldershot.

Taylor, I. (1997) *Developing Learning in Professional Education,* The Society for Research into Higher Education and Open University Press, Buckingham.

Taylor, P. G. (1999) *Making Sense of Academic Life,* SHRE and Open University Press, Buckingham.

Taylor, I. (2004) 'Multiprofessional teams and the learning organisation' in N. Gould and M. Baldwin (eds) *Social Work, Critical Reflection and the Learning Organisation,* Ashgate, Aldershot, pp. 75–86.

Taylor, I., Thomas, J. and Sage, H. (1999) 'Portfolios for learning and assessment: laying the foundations for continuing professional development', *Social Work Education,* 18 (2), pp. 147–60.

Taylor, P. G. (1999) *Making Sense of Academic Life,* Open University Press, Buckingham.

Teeple, G. (2000) *Globalization and the Decline of Social Reform into the 21st Century,* 2nd edn, Garamond Press, Aurora, Ontario.

Thoburn, J. (1999) *The UEA Doctor of Social Work Degree, Theorising Social Work Research,* ESRC Seminar Series, JUC/SWEC, NISW, London.

Thompson, G. (1997) 'Changing universities: from evolution to revolution' in S. Armstrong, G. Thompson and S. Brown (eds) *Facing up to Radical Changes in Universities and Colleges,* Kogan Page, London.

Thompson, N. (2001) *Anti-discriminatory Practice,* Macmillan, Basingstoke.

Thompson, N., Osada, M. and Anderson, B. (1994) *Practice Teaching in Social Work,* 2nd edn, PEPAR, Birmingham.

Thompson, S. and Marsh, P. (1991) *The Management of Practice Teaching,* Universities of Edinburgh and Sheffield, Sheffield.

Three Centre Research on Interprofessional Practice in Learning and Education (TRIPLE) www.triple-ltsn.kcl.ac.uk.

Times Higher Education Supplement (2000) Editorial 'Year on year, the students and the changes add up', 22 September.

Times Higher Education Supplement (2002) 20 September, pp. 26–7.

Toffler, A. (1980) *The Third Wave,* William Morrow, New York, www.toffler.com/publications/pub_aboutta_1122.shtml.

Toohey, S. (1999) *Designing Courses for Higher Education,* Society for Research in Higher Education and Open University Press, Buckingham.

TOPSS England (2000) *Modernising the Social Care Workforce,* TOPSS England, Leeds.

TOPSS England (2002) *National Occupational Standards for Social Work,* www.topss.org.uk/.

Torkington, C., Lymbery, M., Millward, A., Murfin, M. and Richell, B. (2003) 'Shared practice learning: social work and district nurse students learning together', *Social Work Education,* 22 (2), pp. 165–76.

Tosey, P. (2002) *Complexity Theory: A Perspective on Education,* LTSN Imaginative Curriculum knowledge development paper, www.ltsn.ac.uk.

Trevillion, S. and Bedford, L. (2003) 'Utopianism and pragmatism in interprofessional education', *Social Work Education,* 22 (2), pp. 215–27.

Trevillion, S. (2004) *Proposals for a New Framework of Post-Qualifying Education and Training: Some Key Decisions,* General Social Care Council, London.

Trevithick, P., Richards, S., Ruch, G. and Moss, B. (2004) *Teaching and Learning Communication Skills in Social Work Education, Knowledge Review 6*, Social Care Institute for Excellence, London.

Trigwell, K., Martin, E., Benjamin, J. and Prosser, M. (1999) 'Why and how can teaching be scholarly?' in C. Rust, *Improving Student Learning*, Oxford Vrookes, Oxford.

Trigwell, K., Martin, E., Benjamin, J. and Prosser, M. (2000) 'Scholarship of teaching: a model', *Higher Education Research and Development*, 19 (2), pp. 155–68.

Trotter, J. and Leech, N. (2003) 'Linking research, theory and practice in personal and professional development', *Social Work Education*, 22 (2), pp. 203–14.

Trow, M. (1992) 'Uncertainties in Britain's transition from elite to mass higher education' in T. G. Whiston and R. L. Geiger (eds) *Research and Higher Education: the United Kingdom and the United States*, Society for Research in Higher Education (SRHE) and Open University, Buckingham.

Tsang, A. K. and Yan, M-C. (2001) 'Chinese corpus, Western application: the Chinese strategy of engagement with Western social work discourse', *International Social Work*, 44 (4), pp. 433–54.

Universities UK (2002) *Enhancing Employability, Recognising Diversity: Making Links Between Higher Education and the World of Work*, Universities UK, London.

University of Birmingham, *Community Mental Health Programmes*, Interdisciplinary RECOVER Programme in Community Mental Health, 2004, www.cmh.bham.ac.uk [accessed 17 August 2003].

University of Stirling (2003) *Study*, www.stir.ac.uk/Departments/HumanSciences/AppSocSci/DRUGS/Study.htm [accessed 6 July 2003].

Van Wormer, K. M. (1997) *Social Welfare: A World View*, Nelson-Hall, Chicago.

Visvesvaran, P. K. (2000) 'Admission criteria and internal assessment in a school of social work: an analysis', *The Indian Journal of Social Work*, 61 (2), pp. 255–68.

Wagner, L. (2003) 'The Higher Education Academy', Keynote Presentation to National Teaching Fellows, Oxford.

Waldman, J. (2002) *Report of SWAPltsn Network Survey*, SWAPltsn Subject Centre for Social Policy and Social Work, *Baseline Report July 2000–July 2001*, www.swap.ac.uk/SWAP/Survey/aims.asp [accessed 16 February 2004].

Waldman, J., Glover, N. and King, E. (1999) Readiness to learn: an experiential perspective, *Social Work Education*, 18 (2), pp. 219–34.

Walker, J., McCarthy, P., Morgan, W. and Timms, N. (1995) *In Pursuit of Quality: Improving Practice Teaching in Social Work*, Relate Centre for Family Studies, The University of Newcastle, Newcastle upon Tyne.

Walsh, J. (1998) 'A model for integrating research, practice, and field instruction in the undergraduate curriculum', *Journal of Teaching in Social Work*, 17 (1–2), pp. 49–63.

Walton, G. (1993) 'Working for change as a service user' in P. Beresford and T. Harding (eds) *A Challenge to Change: Practical Experiences of Building User Led Services*, pp. 157–63, National Institute for Social Work, London.

Watts, T. D., Elliott, D. and Mayadas, N. S., (eds) (1996) *International Handbook on Social Work Education*, Greenwood, Westport, Connecticut.

Wenger, E. (1998) *Communities of Practice: Learning, Meaning and Identity*, Cambridge University Press, Cambridge.

Wergin, J. F. (1988) 'Basic issues and principles in classroom assessment' in J. H. McMillan (ed.) *Assessing Students' Learning*, Jossey-Bass, San Francisco.

Whittington, C. (2003a) *Learning for Collaborative Practice with other Professions and Agencies*, Department of Health, London.

Whittington, C. (2003b) *Learning for Collaborative Practice: A Study to Inform Development of the Degree in Social Work*, Department of Health, London.

Wiles, K. (2002) 'Accessibility and computer-based assessment: a whole set of issues' in L. Phipps, A. Sutherland and J. Seale (eds) *Access All Areas: Disability, Technology and Learning*, JISC, TechDis and ALT.

Williams, C. (1999) 'Connecting anti-racist and anti-oppressive theory and practice: retrenchment or reappraisal?', *British Journal of Social Work*, 29 (2), pp. 211–30.

Williams, F. (1989) *Social Policy: A Critical Introduction*, Polity Press, Oxford.

Williams, F. (1997) 'Women and community' in J. Bornat, J. Johnson, C. Pereira, D. Pilgrim and F. Williams (eds) *Community Care: A Reader*, Macmillan, Basingstoke, pp. 34–44.

Wolcott, H. F. (1995) *The Art of Fieldwork*, Walnut Creek, Altamira, California.

Worcester University College/Quality Assurance Agency (2003) *Inclusivity Toolkit Project*, www.worc.ac.uk.

World Universities Network (undated) 'Aims', www.wun.ac.uk/news/article.php?id=19 [accessed 7 January 2003].

Yeates, N. (2001) *Globalization and Social Policy*, Sage, London.

Yorke, M. (2001) *Assessment: A Guide for Senior Managers*, LTSN Generic Centre, York.

Yorke, M. (2003) 'Pedagogical research in UK higher education: an emerging policy framework' in H. Eggins and R. Macdonald (eds) *The Scholarship of Academic Development*, Society for Research in Higher Education and Open University Press, Buckingham.

Younes, M. N. (1998) 'The gatekeeping dilemma in undergraduate social work programs: collision of ideal and reality', *International Social Work*, 41 (2), pp. 145–53.

Young, P. (1967) *The Student and Supervision in Social Work Education*, Routledge & Kegan Paul, London.

Young, P. (2003) *'Evolution or Revolution? An Analysis of Teaching Practices in Undergraduate Social Policy Programmes in the Context of Change in UK Higher Education'*, unpublished PhD dissertation, University of Lancaster, Lancaster.

Young, P. and Irving, Z. (2003) *Changing Practices in Teaching Undergraduate Social Policy*, presentation to the Social Policy Association Annual Conference, University of Teesside, July 2003.

Young, P. and Irving, Z. (2004) 'Changing practices in undergraduate teaching of social policy: research report', www.swap.ac.uk

Yuen-Tsang, A. and Wang, S. (2002) 'Tensions confronting the development of social work education in China: challenges and opportunities', *International Social Work*, 45 (3), pp. 375–88.

Index

All references to boxed information, figures or tables are in *italic* print